Hausa Women in the Twentieth Century

Hausa Women
in the Twentieth Century

Edited by

Catherine Coles and Beverly Mack

THE UNIVERSITY OF WISCONSIN PRESS

The University of Wisconsin Press
114 North Murray Street
Madison, Wisconsin 53715

3 Henrietta Street
London WC2E 8LU, England

5 4 3 2 1

Printed in the United States of America

Library of Congress Cataloging-in-Publication Data
Hausa women in the twentieth century/edited by Catherine Coles
   and Beverly Mack.
   310 pp.   cm.
      Includes bibliographical references and index.
      ISBN 0-299-13020-7   ISBN 0-299-13024-X (pbk.)
      1. Women, Hausa (African people) 2. Women, Muslim.
   I. Coles, Catherine M.   II. Mack, Beverly B. (Beverly Blow), 1952–
   DT515.45.H38H38   1991
   305.48′8937–dc20   91-14182
                       CIP

Contents

Foreword

Two generations ago Isa Wali, a bright young intellectual of orthodox Muslim background but educated in the colonial schools of Northern Nigeria, wrote a series of articles on the position of women in Islam. This started a ferment that has continued in postcolonial Hausaland among the intelligentsia through coups and counter-coups, periods of military rule and periods of "politics," boom and slump, glad striving after Western materialism and the rise of the new fundamentalism. In those days, except for *Baba of Karo*, the only women's words that found themselves in print were in the dialogue of plays like Shu'aibu Maƙarfi's *Jatau na Kyallu*. In this, and subsequent similar plays about domestic conflict, the women do not mince words when they talk about male tyranny and irresponsibility. But the writers were men, albeit persons of sensibility and imagination.

More recently, women have spoken for themselves in print. They do so eloquently in this volume, with some assistance from men whose fields of study are relevant. It is hoped that in another couple of generations, the balance of Hausa to non-Hausa writers may shift. But then they might not write in English! I have heard a fundamentalist Muslim criticize an American scholar for her "interference" in the affairs of Muslim women—not in Nigeria, much further east—and I was happy to remind him that, if the Prophet's successors and their armies had not "interfered," somewhat forcefully, in his homeland, he would still be sunk in fire worship or worse. In some matters, an outside viewpoint helps. It still, of course, behooves a foreign scholar to be more than usually scrupulous in how she interprets data, and wherever possible to quote informants' own words. And that is what has been done here.

"Me aka samu?" "Mace." "Allah ya raya, amin!" Or, roughly, "God bless this ship, and all who sail in her!"

Neil Skinner
Madison, Wisconsin

Acknowledgments

None of the research discussed in this volume, nor the chapters themselves, would have been possible without the hospitality, generosity, and assistance of the Hausa women about whom we have written, and of their families and friends. Our thanks are inadequate for what they have given us in terms of time, interest, and support of many kinds. Whenever we have expressed to them reticence about our work, fearing that it might interfere with their privacy, their response has overwhelmingly been to encourage us to interfere, if that is what is required to tell their stories. They may be secluded, but they are not without concern about the world beyond their own lives, or interest in having the world know about them. We hope that another such volume might include far more work by Hausa scholars, whose intimate knowledge of the culture can yield great insight into Hausa women's lives.

Funding for the preparation of the volume was provided by the Department of Anthropology and a Faculty Research Grant at Dartmouth College, for which we are grateful. We thank Debbie Hodges for her editing and typing, and Christina Richards, who worked as a research assistant at Dartmouth.

We also thank Dr. Paul Lovejoy for his comments on the volume, and the editors at the University of Wisconsin Press, especially Barbara Hanrahan, Raphael Kadushin, and Jack Kirshbaum.

Our husbands, George Kelling and Bob Henry, have provided support and tolerance through the long process of preparing this manuscript for publication. Although they are not Hausa men, their patience approaches the level of *hakuri* that is considered a virtue, and we are grateful to them for it.

Among Hausa praise singers, such a litany of thanks as this is mere stock in trade; usually their lists of praise ephitets approach Homeric lengths. There can be no competing with that, but we must acknowledge that over several years of production it is inevitable that many people omitted here have assisted us along the way. The energies of everyone involved in this volume will have been rewarded if it can replace at least some stereotypes with enlightenment, and inspire further research of its kind.

Note on Foreign Terms

Many Arabic terms have become a part of the Hausa language, in which a glottal stop is marked in roman script by an apostrophe. Because this study focuses on Hausa, glottal stops for vowels are marked in this way. Ayns and hamzas are not distinguished in Arabic terms used here, but are only indicated by an apostrophe.

The Hausa language has several "hooked" letters that are known as glottalized consonants. These include: Ɓ, ɗ, ƙ, and 'y (the upper case are Ɓ Ɗ Ƙ 'Y), and are distinct from the letters b, d, k, and y. Throughout this text, such letters represent glottal sounds and are shown in both upper and lower cases as designated above.

Throughout the text foreign words are always italicized. Their origin is given only the first time they appear, and only when they are not Hausa terms. The glossary is a listing of Hausa and other foreign terms. The origin of certain terms is given when the word (usually Arabic) does not appear in the Hausa lexicon. Otherwise it is treated as a Hausa term.

Hausa Women in the Twentieth Century

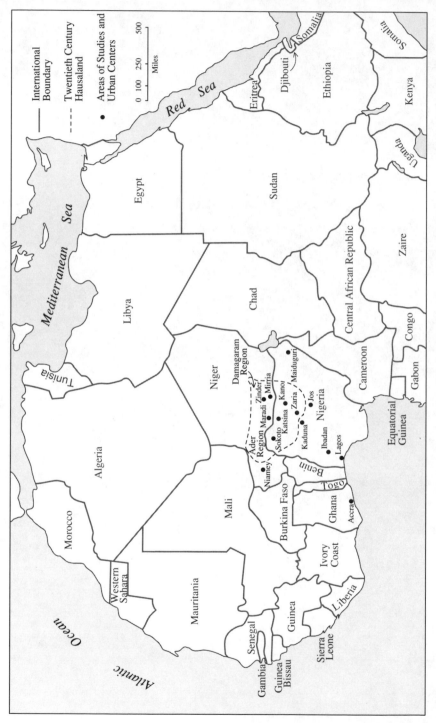

Map of Western Africa

1 *Catherine Coles and Beverly Mack*

Women in Twentieth-Century Hausa Society

This collection of articles presents data and analyses from recent scholarly research on women in twentieth-century Hausa society. Specifically it emanates from two panels organized for the 1984 meetings of the African Studies Association in Los Angeles, to which scholars who had conducted research into all aspects of Hausa society were invited. The panelists explored the current state of knowledge and directions of research on women and gender in Hausa society, and they initiated a dialogue that could lead to the integration of such research with earlier historical and contemporary accounts of political, economic, social, and ritual-religious life. Participants presented original material from their recent research, addressing whatever problems they deemed important within the framework of their own academic disciplines (history, anthropology, African languages and literature, economics, political science). No attempt was made at imposing particular perspectives or directing papers toward specific topics. Rather, an explicit goal of the entire process was to identify and explore different interpretations, issues, and points of agreement and disagreement as they emerged.

This volume brings these papers together with additional manuscripts which were solicited from individuals unable to attend the panels. All chapters are previously unpublished. The chapter by Bilkisu Yusuf is the only contribution from outside academia. Yusuf is a journalist and recently served as editor of the *New Nigerian*, a prominent newspaper in northern Nigeria; as a Hausa woman

3

she speaks personally to many of the issues discussed in other chapters, as do Balaraba Sule and Ayesha Imam.

Most Hausa today live in West Africa, in northern Nigeria, or southern Niger. They constitute one of the largest and most influential ethnic groups in Africa, and their language, Hausa, is the lingua franca of West Africa, spoken by at least fifty million people. Although a small number of Hausa, known as Maguzawa, are Christian or animist, Hausa culture and society are overwhelmingly Islamic. Hausa women are among the most strictly secluded Muslim women in Africa. The increasing identification of Muslim Hausa with the Islamic world in the last decade has created political tensions within Nigeria. For those who study Hausa women this change brings to the forefront the question of the specific impact of Islam on women's lives.

Hausa culture and society are complex and include many extremes of experience: urban and rural communities, agricultural systems and highly specialized craft production, Muslim and non-Muslim religious and ritual systems, and a highly elaborated status system based upon occupation and birth. Hausaland itself has been a center of trade and cosmopolitan activity for many centuries, with Hausa traders traveling as far south as Zaire, and to the north, west, and east coasts of the continent; Muslim pilgrims journeyed east and north for the hajj to Mecca (Lovejoy 1970, 1971; Works 1976). Both traders and pilgrims carried Hausa cultural practices along with them, influencing social and cultural life in, and spreading the Hausa language to, communities in which they settled. Within Hausaland itself, indigenous peoples at various times were influenced or ruled by immigrants such as the Wangarawa, the Kanuri, the Fulani (Hiskett 1984), and under colonial administrations the British (in Nigeria) and French (in Niger). In the face of all such challenges to its traditions, Hausa culture has maintained its own language and cultural attributes, assimilating the new and useful, and defusing whatever threatened its cohesiveness.

Not surprisingly, the Hausa have been studied extensively, attracting the attention of travelers, Islamic scholars, colonial officials, historians, linguists, and anthropologists. Accounts have focused especially on the development of the Hausa city-states in northern Nigeria and southern Niger with their complex bureaucracies and highly developed economies (M. G. Smith 1960, 1978; Hogben and Kirk-Greene 1966; Dunbar 1970), the wide-ranging activities of Hausa traders, and the nineteenth-century creation of an extensive Islamic empire in Hausaland—the Sokoto Caliphate (Last 1967; Hiskett 1973). Up until the 1970s, much of this published literature touched only peripherally, if at all, upon women. In fact, much of the early scholarship on "Hausa soceity" actually documented and analyzed the activities, perceptions, and ideals of Hausa males.

A significant exception to this tendency was Mary Smith's biography, *Baba of Karo: A Woman of the Muslim Hausa* (1954). The first published work in which women were the specific focus of inquiry, it may be considered a counterpart to (her husband) Michael Smith's extensive anthropological studies of Nigerian Hausa society, in which he presented a substantial amount of descriptive information on female activities without attempting to set forth women's perspectives (M. G. Smith 1955). Following this, Rachel Yeld's research on status in Hausa society (1960) considered women as well as men, and a situation similar to that of the Smiths occurred later when Abner Cohen and his wife collected data on women for a single chapter in his analysis of the strategies of Hausa traders in Ibadan (1969).

Beginning in the late 1960s and early 1970s a virtual explosion occurred in research on Hausa society, and intense efforts began which led to more widespread collection of data on females as well as males. This has continued through the 1980s. For the most part scholars involved in research during this twenty-year period of heightened activity have framed their questions and directed their efforts toward *either* males *or* females, with little attempt made at including both. Descriptions of Hausa society have emphasized discrete gender-specific social and economic spheres, linking these with the widespread seclusion of adult women of childbearing age. This polarization in research foci clearly reflects the paradigms within which scholars were trained and which continue to shape their research as much as any "reality" in Hausa society. To investigate power and authority in a society, for example, they have examined formal political hierarchies and roles clearly dominated by males (M. G. Smith 1960, 1978; Last 1967; Hiskett 1973), rather than ways in which power is dispersed throughout society and exercised by individuals and groups (some female) over others.

This trend is certainly not absolute: Polly Hill's studies of agriculture and rural Hausa life include substantial sections on women (1969, 1972, 1977), as do those of Michael Smith (1955). Yet these examples are not typical of most research conducted during this period, in which a definite polarization exists between studies which focus upon males and those which examine "female-associated" topics.

Together the chapters in this volume chronicle a broad range of women's experiences in Hausa society, expanding a more narrow conception of their lives that might easily be construed from a reading of the existing published literature. For example, not all Hausa women live in the old walled cities (*birni*): the behavior and economic activities of Hausa women in Kaduna (Nigeria), a colonial city, and Accra (Ghana) are described by contributors Catherine Coles and Deborah Pellow. Of necessity there are omissions, some significant, in the coverage of Hausa women's lives presented: for example, rural women are not well represented, yet they play crucial roles in agriculture and development processes in many areas of Hausaland (Simmons 1975, 1976). Neither are non-Muslim women treated, although Nicole Echard's chapter on *bori* addresses a set of non-Islamic religious practices. Case studies do include women from both Nigeria and Niger. Furthermore, they concentrate on what we should more accurately refer to as "Hausa-Fulani" women, whose families represent the indigenous Hausa, or Haɓe, element of society as well as Fulani who have intermarried with Hausa, especially since the time of the Fulani jihad and Sokoto Caliphate in the early nineteenth century.

The dominant approach toward gender in Hausa society in scholarship to date has been to emphasize the subordination of women to men arising from the intersection of a patriarchal Islam and Hausa cultural values which were in place prior to colonization. Yet a preconceived assumption of gender asymmetry actually distorts many analyses, since it precludes the exploration of gender as a fundamental component of social relations, inequality, processes of production and reproduction, and ideology (Ortner and Whitehead 1981; Lamphere 1987). We suggest that this exploration should be a high priority in future research on and analysis of Hausa society, and prior to any assumptions or findings on gender asymmetry. We further propose that Hausa women's current "invisibility" arises out of a lack of understanding of the nature and importance of their participation in basic social processes; indeed, the redefinition of particular processes may be required in order to make visible their participation. This approach is discussed more fully in the pages which follow. The first step toward its implementation has already been initiated through documentation and analysis of actual female behavior and interaction of Hausa women with different social identities and at different stages in the ᴧᴉᴇ cycle (Schildkrout 1988; Mack 1988; Potash 1989; Morgen 1989:6–7; Coles 1990b).

Many of the chapters in this volume do not address the theoretical perspective set out in this introduction, nor would all the authors necessarily accept or choose to work within it. Each chapter does offer new data on women's participation in one of four arenas of Hausa society that form the basis for the volume's organization: Hausa women in Islam; the power of women; women in a changing economy; and feminine gender in ritual, the arts, and media. Chapters included in each section contribute differing and even conflicting interpretations and conclusions. They are introduced in the following discussion, which summarizes data on women currently available in each arena, and suggests ways in which future research and analysis could move beyond limiting stereotypes that have persisted.

Hausa Women in Islam

The specific impact of Islam on women's roles in Hausaland is not as apparent as is often assumed. Here, as elsewhere in the Muslim world, a syncretistic blend of Islam and local cultural features shapes women's lives—sometimes in the direction of patriarchal systems and practices which emanate culturally from the Middle East and those societies in which Islam originated, at other times reflecting (sometimes equally patriarchal) local custom—often making it difficult to distinguish traits or behaviors arising out of Islam from those that were originally "Hausa." However, a careful investigation of gender roles in Hausa society before and after the adoption of Islam shows quite clearly that the spread of Islam, and particularly the Fulani jihad (holy war) early in the nineteenth century, changed profoundly the social, political, and cultural conditions of Hausaland for women (Hiskett 1973, 1984; Mary Smith 1981; Boyd and Last 1985).

Although Islam originally entered Hausaland in the late eighth century, data from origin myths, king lists, and historical sources such as the Kano Chronicle indicate that several centuries before widespread conversion to Islam occurred females appear to have participated actively in formal public affairs, may have held positions of leadership, and seem to have been no more legally constrained than men by their gender (Palmer 1928:142–43). Data on the non-Muslim Maguzawa (although they must be critically evaluated and used with care) provide an important source of information on the status and roles of free women in rural Hausa society prior to the establishment of Islam. Jerome Barkow (1970, 1972, 1973) and Joseph Greenberg (1946, 1947) assume that the Maguzawa religious system, clan organization, and other aspects of social life including gender roles may be representative of earlier Hausa society. They describe mid-twentieth-century communities of Maguzawa in which women are not secluded but rather interact freely with men, where Maguzawa females marry later than do Muslim Hausa girls and to men closer to their own age, and where women farm their own plots from which they feed their families (in addition to participating in communal family farming). Maguzawa females also play significant roles in the spirit possession cult of *bori* as well as minor roles in clan and domestic group rituals.

Eighteenth-century European traveler's accounts of Hausaland also describe women in town, some of whom sold wares in Hausa markets (Denham et al. 1826; Clapperton 1829; Lander 1830; Barth 1857; Robinson 1896; Moody 1967). Although the wives of Hausa kings were sometimes restricted to the women's quarters—the *harem*—most other women were free to move about. Such liberalism was challenged by the Sokoto jihad, a campaign of Islamic religious reform that swept Hausaland from 1804 to 1812, spread by the armies of the Fulani cleric Usman dan Fodio. In his account of dan Fodio's life, Hiskett details the reasons for the conflict between Fulani evangelists and the nominally Muslim Hausa, making it quite clear that a major portion of the reformation affected women's lives:

> The kinds of things [the Fulani Muslims] objected to were idolatrous rites of animism . . . failure to observe the Islamic food prohibitions and prohibited degrees of marriage; the survival of inheritance through the female line in defiance of Islamic law

prescribing inheritance through the male line. . . . Particularly offensive to [the Shehu] was what he called "nakedness with women" by which he meant failure to adopt the long Muslim robe and veil; as well, of course, as the un-Islamic practice of the mingling of the sexes in public, at celebrations, dances and the like. Another of his accusations was that people who claimed to be Muslims made their own rules concerning private and public behavior instead of referring to the learned scholars for an authoritative ruling. (1973:8)

With the jihad, characteristic features of female behavior and feminine gender roles that had been expressed in rural Maguzawa society, and among "nominal" Muslims, were altered significantly. Norms for acceptable behavior by Muslim women were forcefully introduced, stressing their proper place as the home. Here they were expected to remain secluded, carrying out domestic labor and childcare responsibilities, engaging in income-earning activities, praying alone, and participating in a social life involving them in relations with other females, children, and kin. Seclusion also led to fundamental changes in the nature of Hausa women's productive roles, which Barkow characterizes as follows:

Islamization provided Hausa women with an opportunity to forsake laboring in the fields and to develop craft skills. Men encouraged or at least accepted wife seclusion because it increased individual prestige and was associated with piety. This increased the men's burden and permitted women to acquire individual wealth. Since much of their activity involves the preparation of cooked foods, an economy based on a high degree of labor specialization arose. (1972:327)

Today the observance of seclusion coincides with class and educational distinctions. In rural areas with dispersed compounds or small villages, where the need for their labor continues to involve many peasant women directly in subsistence agricultural production on family farms, seclusion is practiced minimally, if at all. Where such work is available, women may even seek jobs as paid agricultural laborers (Jackson 1978; Longhurst 1982). Here only religious teachers (*malamai,* pl.), and wealthy merchants or farmers can afford to and do seclude their wives. In large villages women are more likely to experience confinement; yet even those who are secluded are likely to engage in craft production, trade, or other productive activities from within compounds (Hill 1969, 1972; Simmons 1975, 1976). Poor urban women live in conditions under which seclusion is difficult if not impossible to maintain: they share compounds with other unrelated families and find mobility necessary to carry out income-earning subsistence activities (Schildkrout 1983). On the other hand, seclusion has increased during this century for middle-class women, wives of merchants, traders, and craftsmen, among whom imposing seclusion may represent an attempt at increasing male prestige by showing that a man is sufficiently wealthy to meet all his wife's and family's needs without her going out. Among members of the upper class, increasing numbers of whom are Western educated, women may or may not be secluded; in some cases women who have professions which take them outside of the home observe seclusion except during working hours (Coles fieldnotes; Mack fieldnotes).

It is clear that through the seclusion of women, and under the Maliki legal code (by which women inherit one-half the shares of males within the family and are declared legal minors requiring adult male representation in all legal matters; Ruxton 1978), the behavior and autonomy of many women are constrained in Hausaland. Yet Hausa women do not exclusively follow Islamic norms in their behavior any more than do Hausa men. A discrepancy between norms and actual behavior is particularly clear in women's observance of seclusion, in procedures for divorce, and in child custody after divorce. Hausa interpretations of Islam stress norms that preclude adult women of child-bearing age from remaining unmarried or unsecluded. Yet among married women themselves, many who claim to be secluded actually move about relatively freely. Furthermore, most Hausa women recognize a status for adult females who neither remarry after divorce, nor engage in prostitution, but support themselves through other types of income-earning activities and live with their families. Hausa women use a distinct term, *bazawara,* for such women; Hausa men, however, apply this term only to their immediate female kin, referring to strangers as *karuwai* (courtesans) (Pittin 1979a, 1983, 1984b; Coles 1983a, 1983b).

In two other instances Islamic prescriptions and Hausa cultural norms conflict, and the latter prevail. In cases involving Hausa women who wish to leave a marriage but fail to obtain a divorce through their husband's pronouncement of the *talaq* (the standard phrase repeated three times by which a husband divorces his wife) and seek one in court, judges have increasingly found in favor of the women, in accord with Hausa beliefs that a woman cannot be forced to stay with a husband if she is genuinely against him (Pittin 1979b). Maliki law also stipulates that after divorce women have custody rights to children until males attain the age of puberty or females marry (Ruxton 1978:155). Yet Hausa fathers generally claim their children upon weaning. Clearly both men and women in Hausa society selectively apply Hausa cultural norms, as opposed to those proposed by Islam, when it is advantageous for them to do so. Women have developed workable strategies for manipulating seclusion and divorce procedures for their own ends. They have been less successful in doing so in the area of child custody, where their rights remain severely limited and where Hausa norms prevail.

Knowledge of Islam is passed along in Hausaland through a formal educational system, beginning with Qur'anic schools attended by young children, progressing through more advanced Arabic and Islamic schools, and on to universities, which smaller numbers attend. For adult Hausa women, Islamic

with Sule and Starratt that Muslim women themselves have an acceptable, important, and necessary role to play in determining the course and goals of the development process.

The debate currently raging among scholars and Muslims themselves over whether Islam constrains and oppresses women or provides them a different path toward exercising power and authority, toward involvement in public affairs, and toward the achievement of their own goals for development is evident in this volume. One positive result of the exchange of information which has occurred as part of this controversy is the elimination of many stereotypes about Muslim women's lives. For example, findings from research on women in Hausa society have shown that although seclusion imposes limits on the form women's participation takes, it does not cut them off from political, economic, religious, and artistic aspects of life. Neither does Islam preclude the exercise of power and authority in Hausa society.

The Power of Women

The patriarchal nature of Hausa society, the pervasive notion that Muslim Hausa women should be and are subject to control by men, and the seclusion of women have given rise to a view of Hausa women as largely powerless relative to men and entirely lacking any authority in the public realm. Research findings have tended to confirm this male dominant–female subordinate image of Hausa society. This is not surprising since the domain of public affairs has been equated with formal political structures, and Hausa women have been largely absent from these structures since the Fulani jihad. Application in later Hausa research of the "public-private" dichotomy, an analytical framework that explains women's subordination by virtue of their being restricted to the domestic or private sphere, served further to reinforce this image of gender asymmetry. After its introduction by Michelle Rosaldo in 1974 for the study of gender roles, this scheme was subjected to well-deserved criticism and subsequently revised by her (1980). Among the most significant critiques were those which argued that the content of and relations between the public and private spheres, as Western scholars defined them, were inaccurate for many non-Western societies, where power exercised within the kin group could have significant implications for public affairs (C. Nelson 1974; Nicholson 1986; Sudarkasa 1986; Yanagisako and Collier 1987; Comaroff 1987).

Given the continuing importance of kinship and descent in Hausa society this criticism of the public-private dichotomy seems particularly appropriate. Yet while critical debate over it goes on, the framework has consistently been applied in its earliest form to compare and contrast Hausa women's and men's roles and to illustrate women's subordinate status. If one examines the power which women exercise in Hausa society, however, it becomes clear that they do not share a single, subordinate status. Women's power is visible in their ability to control and influence the lives of others; its sources are many, as are examples of its use during this century. Aristocratic women of high status (by virtue of descent and kinship) have had an effect on public affairs through direct involvement and indirectly by influencing their male kin or affines (Mack 1988). Earlier in the century, women of sufficient means owned and controlled the labor of slaves; such relationships have not completely disappeared today, although they are not sanctioned legally and the terminology has changed to "servants" (Christelow, this volume). Virtually all women gain influence over other individuals through prestige which accrues to them from the bearing and socialization of children, seniority accorded through age and generation (Coles 1990a), secular or Islamic learning, and the exercise of ritual power and authority. Wealth, whether achieved individually or inherited, brings both prestige and the ability to control others through its use. These attributes endow individual Hausa women with different degrees and forms of power in their relationships with other women and men, and determine women's positions relative to others in terms of prestige. Women's status clearly cannot be measured unidimensionally (see Whyte 1978; Ortner and Whitehead 1981; Mukhopadhyay and Higgins 1988).

Just as Hausa women are not uniformly powerless and subordinate, neither are their lives and activities irrelevant to public affairs and "politics." When wealthy women own property, contribute money to particular community development activities, and serve as patrons to younger women, when elder women command the labor of junior male and female kin, control local ritual activities, and offer innovative behavior as role models for younger females, when married women bear and socialize children and monopolize certain occupations in a local economy, their acts have implications for the entire society. Recent trends in feminist thought suggest the need to broaden a conception of politics to incorporate many of the types of activities and forms of control that Hausa women perform, "activities that are carried on in the daily lives of ordinary people and are enmeshed in the social institutions and political-economic processes of their society. When there is an attempt to change the social and economic institutions that embody the basic power relations in our society— that is politics" (Morgen and Bookman 1988:4; see also Collier 1974). Recognizing Hausa women as political actors, whose behavior affects particular outcomes in the public realm, and who participate in processes of social change, offers the potential both to improve our understanding of women's roles in shaping society and to construct a more comprehensive account of the political history of an era than can be obtained from a focus limited to formal political structures. It does not deny the existence of patriarchy in Muslim Hausa society, but because of its emphasis on women's active participation in society, prods us to ask how and why women accept or resist patriarchal elements.

Nor does such an approach deny that gender may be an important element in status and prestige rankings within particular social contexts, in relationships of inequality, and in the access to, allocation, and distribution of resources.

Hausa society today remains highly stratified. The formal system of social classes that originated in precolonial society has changed with the upheavals of the Fulani jihad, colonial rule, and the creation of a Nigerian state, yet it remains strong. Based primarily upon descent and occupation, and including a distinction between *masu sarauta* (rulers, by virtue of birth, and by achievement or appointment) and *talakawa* (common people), it is an important part of the overall status-prestige system (M. G. Smith 1959; Yeld 1960). Women's positions in the class hierarchy are determined primarily by their kinship–descent group affiliations. Traditionally they could move upward within this system through marriage; marrying a husband of a lower rank did not result in the lowering of a woman's own status (Yeld 1960). Women's power and autonomy, their overall position in the Hausa status-prestige scale, and their standing relative to males reflect both their social class and other personal attributes noted above, such as age, generation, education, and children.

To some degree the old Hausa-Fulani aristocracy has been able to maintain power and privilege alongside new political structures in Nigeria and Niger through its access to resources, secular education (Trevor 1975a; Tibenderana 1985), and channels to various levels of government. Yet the overall system has been altered with the emergence of new sources of power, prestige, and status available to women as well as men. One of the most important has been the introduction of Western secular education. Although fewer Hausa females than males were educated in secular schools during the colonial period, the establishment of Universal Primary Education (UPE) in 1976 validated the legitimacy of women's education at both the political and sociocultural level (Bray 1981). Many Hausa parents still resisted sending their daughters to Western schools, and even today female attendance at secular school in northern Nigeria remains below that of males at every level, substantially below males at levels above primary school (Callaway and Schildkrout 1985). The contact of most young Hausa women with Western secular education ends upon marriage in their early teens. Yet increasing numbers have experienced education of various types and have entered new occupations as a result of their training, becoming teachers, entering the commercial work force, and giving voice to their creative talents to an extent unprecedented in the region's history (C. Martin 1983). Western-educated females from all social classes marry into the aristocratic class (Knipp 1987) or enter it through education and subsequent occupational positions.

Relations of inequality in Hausa society are rooted in the traditional hierarchy of classes and in the wider status-prestige system. Gender was, and is, an element in these relations. Muslim Hausa society itself contains many patriarchal elements; similarly, structural conditions resulting from colonialism, the spread of capitalism, political independence, and greater integration into a world economy have had many adverse effects on women (Remy 1975; C. Martin 1983; Okonjo 1983; Knipp 1987). Grounding patriarchy in material relations in society, Jeanne Henn draws a picture of the articulation of patriarchal and capitalist modes of production that mirrors many aspects of Hausa women's experiences: male heads of households attempt to expropriate the surplus labor of women and male dependents through their control of economic resources, the reproduction of the sexual division of labor, the production and distribution of food, and the arrangement of marriages (Bujra 1986; see also Stichter and Parpart 1988; Henn 1988:42). This model approximates more closely to rural than urban Hausa society. Yet even in urban settings women's access to wage labor (movement outside the patriarchal mode) has been limited. Opportunities for them to enter the cash economy exist within the informal sector, but earnings are often not "sufficient to free them from patriarchal dependence" (Henn 1988:49). Whether or not one accepts the explanations for women's subordination provided in current Marxist feminist writings, Hausa women's much reduced access to the cash economy compared to males, their limited ability to enter occupations that bring greater material return, and limits imposed through Maliki law on female inheritance, all hinder the control of wealth, and the corresponding influence it brings, for most women in society.

Yet Hausa women have not been altogether unsuccessful in developing strategies to counter the control of men—manipulating seclusion, retaining control over their own income, seeking divorce and remarriage, or even remaining unmarried. Because women's primary allegiances remain with kin and descent groups, female solidarity and a common class identification have not emerged among most Hausa women. Thus it should not be surprising that older, more powerful, wealthier women exploit younger, less powerful, poorer females in their own interests, and in doing so they seem to be supporting the system of patriarchy by which men attempt to control women. These divisions among women are a major factor in their slow progress toward challenging patriarchy at the state level. State structures in Nigeria that institutionalized both indigenous and western elements of patriarchy, set up initially under British colonial rule, have undergone many changes with alternating periods of civilian and military rule. Barbara Callaway (1987) and Bilkisu Yusuf (this volume) document the difficulties women have faced in the north in obtaining the franchise, participating in formal political processes, gaining access to state structures through employment, seeking involvement in development planning, and receiving allocations of state-controlled resources (see also Silverblatt 1988; Parpart and Staudt 1989). Yet in a recent article Nina Mba describes a "military commitment to the incorporation of women into the militarized state at least at the local, state, and institutional levels [that] is strong enough to overcome the ethnic, cultural, and sexist prejudices which would handicap a civilian government in Nigeria" (1989:88).

Each chapter in this volume explores the extent, and limits, of Hausa women's power in varied circumstances; indeed, some authors have incorporated the public-private dichotomy into their analyses. Three chapters in particular deal specifically with issues of women's power and authority. In her chapter on royal wives in Kano, Beverly Mack traces a portrait of women as rulers and conquering warriors from legends and other historical sources. After the sixteenth century, with the spread of Islam, and especially after the Fulani jihad and establishment of the Sokoto Caliphate, evidence of such roles for women in Hausaland decreases considerably. Mack contrasts these earlier images with the experiences of royal women today. Contemporary women's roles, she maintains, reflect the loss of earlier political standing and a transformation in the exercise of power to more indirect forms. Secluded in the palace of the emir, royal wives would seem to be cut off from public affairs. Yet Mack contends that they hold significant power over other individuals, male and female, outside as well as inside the palace. She cites historical incidents in which royal mothers and wives played major roles in succession disputes, in starting or preventing wars, and in this century in their husbands' dealings with British colonial officials. Today such women act as conduits of particular information to the emirs, developing and advocating specific interests such as education and advising and pressing their concerns with the emirs.

Against this account of royal women's concerns and powers, Allan Christelow's contribution brings into sharp focus the experiences of nonroyal Hausa women in the early 1900s, in particular their legal freedom and power struggles as widows. He points out that free women who were widowed were frequently in an opportune position to maintain the property and estate left by their husbands. Christelow traces this fact to social policy emanating from the emir's judicial council which aimed at preventing the breakup of household property rather than explicitly protecting the rights of women. Widows with children were often able to hold their husband's estate in trust for them, although they could not alienate any portion of the estate. Unable to marry again and maintain possession of the trust, such women relied upon the labor of slaves to manage their land and houses, and kept slave women who bore children to increase the size of their households. However, there were several limitations on the power of women in this situation. Women without children often found it difficult to maintain their land rights against encroachers, and even those with children were less able to resist the loss of land and houses that were part of family holdings when the availability of slaves decreased after British declarations took effect. Furthermore, inheritance rules and property rights were ineffective in preventing acts of violence sometimes committed when co-wives, concubines, or members of the husband's family contested a widow's legal rights.

Concentrating on the fundamental transformation of the formal political system underway today in Nigeria, Barbara Callaway's chapter chronicles many of the major changes which occurred in Kano City from the 1950s into the 1980s, and their relevance for the interests of Hausa women. In particular she stresses the role of Mallam Aminu Kano and the People's Redemption Party (PRP) in challenging the exclusion of women from public life and formal political processes. Before the franchise was extended to women in the north, women's wings of the major political parties were established, although it was popularly believed that prostitutes made up a majority of the members, and no real power or leadership was exercised by women in them. Callaway notes that many male leaders opposed the vote for women, which was extended by a military decree in 1976; only later did they realize the importance of women's votes for advancing northern interests in federal elections. Callaway's analysis rests on the notion that advances for women in the north can only be won through justification of their worth within Islam. She further suggests that fundamental changes in society are needed to prepare women to take up the roles in public office and government for which Aminu Kano and the PRP fought.

Callaway clearly sets out the challenge that Hausa women face in both Nigeria and Niger today: how to advance their interests and gain access to the channels of public policy making while maintaining their cultural and religious identity. It is a difficult prospect for both the educated, elite Hausa woman and her illiterate rural counterpart. There is ample evidence to suggest that a trend may be in motion that will challenge the severe restrictions imposed on women in Hausaland since the jihad in 1804. Although not in control of the reins of government, Muslim Hausa women are increasing their presence in public life. At the same time, they continue to exert power within their households, and many have indicated that they do not view their domestic activities as separate from new roles they may be assuming outside the home.

Women in a Changing Economy

Many estimates of Hausa women's participation in the economy have suffered from the inaccuracies that have plagued quantitative analyses of African women's work generally (Stichter 1984). Reliable census data and economic statistics either are lacking, or focus entirely on the formal sector of the economy in which women participate only to a limited degree. Furthermore, much of the labor carried out by women, such as unpaid domestic labor and income-generating activities conducted in or from the home, is not recognized as work and is not amenable to measurement through the application of concepts (such as active labor) currently in use (Fapohunda 1978; Beneria 1981).

The underestimation of Hausa women's work and contributions to the economy, particularly as represented in Nigerian census data collected since 1911, is a particular problem. Renee Pittin finds that in censuses from 1921 through 1963 (from which the last official census figures date) women's work categories were frequently confused and their work activities inaccurately recorded (1987: 30–36), resulting in "gross undervaluation of Northern women's labour in the statistics. A mere 12.8 per cent of the adult female population in the North was included in the labour force, compared with 32.4 per cent in the Eastern Region, and 62.1 per cent in the (largely Yoruba) Western Region with its long tradition of female traders" (1984a:479). This undervaluation has serious implications. First, it produces an inaccurate view of women's—and by implication, men's—actual activities and behaviors. Equally important, however, is that ignoring Hausa women's contributions to the economy could lead to gross underestimation of total economic activity in the area and thus to potentially inaccurate data that would be of questionable use in development planning.

Fortunately, qualitative studies have at least partially offset the shortcomings of census data by providing detailed accounts of women's work in income-earning occupations and as unpaid domestic and family farm laborers. Polly Hill has described the "hidden" trading activities of rural Hausa women in the village of Batagarawa (northern Katsina Emirate), portraying a "honeycomb-market" in which women trade in grain and other commodities from inside their compounds in a fully competitive system which (she maintains) is the equivalent of a marketplace (1969, 1972:268–69; see also Mary Smith 1981; M. G. Smith 1955). Emmy Simmons has studied Hausa women's occupations in rural Zaria, particularly food processing, and addresses the problems of measuring and documenting female productive activities (1975, 1976). Renee Pittin's original study (1979a) attacks the dominant perspective of marriage as a Hausa woman's sole "career" option, arguing that unmarried adult women in the old city of Katsina select from among a number of income-earning activities both inside and outside of marriage. Benson and Duffield (1979) find that in Gwagwarwa, a community near Kano City, women's occupational opportunities and potential for capital accumulation are limited by poverty and competition with women of other ethnic groups. Other scholars have added to our knowledge of Hausa women's productive activities in both rural and urban contexts, for women of different ages and classes (Remy 1975; Pittin 1976; Jackson 1978; Schildkrout 1979, 1983; Longhurst 1982; Coles 1983a, 1983b). A few have considered the effect of colonial rule and associated economic changes on women's labor, pointing out both the negative and positive influences (C. Martin 1983; Knipp 1987).

One occupation not yet systematically studied, but which appears to provide opportunities for substantial income, savings, and a certain degree of social mobility for Hausa women, is prostitution (Barkow 1971; Pittin 1983). In many locations Hausa women move back and forth from marriage to independent status as prostitutes (Cohen 1969). Little or no information exists on specific numbers or income levels of prostitutes (Frishman, this volume). However, their socioeconomic position is vulnerable in times of social stress, such as during droughts or other disasters, when they have been ordered by officials to either marry or leave the community (Pittin 1984b).

Clearly, women in Hausa society today are active in income-earning occupations. Most earn income through the preparation and sale of cooked food, sewing, weaving, trade (both petty and large-scale), midwifery, herbalism, and prostitution. Children, older women, and males assist secluded women by procuring needed items or selling their products outside compounds. Earnings are low for many of these activities, and the more lucrative occupations are frequently carried out by older women no longer secluded, as they tend to require mobility or the exercise of ritual power. In rural Hausaland, as elsewhere, women have not benefited from agricultural extension services and efforts to improve productivity directed at their male counterparts, and their agricultural wage labor is poorly paid and frequently insecure (Jackson 1985).

Closely related to the productive work of Hausa women are activities involved in reproduction and domestic labor. Childbearing and childrearing may actually increase the demands on Hausa women to earn an income. In a study in Kano City, Judith Harrington found a correlation between high fertility and a woman's assumption of responsibility for the provision of basic household subsistence necessities: about half of those women with the highest nutritional burdens from frequent pregnancy and lactation contributed most toward the family's subsistence needs (1983). Studying a rural Hausa village in Niger, Ralph Faulkingham notes a probable decline in female fertility associated with periods of poor nutrition (1977). The precise relationship between the demands of childbearing and other reproductive activities on women and their occupational activities remains to be adequately researched, though Barbara Entwisle and Catherine Coles suggest that family planning and fertility surveys provide a potential source of data already in existence but previously unused in consideration of such questions (1990). But the heavy burdens on women resulting from the demands of income-earning occupational activities, reproduction, and domestic labor, if not addressed and alleviated, may result in a decline in the subsistence levels of children and men as well as being detrimental to women themselves.

In this volume two chapters present data on Muslim Hausa women's occupational activities, emphasizing the important contributions which women make to basic subsistence, particularly to families living in poverty. Catherine Coles's study of women in Kaduna examines women's occupations in a Hausa community outside of Hausaland. Living among Ibo, Yoruba, and other migrants from around the country, in a city that was created under colonial rule, Hausa residents in Kaduna live in compounds that are not kin-based but rather include nuclear families renting rooms. Strict seclusion is not possible for

Hausa women under these circumstances, although many claim to be secluded. Kaduna women carry out many of the same activities that are performed in the old cities of Kano, Katsina, and other locations from which they have come, but competition and poverty have caused some occupations, such as weaving of cloth, to be dropped. Coles documents a division of female occupations on the basis of age and seclusion status, noting that middle-aged and older women frequently have higher incomes and practice occupations that provide them with high status and prestige in the community. Such occupations invariably involve the exercise of ritual powers or mobility or both. Yet it is frequently younger women of childbearing age, more constrained in their movement and occupational choices, who must help meet the subsistence needs of their family in a worsening economy.

Alan Frishman's chapter on Kano City deals with a setting in which a majority of households live below the poverty level (see also Mack 1980). In these households, as in Kaduna, women's informal sector earnings are crucial to basic subsistence, providing up to a third of total family income. Yet Frishman finds that many of women's informal sector occupations have been either eliminated or severely restricted in the course of industrialization and implementation of "capital-intensive production," illustrating how vulnerable their position is in the economy. Using data from several surveys of workers, Frishman estimates what he believes to be typical incomes for households to which women contribute; and using Enid Schildkrout's (1981) figures on earnings of Kano women, he estimates approximately 135 naira per year for women in seclusion and up to 190 naira for women in small-scale industries. (Both figures are lower than those found by Coles for Hausa women in Kaduna.) Participation by women as manager-owners in small-scale industries in the informal sector and in formal sector industrial work bring considerably higher earnings, but he found few women working in this capacity.

A goal of development efforts in many locations including Nigeria has been to increase women's access to formal sector activities. Such a priority appears especially important in Hausa society given the evidence provided by Coles, Frishman, and others concerning women's contributions to basic family subsistence. Largely as a result of Western secular education and new occupational opportunities associated with a modernizing, industrializing economy, the movement of Hausa women into the formal economy is occurring, albeit slowly. However, their lack of involvement in formal efforts to plan and implement economic development programs is directly related to women's absence from formal political processes and public policy making.

Different Voices: Feminine Gender in Ritual, the Arts, and Media

Among the Hausa, the traditional separation of the sexes has meant that women's roles as artist and audience have been relatively inaccessible to researchers. Consequently women's artistic roles are as little documented as their historical and socioeconomic roles. In addition, cultural expressions of gender in *bori* and the arts have not produced a uniform image of women's position in society.

In fact, Hausa women are indeed creative artists, performing and producing music, praise song, and written poetry, and working in various communication media. Those who earn their living by dancing, singing extemporaneously, and creating oral poetry for celebratory events are often marginal members of society, neither deferring to nor enjoying the financial support of a husband in accord with Islamic tenets. Nevertheless, they are much in demand among devout Muslim audiences and are well compensated for their endeavors. Their social status and financial status are often inversely proportional. Others whose creative work takes them out of their homes are proper, married women whose liberal husbands condone their writing poetry for teaching purposes, editing a newspaper column, broadcasting television and radio shows, or acting in itinerant drama troupes (Mack 1981, 1983, 1986; Beik 1987). Finally, among traditional secluded Hausa women there are many nonprofessional artists who paint or compose verse only for their own pleasure and that of close friends (Mack 1986). The habit of Hausa women's writing religious and topical verse in Arabic form was begun by Nana Asma'u, the jihad leader's own daughter, who used verse to teach men and women religion (Hiskett 1973; Boyd and Last 1985; Boyd 1989). Thus Hausa Muslim women are indeed literary and performing artists; neither the custom of wife seclusion nor religious philosophy precludes their creative expression.

Hausa celebratory events are often, though not exclusively, keyed to Muslim festivals of collective and individual import. The nature of participation in such festivities depends on both the festival itself and one's gender. Celebrations like the annual *salla* processions that follow the month of Ramadan are male-oriented. Women's celebrations take place within homes, usually in larger, more affluent households with their greater numbers of regular women residents; other women from throughout the neighborhood are invited to attend. Royal women celebrate *salla* festivities inside the palace (Mack 1981). Weddings and naming days provide other opportunities for women to leave their chores and gather for a day of feasting, gift giving, music, and dance. Women musicians are hired for these occasions, and singing and dancing continue on into the night. Women's festivities, as much as men's, mark important events on the Muslim calendar.

If the celebratory events mandated by Islam reflect the gender division inherent in Muslim beliefs, one might logically look to non-Islamic celebratory events as arenas for more egalitarian performance among men and women. Ostensibly, this is the situation provided by the *bori* cult of spirit possession, which relies on music, song, and dance to effect its curative aim. In *bori* both men and women act as audience and participants. Illness is "cured" through possession of a patient by a spirit capable of purging him or her of the particular affliction (Palmer 1914; Besmer 1973a, 1973b, 1975, 1983; Bourguignon 1973). The origins of *bori* are not clear: some sources explain the cult as a remnant of pre-jihad Maguzawa spirit worship (Tremearne 1914; Greenberg 1946). Others argue for its post-jihad evolution, as a reaction to Islam's strictures on women's social roles (Nicolas 1967; Broustra 1972). Through curing, an individual is relieved of marginality by becoming integrated into an alternative social order; participation in the cult is thus viewed as a means of expressing grievances linked with subordinate social status (I. M. Lewis 1966, 1971; Beattie and Middleton 1969). Yet other scholars focus on the very real physical complaints that are cured through spirit possession rites, specifically for women (Berger 1976; Spring 1978). Murray Last's study of a "stereotyped" illness among the non-Muslim Maguzawa allows for both interpretations, suggesting that the kinds of illnesses cured through *bori* and similar rites are, for women, primarily strategies against role expectations associated with particular stages in the life cycle and only secondarily against men (Last 1979b).

Among the Hausa the *bori* cult has been assumed by many to be practiced through an egalitarian, if not an inverted, social and gender hierarchy, in which deviants and inferiors assume positions of power. Female adepts, some of them prostitutes, are instrumental in the performance and maintenance of *bori* (King 1966, 1967; Besmer 1983). Nicole Echard's chapter here on *bori* in the Ader region of Niger reveals, however, that the rules of the cult's functioning only appear to assert the equality of the sexes. The cult seems to provide a rare context for male-female social relation in that some female spirits hold places of importance in the pantheon, and women in *bori* supposedly move beyond their normative role expectations in society. But Echard demonstrates that *bori* actually reinforces the masculine dominance that characterizes Hausa society in Ader: there are greater numbers of male versus female spirits in the pantheon, and those deemed most important are male. Furthermore, male adepts tend to be possessed by more important spirits associated with social positions relatively recent in origin and are more likely to be the chief of *bori*.

In rural Ader, as elsewhere in Hausaland, *bori* is an integral part of social organization. New spirits are added to the pantheon as the figures they represent emerge in a modernizing and changing society. Clearly Echard's findings need to be tested in other locations and contexts, especially those in which Hausa women can and do maintain themselves through productive activities, apart from their roles as wives and mothers. For example, in large urban centers, where processes of social change may be occurring more quickly and with consequently varied forms, it is possible that the functioning of *bori* and the pantheon itself might represent different aspects of gender relations. Nevertheless, her conclusions are of paramount importance to future research on *bori* and should result in a reexamination of many previous studies.

As with their active involvement in *bori,* Hausa women have also long been literary artists. Some women, often daughters of Muslim scholars, are trained in Islamic literary traditions and write long verse in Arabic literary style. Their subjects include eulogy, religious instruction, historical accounts, politics, and explanation of widespread social change. Although such poetry by men has been published in Hausa for over sixty years, the first volume by women was produced in 1983 by Hauwa Gwaram and 'Yar Shehu. Entitled *'Alƙalami a Hannun Mata'—A Pen in the Hands of Women,* this anthology of verse has been popular since its appearance, especially for use in literacy classes for adult women. Other women, often nonliterate, are performing artists whose extemporaneous chanting may be a praise song for an emir, or, embellished with body gesture, a song for wedding and naming ceremonies (Mack 1981, 1983, 1986). Both written and oral poetry are known as *waƙa* (pl. *waƙoƙi*).

Oral narratives satisfy and shape an audience's aesthetic sensibilities and effect social change through the messages conveyed (Skinner 1969, 1977a, 1977b). Through the telling of them women pass a perception of their own capability along to the next generation. Children are socialized as well as entertained by these tales in which women are cast in traditional domestic roles, yet are not portrayed as dependent. Rather, they actively seek ways to challenge their husbands, and regularly triumph in the ensuing intramarital competition. Underlining their superiority in the tales' competitions is the fact that these female antagonists are in alliance with both natural and supernatural forces.

Connie Stephens' analysis of four oral narratives (*tatsuniya, tatsuniyoyi* [pl.]) proposes that they offer a counterpoint to the ideology of gender portrayed in Islam. A pre-Islamic tradition that carries many images long present in Hausaland, *tatsuniyoyi* nevertheless contain many Islamic themes acquired through the history of their telling. The image of women presented in them is of independence and even superiority to men. Women's cultural roles are expressed in and sustained by their culinary and reproductive activities—traditional aspects of their roles. Yet Stephens demonstrates that in the narratives when these cultural roles are combined with women's natural and supernatural powers, their husbands, representing worldly political authority, have no chance against women. Although it might be argued that the narratives' feminist symbolism is mere response to patriarchal constraints on women, Stephens argues effectively that such symbolism reflects a degree of power not recognized overtly in a Muslim framework. Furthermore, the fact that narratives told by Hausa women have rarely received the attention they deserve as literary artistry has precluded an appreciation of the messages they contain. As political satire and mechanisms of socialization and entertainment, narratives offer commentary on gender roles and categories that does not translate into female subordination and male domination.

Hausa drama (*wasan kwaikwayo*) is popular in different forms throughout

the means of production have a great deal to offer in increasing our general understanding of Hausa society. Yet they have been largely ignored by scholars studying the Hausa. Claire Robertson describes the dangers of such a course: "When women's studies is ghettoized by some who work in it but by more who work outside of it, separate becomes not only unequal in influence but also inaccurate" (1987:97).

The contributions here provide perspectives on women's lives as Muslims, on their power and positions in the status-prestige system, on their participation in the economy, and on feminine gender as it is represented in the arts, media, and ritual. The analyses offered move beyond norms, ideology, and formal structures to examine actual behavior, showing that the degree and limitations of women's power and authority vary by age, class, ethnic identity, and particular context. This is an important first step not only toward understanding women's experiences, but also toward reinterpreting how power is distributed and exercised within Hausa society as a whole. We hope this volume serves to encourage further research toward these ends.

PART 1. HAUSA WOMEN IN ISLAM

2 *Balaraba B. M. Sule and Priscilla E. Starratt*

Islamic Leadership Positions for Women in Contemporary Kano Society

This chapter reports on the lives of several contemporary women in Kano, Nigeria, who occupy significant leadership roles of an Islamic nature. Although it is premature to base any generalizations about the society as a whole on such a small sampling, we will indicate new directions for further research. Earlier studies have been criticized for giving excessive attention to the role of women in spirit possession cults and the use of Islam to socialize women to accept their subordination to men (Boyd and Last 1985:284).[1] In a plea for research on female scholars, saints, poets, teachers, and leaders in Muslim Africa, Boyd and Last asked, "If women in these Islamic societies really are so concerned with things religious, is it not very probable that a proportion of women will also prove to be pious Muslims—a category admittedly harder (and less exciting) to research?" (1985:284). Such pious Muslim women certainly do exist, and among them are a number who have leadership roles of a specifically Islamic nature, suggesting that women are not just marginally involved in the Islamic faith. The roles of these women as scholars, teachers, mystics, and social workers necessitates a reexamination of the previous, stereotyped descriptions of Muslim women in Nigeria on a much wider basis.

1. For example, "*Bori* thus provides women with a symbolic escape from the pervasive 'maleness' of Islam . . ." and "Extensive survey research in Kano clearly establishes that women support the 'Islamic way of life' and by implication their subordinate status." (Callaway 1984: 438, 444–45).

We begin this study with a look at opinions about the position of women in Islam. Unless the controversial nature of women's actual position in Islam is understood, the implications of Islam for future roles of Kano women will not be appreciated.[2] We will then present the results of our field research concerning contemporary Kano women in Islamic leadership roles.

The Position of Women in Islam

The status accorded to women by the Muslim faith is much disputed, even or rather especially, among Muslims themselves. The Moroccan sociologist Fatima Mernissi noted, "The controversy has raged throughout this century between traditionalists, who claim Islam prohibits any changes in the sexes' roles, and the modernists, who claim that Islam allows for the liberation of women, the desegregation of the society and the equality of the sexes" (1975:xv). The opinions of other Muslim scholars and intellectuals can be found somewhere between the two poles. Depending on which scholar is consulted, which country or culture is observed, and which century or decade is represented, the Islamic view on the role of women can be radically different. Why is this? First, today there is no central legal authority in Islam that dispenses and enforces legal uniformity. There are four major Islamic law schools, which sometimes treat issues differently. Even within any one law school, individual jurists and scholars may interpret laws differently. Advanced Muslim scholars are allowed to reinterpret the evidence of the four sources of law (the Qur'an, the Prophet's acts and sayings, analogy, and the consensus of the scholarly community) in order to arrive at their own, fresh conclusions through the process of independent reasoning (Ar. *ijtihad*). There are several biographies of the Prophet Muhammad (Ar. *sira*) and many divergent collections of his reputed sayings (Ar. *hadith*). Contemporary and local thinking are injected into Islamic law through the principles of the consensus of the region's scholars (Ar. *ijma'*) and analogy (Ar. *qiyas*) of old laws with new situations. The wide geographical distribution and range of cultures of Islamic societies owes much to the flexibility of its laws and tenets in the face of local culture and belief. Islam is found in such diverse countries as Iran, the Soviet Union, Sudan, Morocco, Zanzibar, Syria, the United States, Great Britain, South Africa, Malaysia, India, France,

2. The term "Kano women" is preferable to "Hausa women of Kano," for although most women in Kano City can speak Hausa, they may not be of strictly Hausa backgrounds. Hausa culture no doubt has a strong influence, but since Kano has been a huge trading emporium for centuries, its culture is blended with elements from North Africa, Mali, the Sahara, Borno, southern Nigeria, and the Sudan. There is also a strong Fulani effect on Kano culture: the Fulani have provided the traditional rulers since 1807 and have intermarried with Kano women. Attitudes about the correct position of women in Islam may vary from city quarter to city quarter because of the different backgrounds of Kano people.

Turkey, the Philippines, Israel, Libya, Saudi Arabia, China, and Malawi. Unless they directly contravene one of the five basic pillars of the faith—witness that there is one God and Muhammad is His Prophet; fasting for the month of Ramadan; pilgrimage to Mecca, if one can afford it; tithing; and prayer five times a day—most local customs (*al'ada*), are initially tolerated and are often respected as social laws. The position of Islam on women's roles and rights has often reflected these customs rather than the actual legal recommendations of Islam (Ar. *shari'a*), in many areas of the Muslim world.

For example, Abdur Rahman I. Doi argues that veils and seclusion were not originally part of Islam but were adopted as Islamic culture when Islam spread to other Middle Eastern and Asian countries beyond Arabia (1984:291). Then Islamic laws were interpreted to support veiling and seclusion, just as today they are being reinterpreted to end these practices. As another instance, in Kano, Nigeria, it is widely believed that Islam awards custody of children to the father in case of divorce, despite the fact that Islamic law clearly states that the mother is the first person to be given custody of the children (Lemu 1986:20). The husband is supposed to be the seventh person considered. Furthermore, in Kano it is widely believed that most men would not support another man's children in their home and that few men would pay child support for children being raised in another man's home. So it is assumed that children "must" belong to the father or the father's side of the family. The father's family is thus considered the relevant family. Given these beliefs, it is not surprising that some local religious scholars and judges say that Islam awards custody of children to the father, for the function of all courts everywhere is to uphold the beliefs and values of the society. Local customs and marriage patterns have in this case distorted the original intention of Islamic law. Women do not usually form a new, solid family unit with their husbands when they marry. Serial marriage is common and most marriages are polygynous. Divorce is also common, and the tradition of marrying young girls to older men leaves many young widows in the society. Whether divorced or widowed, young women are pressured to remarry quickly. It is not unusual for a woman to have had from three to eight marriages during her life and to spend her later years with no husband at all. Between and after her marriages, a woman usually returns to live with her father, elder brother, or eventually a grown son. So it is this patriarchial nature of the society reflected in local custom that has more influence on the domestic lives of women than the *shari'a*. Family life in some other Muslim countries looks entirely different.

As an Asian Muslim, Doi found much to criticize about the treatment of Muslim women in Nigeria. From his position as director of the Centre for Islamic Legal Studies at Ahmadu Bello University in Zaria, Doi expressed regret at the role of women in the Muslim Bamidele community of western Nigeria:

It is a pity that Alhaji Bamidele is unaware of the status of equality conferred upon women in Islam. In Yorubaland, where women along with men are bread winners for their families, the Bamidele women are forced to remain in purdah (Eleha). In fact, the Bamidele women, too, are deplorably ignorant of their equal social status and the legal rights conferred upon them by the religion of Islam. Times have changed. Social thought has advanced and the progressive Muslim nations have adjusted themselves to the changes in their environment, except a few Indo-Pakistani Muslims and some extremists in the Middle East who are ignorant of the fact that the true Islam enjoins on women a modest conduct and not that type of seclusion behind veils. . . . The Qur'an, by using the words for the type of dress regarded as decent by the Arabs, merely emphasizes the idea of decency and not some particular type of dress. It is not the literal meaning of the words but the spirit behind them that the Qur'an wishes to bring home to Muslim women. . . . Islam requires the equal observance of modesty and chastity by both sexes, and does not demand the rigid segregation of men and women, as is sometimes wrongly suggested. It is true that the Qur'an demands careful behaviour in the presence of opposite sexes, which means that there may arise obvious dangers to virtues when a man and a woman, not closely related to each other, associate in private and informally, but there is no Islamic reason why men and women should not meet and co-operate under conditions, for religious, cultural, social, educational or occupational purposes. (1984:289–91)

It is clear from Doi's statement that Alhaji Salami Bamidele believes Islam requires women to be fully veiled and secluded; Doi does not. Both men are well-educated scholars, but their opinions about what Islam decrees for women differ sharply. The role accorded to women by Islam then is very ambiguous and a subject of controversy among Muslim scholars. A whole range of opinions about women could be found in Nigeria today, and women there who wish to expand their traditional roles can ally themselves with those scholars who support the equality of women. The fact that Kano women today are using Islam to justify their bid for a larger public role in life means they are increasing the likelihood of achieving their goals. If they used Western feminism or secular socialism as the framework of their aspirations, their chances for success would be diminished.

Although the situation of women in Kano is strongly influenced by local custom, which may prevail over Islamic law, Islam nevertheless has a pervasive effect on women's lives. It shapes women's views about birth, childhood, marriage, and death, and it answers their questions about the supernatural and what happens after death. Their religion affects the way Kano women eat, cook, wash, dress, recreate, and do their marketing. It is certain that there are women (and men) in Kano who consult *bori* specialists. Yet many *bori* specialists consider themselves Muslims, and some of the people who consult them for medicine or advice are devout Muslims who also fulfill their Islamic religious obligations. Just like men, Kano Muslim women are assiduous in their ablutions, prayers, and fasting, and they place great importance on making the pilgrimage to Mecca (Ar. *hajj*). Women do much of the special work associated with the month of fasting, including the preparation of heavy meals of special foods for fast-breaking. They also look forward to the two great Muslim holiday celebrations (*salla*), when they send gifts and food to others.

Women in Kano are not isolated from the rest of the world. Some attend conferences at home and abroad, traveling to nearby Minna or Kaduna or as far as Iran, Libya, the Sudan, Germany, or Great Britain. They read international Islamic magazines and books and share what they read with their Muslim sisters. The local media are also being used by Muslim women to improve their status. In an article entitled "The Ideal Muslim Husband," Hajiya Aisha Lemu, the president of the Federation of Muslim Women's Associations in Nigeria, sought to explain the rights of Muslim women by stressing the way the Prophet Muhammad treated his wives. She referred to passages of the Qur'an and *hadith* literature to support a woman's right to go out of the home for valid reasons, to retain custody of her children in case of divorce, to discuss serious issues on an equal footing with her husband, to claim a divorce for a host of good reasons, and to expect kind and amusing company from her husband without any threat of physical brutality (Lemu 1986).

Access to international publications and the written opinions of respected Muslim figures like Professor Doi or Hajiya Lemu give Kano women the necessary support to challenge their customary roles. Foreign and national television and radio play a part too. Radio Kano broadcasts have included a weekly program by Alƙali Ali Gaya Yusuf on the rights of wives and husbands in Islamic marriage. One young girl who was given in marriage to an old man against her wishes because the bridegroom brought a large gift to her father ran away and appeared at the radio station for help. Alƙali Yusuf and radio staff member Hajiya Mairo Muhammed took the girl home and tried to instruct the father that it was not Islamic to give a daughter in marriage without her consent (interview, Alƙali Yusuf, February 23, 1986).[3]

Through better education and the media, Kano women hear views that they can use to improve their positions substantially and increase their control over the major decisions affecting their lives. Every day they see more examples of women working outside the home, occupying leadership roles in the society. It is in this wider framework of Islam and the status of women that the following research on women's Islamic leadership positions in Kano needs to be placed in order to evaluate its implications for the society as a whole. Although a wider

3. For a view on forced marriage, see Baveja (1979:59–60): "All these Traditions go to establish the fact that no person can give away a girl in marriage without her consent, and if he does so, the girl has a right to get the marriage cancelled by applying to a Court of Law."

and more public role for women is still much debated among Muslim scholars, the above discussion indicates that there are many progressive Muslim voices for Kano women to draw upon to justify desired changes.

Contemporary Islamic Leadership Positions among Kano Women

In the Kano Muslim community certain Islamic leadership positions for women have emerged. By focusing on these leadership roles, we will see that Islam in Kano does not reject female leaders and their participation in religious activities. Evidence suggests that this has been true at least since the early nineteenth century.

The Muslim women considered here—scholars, mystics, and social workers—occupy roles that may exist in other contemporary Muslim societies.[4] They are roles currently in existence, not carryovers from pre-Islamic Kano society. Attention to them provides an important perspective on the variety of options open to devout Muslim Hausa-Fulani women.

Women in Kano possess a full range of educational standards. Although some girls in rural areas may not even be sent to Qur'anic school, many girls do attend, especially in the cities. A child is literate once he or she learns the Arabic alphabet, which is phonetic, for this enables one to write any spoken language in the Arabic script. Throughout Muslim Africa, converts to Islam were able to read and write their own local languages in Arabic script just by spending a few weeks learning the Arabic alphabet. Arabic script used in writing other languages like Hausa or Fulfulde is called *ajami* or "foreign." Therefore these students become literate in *ajami,* even though they may never finish reading the Qur'an. The women scholars in this study, however, have gone much further than this stage.

Among the women scholars interviewed, almost all had achieved an advanced understanding of Arabic grammar and vocabulary, thus they need not depend on their teachers or husbands for definitions or translations but could form their own ideas about religion. Less well educated women in the study had all attended Qur'anic school to some extent, even though they did not learn Arabic. Some women also attended western or European (*boko*) schools as well. The scholars interviewed had all acquired much more education than the average Hausa-Fulani individual in Kano, but four of the other women in the study are more typical in not having completed their Qur'anic educations.

4. Research for this study was conducted between March and August 1986 by taped oral interviews. The women interviewed were: Hajiya Rabi Wali (March 31 and April 5), Hajiya Aisha Mahmoud (April 13), Hajiya Sadiya dan Iya Aminu (April 23), Hajiya Hassana Sufi (April 26), Hajiya Iya Isiyaku (April 29), Hajiya Maria Mai Tafsiri (May 1), Hajiya Yelwa Ina (May 4), Hajiya Hauwa Idi Kabara (June 21), Hajiya Laraba Kabara (June 21), Hajiya Saude Datti (July 28), and Hajiya Hauwa Adamu (August 14).

The Scholars

One of the most prominent features of the Islamic religion is its emphasis on learning and literacy as a religious obligation. This admonition applies equally to men and women. A famous saying from the *hadith* states, "The seeking of knowledge is obligatory upon every Muslim man and woman" (quoted in Doi 1970:115). Another *hadith* says, "Whoever brings up two sisters or two daughters and gives them a broad education and treats them well and gives them in marriage, for him is Paradise" (quoted in Lemu 1986:20).

Among the Prophet's wives, Aisha was responsible for transmitting 1,210 *hadith* by teaching them to scholars and jurists who came to consult her, and Hafsa was a Qur'anic scholar who was made the official guardian of the authentic Qur'anic manuscripts for the Muslim community (Galadanci 1971:6–7). Thus in eighth-century Arabia, when Islam was still a new religion, it encouraged the education of women and respected its female scholars. Ten centuries later, jihad leader Usman dan Fodio claimed that one of the errors of the Hausa *malamai* was that they left their wives in ignorance:

(Help is with God) A chapter relating the matters which have become a general misfortune in this land, I mean the land of the Hausa, which are getting worse, and indeed which are a general calamity in the lands. For example, what many of the 'ulama' of this land do in leaving wives, daughters, and servants neglected in the way of their beliefs and the rules of their ablutions, and their prayers and their fasting, and other things whose learning God has obligated for them, and what is allowed them and permitted for them, such as questions of their business transactions, and what is similar to their business transactions, and this is a great error, and a forbidden innovation. They have made them like a dish which they use until it is broken, and then they throw it away in a trash pile or an unclean place. O how astonishing! How they leave their wives and daughters and slaves in the darkness of ignorance and shadow, and yet they teach their students morning and evening. And what is this but their own error because they teach their students hypocrisy and pride. And this is a great error because the teaching of wives and daughters and slaves is obligatory, and the teaching of students is voluntary. And the teaching of students is not obligatory for the teacher unless there is no other teacher, then it is obligatory for him to teach, but only after teaching his people, because the priority is first before everything else. O Muslim women, do not listen to the misleading words of those in error, who deceive you by commanding you to'obey your husbands without commanding you to obey God and His Apostle (may God bless him and grant him salvation). And they say that the happiness of a woman is in obedience to her husband. This is nothing but seeking their desire and their wish from you.

And they require of you what neither God nor His messenger make obligatory for you by birth, such as cooking, washing clothes, and other things which are mostly what they desire; while not requiring of you what God and His Apostle (may God bless him and grant him salvation) oblige for you in the way of obedience to God and obedience to His Apostle. Yes, it is obligatory for the wife to obey her husband both in private and in public, even if her husband is very wretched or a slave. And it is forbidden for her to go against her husband except when he commands her to disobey God Most High. Then it becomes necessary for her to refuse to obey, because there is no obedience to the created in disobedience to the Creator. And also when a woman obeys her husband, her reward is double, but after obeying God and His Prophet. (Quoted in Wali 1980:14).

By contrast, the Shehu educated his wives and daughters and strictly defended the right of women to attend public preaching and instruction together with men, provided that they were modestly dressed and sat slightly apart (Doi 1984:322). Many of the Shehu's daughters were famous scholars, including Khadija, who translated the noted law book, the *Mukhtasar* of Khalil, from Arabic into Fulfulde, and Nana Asma'u, who was an authority on the Qur'an and *hadith* and preached in Arabic, Tamasheq, and Hausa in addition to her mother tongue, Fulfulde (Galadanci 1971:9; *Research Bulletin* 1972:33–34). The women of the jihad community organized teams called "Yan Taru," which traveled in caravans to bring Islamic knowledge to women in rural areas; their successors exist in the region today (Boyd and Last 1985:289–92). Thus the religious tradition of the Sokoto caliphate clearly endorsed the education of women.

In this system of traditional Islamic education, children start at local Qur'anic schools (*makarantun allo*). From ages three to twelve, they learn to read the alphabet and go on to read the full sixty portions into which the 114 chapters of the Qur'an are divided. When this is complete, they are exposed to introductory works in Islamic fields of scholarship, including law (*fikihu*), traditions (*hadisi*), belief in the oneness of Allah (*tauhidi*), biography of the Prophet (*sira*), and Arabic grammar (*nahawu*).[5] The study of these works is often followed or accompanied by a second reading or revision of the reading of the Qur'an for better pronunciation, recitation, and understanding. This introduction to the various subjects of Islamic learning takes place in the upper-level Muslim schools and can last until age twenty or so.[6] Some students then start more advanced work with *malamai* who have specialized in particular fields to study famous books one by one. When they have mastered a book, the *malam* writes a diploma for that work which entitles them, in turn, to teach it to others. Some advanced students take up the study of Qur'anic exegesis of *tafsiri*, the careful analysis of the Qur'an according to linguistic, historical, theological, and other criteria.

Although it is not unusual to see very young girls studying their Qur'anic slates along with boys, after a certain age the girls disappear from public, giving the impression that girls cease to be taught above a certain level. But,

---

5. See the list of books studied by these women in the chapter appendix for an example of what is meant by a selection of introductory works in the various fields of Islamic knowledge.

6. For a description of the traditional Islamic educational system, see Abdurrahman and Canham 1978:50–56; U. Hassan 1978; Hiskett 1973:33–39; Paden 1986:75–80.

in fact, as in most Muslim countries, the advanced education of girls in Kano traditionally is in the hands of fathers, brothers, and husbands, rather than in the higher Islamic instititutions reserved for men: "This disparity in educational facilities for men and women in Muslim communities caused a great deal of misconception with regard to the position of women in Islam; and this subsequently led some people to believe erroneously that Islam abhors and discourages female education" (Galadanci 1971:5).

Contrary to cliché, the traditional system of Islamic education in Kano has long produced female scholars and teachers. Some of the women interviewed for this study had solely been educated privately; others had combined traditional, private education with some type of public government schooling or employment. Three of the women interviewed had been taught and employed completely privately. Hajiya Iya Isiaku, Hajiya Aisha Mahmoud, and Hajiya Maria Mai Tafsiri are prime examples of female scholars educated in Kano.

Hajiya Iya Isiaku of Rijiyar Lemo was educated in the home of her husband, the late Madakin Kano Alhaji Shehu Ahmad. Her teachers included the children of the Madaki's *malam,* a woman sent from the Emir's Palace named Gwaggo Kahu, and the Madaki's own children. Under their tuition she completed reading the Qur'an (the Hausa expression is *'ta sauki Alkur'an'*—i.e., she graduated), and read *Ahalari* and *Kawa'idi.* After her husband died, she ran an evening Islamiyya school for about thirty married women in Yola Quarter until she remarried.

Hajiya Aisha Mahmoud is a widow living in Galadanci Quarter. She was educated by her father and successive husbands. Even though she had six children, she was able to finish and revise her reading of the Qur'an and read *Kawa'idi, Kurdabi, Ahalari, Ashmawi, Izziyya, Ishriniyyat, Risala, Arba'una Hadisan,* and *Kara'atu Irrashida.* She noted that in the past, big households always had plenty of women relations, aunts and grandmothers and servants to help look after the housework and children to leave her free to read and teach. She was always the teacher of the household and neighborhood children. Now she studies Qur'an, *hadisi, tauhidi,* and *tafsiri* on her own at home.

Of the women interviewed in this study, Hajiya Iya and Hajiya Aisha are probably most typical of the general population. Educated privately, they have also taught privately, never coming into the public limelight. It is likely that there are many such well-educated Kano women who have taught others without public acknowledgment. Hajiya Maria Mai Tafsiri has enjoyed greater renown. Although she was also educated privately, Hajiya Maria Mai Tafsiri is already quite famous in Kano as a female scholar. She was taught Qur'an, *Ahalari, Kawa'idi, Izziyya,* and *Risala* by her father *all* before she was married at age thirteen. During one of her marriages, her husband taught her *tafsiri,* or Qur'anic commentary. Because this is a particularly specialized field, she came to be known as Hajiya Maria Mai Tafsiri or Hajiya Maria, "The One

Who Knows Tafsiri." Tafsiri is usually recited during the Muslim month of fasting [*azumi*]. Hajiya Maria has allowed both the local television and radio stations to record from her home in Sanni Mai Nagge her recitations of *tafsiri*. This has increased people's awareness of her scholarship. In addition, Hajiya Maria runs a large Islamiyya school, located opposite her home. It caters to both married women and children.

Other women scholars either received some education from the Kano state government, worked in government institutions, or both. Therefore they have moved beyond the traditional, private education for women and have entered the more modern, public sphere. Hajiya Yelwa Ina, Hajiya Sadiya 'Dan Iya Aminu, and Hajiya Rabi Wali are recognized for their skills as teachers.

Hajiya Yelwa Ina was taught Qur'an and *hadisi* by her father. Although she was married at fourteen, her father continued coming to her husband's house to teach her until she finished her reading of the Qur'an. She later studied in Sokoto, Katsina, and Zaria with other women and continued her studies with her second and third husbands. In this way she studied the *Ahalari*, *Kurdabi*, *Ashmawi*, *Hayatul Islam*, *Izziyya*, and *Arba'una Hadisan*. For the past fifteen years Hajiya Yelwa has been teaching Islamic Studies and Arabic in Hausa to students on the secondary school level at the Women's Teachers College in Kano. She also learned Hausa in Roman script [*boko*] long ago in a government course. In the evenings, she teaches Qur'an, *hadisi,* and *Ahalari* to women.

A similar personal history was related by Hajiya Sadiya 'Dan Iya Aminu, who has been teaching Arabic and Islamic Studies in Hausa to girls in the Shekara Girls Primary Boarding School for the past sixteen years. She first attended Qur'anic school in the Emir's Palace at the same time she went to the government primary school at Gidan Makama. In her husband's house, she finished reading the Qur'an and read the *Ahalari*, *Kurdabi*, *Izziya*, and part of *Kara'atu Irrashida*. The older children in the house helped her with English, and she read *Risala* on her own after her husband's death. She learned about the lives of the women of early Islam, like the Prophet's daughter Nana Fadimatu, by reading books on Islamic history such as *Nur al-Absari*. Hajiya Sadiya had also taken courses in education for primary school teachers and Arabic at the Kano Educational Resource Centre (K.E.R.C.). In the evenings she sometimes helps teach married women.

Like Hajiya Sadiya, the career of Hajiya Rabi Wali has combined both traditional and modern sources of Islamic education. Hajiya Rabi also began her education in the Emir's Palace Qur'anic school. She continued under the special instruction of Hajiya Saudatu, a teacher at the girls primary boarding Government Girls School in Kano. Hajiya Saudatu was a famous woman Islamic scholar who was known as "*Umma Makaranta,*" the "Mother of the School." After the day's classes were over, Hajiya Rabi studied Qur'an, *Arba'una Hadisan*, and *Ahalari* with Hajiya Saudatu. Then, while married, Hajiya Rabi improved her Arabic and English in the homes of her successive husbands until, at age twenty-eight, she was able to enroll at the Women's Teachers College. She continued her education at Bayero University, where she studied education for her bachelor's degree. Hajiya Rabi now owns and runs the Tarbiya Islamic Nursery School in 'Yan Kaba Quarter. In the afternoons, she runs a separate school for married women. She teaches subjects like Qur'an, *tauhidi, hadisi, fikihu,* good behavior, Islamic history, Arabic, and English. This is a much wider syllabus than these women could receive in a comparable period of two or three years of the traditional system of Islamic education. In recognition of her scholarship and contribution to education, Hajiya Rabi was recently made a councilor on the Kano City Municipal Council. Hajiya Rabi's mother was also an Islamic scholar who was well known for doing *tafsiri*. A historically important insight as to how the learning of the Sokoto women scholars spread to Kano women was revealed in Hajiya Rabi's interview. Her testimony provides concrete evidence that the jihadists' religious ideas were still circulating among Kano women in the mid-twentieth century:

Women have been teachers for a long, long time. Even I have my mother's books with me which she used to write. And they were forming discussion groups because they have prayers. Even in the palace, there are different types of people. There are people who like *bori* and those who like learning don't associate themselves with that *bori*. Like my mother's group—they always gathered together. They discuss books and *kasidas*, you know, poems written by *malams*, or Shehu Usman's poems. They have people from Sokoto, women who used to visit the palace and they stay with my nanny. . . . And all those people who like learning, they will come and stay the day with them discussing all those things like the Shehu was telling people. And most of them live in the *hubbare,* that is where the Shehu's tomb is. They were reading them like the writing of people like Nana [Asma'u]. I think Nana is the only female I hear them speaking of. Only some time they will mention Isa Kware, the youngest child of Shehu Usman, and they mention it. So there have been teachers, women teachers, all along.

Although female scholarship has not been rare among Kano women, neither is it common. It is hard to know what factors caused certain women to become Islamic scholars while others did not. The women interviewed for this study were all in their forties or fifties and were equally divided among those with Qadiriyya (2), Tijjaniyya (2), or no *darika* affiliation (2). All the women scholars discussed in this section had children, and most had been married several times. During the interviews, the women were asked why they had been able to reach such a high level of scholarship. Hajiya Sadiya dan Iya Aminu said that it made a big difference if your parents showed your husband that they had educated you to such a point and that they expected him to continue. She noted that women from the royal family and from urbanized Fulani families are more likely than others to be educated; those with rural backgrounds and lower-class city dwellers have fewer chances to study. Hajiya Maria Mai Tafsiri said that most women in Kano received insufficient support for education from their parents. If the father was not firm in promoting education, the husband would not take the education of his young wife seriously.

Both Hajiya Aisha Mahmoud and Hajiya Hassana Sufi, however, felt that ultimately the chance for a woman to pursue an education depended on luck. One noted that even in a city quarter like Galadanci, famous for its scholars, a woman would be thankful to find herself married to someone who taught her. The other agreed that many men were more serious about educating their children than their wives. Some women find that their husbands think the question of education is over once they marry, regardless of the women's age. Other, luckier women are taught by their husbands, sent to Islamiyya schools, or have teachers brought into the home to teach them, particularly in the houses of royalty.

The jihad reformers made women's education part of their ideology. Shehu Usman dan Fodio pointed out the economic importance of educating women: when women lost their youthful looks and ceased bearing children for their husbands, they would still be considered valuable assets to the family as Islamic teachers, and their husbands would not be tempted to divorce them in favor of younger wives (Boyd and Last 1985:286). Current research does show that this recommendation was adopted among certain Fulani families in Kano:

The general practice here in Nigeria was that learned men would teach their daughters and sometimes their wives at home. More often than not, emphasis would be given on religious instructions. In some cases, widows of learned men regarded it not only meritorious but also obligatory to pass on to their own sex what they themselves had learnt from their husbands. These widows were sometimes privately employed by well-to-do people to teach their families. At times they would have a collection of children, mainly girls, to teach in their homes in addition to teaching grown-ups. (Galadanci 1971:9)

The extent to which the tradition of Islamic scholarship existed among Kano women prior to the jihad or was spread from Fulani to other Kano women needs to be investigated further. Many non-Fulani families and quarters in Kano are famous for their Islamic scholarship, and they may also prove to include women scholars and teachers.

The Mystics

One of the leadership positions of Muslim women in Kano has been in organizations that promote mysticism, a movement in Islam and in many other religions that teaches its followers to experience God directly. Emotional and intuitive knowledge of God is sought through communal prayer, litanies, retreats, fasting, asceticism, and following a daily regimen of piety and contemplation. The members of mystical movements try to establish contact with the source of all existence in preparation for the eventual return to that source at death.

Such Islamic movements have often been referred to as Muslim "brotherhoods" (see, e.g., B. G. Martin 1976), but such a designation is not meant literally; women have been active members and leaders of these mystical movements since their inception. As early as the ninth century A.D., there were famous female mystics, and special convents were set aside for women to pursue mysticism in various parts of the Muslim world, such as Damascus, Baghdad, and Cairo (Trimingham 1971:18). In northern Nigeria during the nineteenth century, Shehu Usman dan Fodio's wife Aisha was a famous mystic, as was one of his female students, Amina bint Ade (Last 1967:20). During the post–World War I period, several women mystics were known in Kano, among them the ascetic *muqaddama* (Ar.) and *hadith* expert Aisha (daughter of Khadija, a *muqaddama* from Morocco), and Safiya Umar Falke, who was also a *muqaddama* (Paden 1973:100). Therefore, instead of the Arabic term for brotherhood (*ikhwan*), it is more accurate to refer to these mystical groups by the Hausa term *darika*, which comes from the Arabic term for "path" (*tariqa*). Members of a *darika* are not defined by gender but by their religious devotion and affiliation.

Of the two largest *darikas* in Kano, the Qadiriyya is said to have predated that of the Tijaniyya by several centuries. Kano traditions claim that either the Algerian visitor Al-Maghili (c. 1492) or the Kano scholar Abdullahi Sikka (c. 1610) introduced the Qadiriyya to Kano (Hiskett 1984:246). Paden reports that "the original contacts in Kano with Tijaniyya came from the early nineteenth century visit of Umar Futi" to the area (1973:68). The movement grew until a Kano ruler, Emir Abbas (1903–19), formally adopted the new *darika* (Paden 1973:73–75). Today both *darikas* are widespread and include scholars renowned throughout the country.

Membership in the *darika* is by personal commitment. Before joining, new members learn special prayers, litanies, and rules and regulations (for example, it is said that Tijaniyya members may not smoke) under the guidance of *darika* leaders. At the present time, both Qadiriyya and Tijaniyya have some female leaders who instruct new women members, like those described here. The women interviewed for this study include those of both *darikas*:

Hajiya Laraba Kabara is the highest ranking Qadiriyya woman leader associated with the Qadiriyya Mosque in Kabara Quarter. She attended Qur'anic school but never finished the first reading of the Qur'an. She tried marriage several times but had no children, and jealousy with her co-wives always broke up the marriages. She joined the *darika* because of her long family association with Alhaji Nasiru Kabara, the present Shaikh of the Kabara Mosque and the most prominent leader of Kano Qadiriyya.

Hajiya Laraba has been on pilgrimage five times and has once visited the tomb of Shaikh Abd al-Qadir Jilani at Baghdad, Iraq. During the annual Qadiriyya procession to the tombs of the *waliyai*, or saints of Kano, Hajiya Laraba is said to cut an impressive figure mounted on horseback in all her finery.[7] The procession takes place on the birthday of Shaikh Abd al-Qadir (*Mauludin Abdulƙadir*) and attracts members from all over the country. As the *Darwisha* of the *dariƙa*, she is in charge of the new women members to teach them how to use the prayer beads to say the *dariƙa*'s special prayers. In addition, she makes sure the women are doing their five daily ablutions and prayers correctly. If the women want to enroll in the Kabara Mosque school for married women, she takes them to register. Since they began keeping records, Hajiya Laraba said she has helped one hundred and seventy women to join the Qadiriyya.

In her work, *Darwisha* Hajiya Laraba is assisted by *Shahusha* Hajiya Hauwa Idi Kabara. She is the only one of five *Shahushas* who lives in the Mosque compound. Hajiya Hauwa had never completed Qur'anic school and joined the *dariƙa* ten years ago. In addition to helping Hajiya Laraba with new women members, she takes responsibility for seeing that the women's Mosque in the Kabara compound is well cleaned for the communal Friday prayers. As the Kabara Mosque is close to the Emir's Palace, both *Darwisha* Laraba and *Shahusha* Hauwa are well-known figures in the palace.

A female leader in the Tijjaniyya is called a *muƙaddama*, whereas a man is referred to as *muƙaddami*. Hajiya Hassana Ahmad Sufi followed her mother, Hajiya Maimuna Ismail, into this work. Her mother had joined the *dariƙa* while on pilgrimage at Medina. Hajiya Hassana became a member in 1950, and when other women asked her how to join, she took instruction under the scholar Shehu Mai Hula. She confers membership to women only. Hajiya Hassana knew of only one other *muƙaddama*, Hajiya Nana Fulanin Rano. But she had just moved to Karaye and so was outside Kano municipality. As there are many strongly Tijjani quarters in Kano, other *muƙaddamas* can likely be found in other areas too.

In addition to being a female *muƙaddama*, Hajiya Hassana is widely known in Kano as an Islamic scholar. Because of her reputation, she was named to the Board of Trustees of the Kano Foundation, a private development fund (she is the only woman so honored, along with fourteen men [*New Nigerian*, October 21, 1986, p. 20,]). Her career is an excellent example of the dual interests in scholarship and mysticism so often combined in West African scholarship. Hajiya Hassana completed her reading of the Qur'an and studied *Ahalari* and *Kara'atu Irrashida* under the guidance of her mother and elder sister, Hajiya Zainab, before being married at age thirteen. Her successive husbands taught her *Risala* and helped her to revise her reading of the Qur'an. Although she had children, none lived beyond childhood. After two marriages ended in divorce, Hajiya Hassana started teaching Arabic and Islamic Studies at the Shekara Girls

7. Conversation with Barden ƊanRimi, Malam Kabiru Abdullahi Kwaru, Emir's Palace, Kano, June 21, 1986.

Darwisha Hajiya Laraba Kabara is the highest ranking Qadiriyya woman leader associated with the Qadiriyya Mosque in the Kabara Quarter of Kano. Photo by P. Starratt.

Darwisha Hajiya Laraba Kabara at the tomb of Kano Muslim saint Wali Allah 'Daya. Photo by P. Starratt.

Primary Boarding School. Because she wanted to receive a recognized certificate in her field, she became the first female student of the School for Arabic
Studies in Kano. She did the coursework on her own in the afternoons after
finishing her teaching, but she was allowed to take the exams with the male
students. Having obtained the Higher Muslim Studies Certificate, she went on
to earn a diploma in Arabic, Hausa, and Islamic Studies at Bayero University
in Kano.

Hajiya Hassana currently teaches the Higher Muslim Studies course for married women at the Gidan Galadima School. In the evenings she teaches married
women in the Islamiyya school she built privately in her home. She has written many books for her students. They include three volumes to clarify the
Islamic religion entitled *Goranfito*. This word is the name of the calabashes
used as flotation devices by fishermen and people who want to cross flooded
rivers during the rainy season. The allegorical meaning of the title is that the
Islamic religion is a life support. She wrote a translation of *Ahalari* and a book
of poems of preaching, including *Igiyar-riƙo*, or "The Rope to Hold On To,"
meaning the correct knowledge and behavior to follow to obtain salvation.
There is also a poem entitled *Waƙar Ilmi* or "Song of Learning."

Paden estimated that in the 1960s 60 percent of the adult men in Kano City
belonged to the Tijjaniyya *dariƙa;* 24 percent were Qadiriyya, and the remainder were unaffiliated (1973:70). Comparable membership figures for women
have not been determined, much less the numbers of women in *dariƙa* leadership positions. There remains much research to be done on these women, as
well as those who belong to Kano *dariƙa*s other than the Qadiriyya and Tijaniyya.

The Social Workers

Other Kano women render an Islamic form of assistance to society. Some
belong to Muslim voluntary associations dedicated to aiding the society, and
others work privately or contribute in the course of their professional careers.
Every year, for example, many women help with the pilgrimage in different
capacities. Hajiya Saude Datti's work was a combination of practical and material assistance, together with spiritual guidance. Hajiya Saude Datti had not
yet completed reading the Qur'an when she was married at ten. She travelled
quite extensively with her husband, living in Niger Republic, Chad, and the
Sudan. She said that when she performed *haji* herself, she saw the need to
assist pilgrims. For four years she had been representing Kano State among
the women employed by the federal government of Nigeria to help with the
Islamic pilgrimage. Government aides are divided between Jidda, Mecca, and
Medina. They help bring the pilgrims to their lodgings, buy them food if they
run out of money before the flight home and look after anyone who falls ill.

Also included in the government team are Islamic scholars, both male and
female, who instruct the pilgrims on the religious aspect of each step of the

pilgrimage. In fact, intensive briefing of pilgrims is done before the pilgrims depart, some of it by media personnel. Hajiya Mairo Muhammed of the Kano State Radio has published a book, *Advice to Women on Performing the Pilgrimage*, based on several years of experience of teaching and accompanying pilgrims (Muhammed 1986). The federal aides find themselves called upon to remind the pilgrims how to perform obligatory rites, such as circumambulations of the Kaaba, the movement between the hills, and the symbolic throwing of pebbles at Satan. They also find themselves encouraging the pilgrims to put forward their best moral behavior while on pilgrimage, as Hajiya Saude warned:

If you steal in Mecca, where will you go to wash away the sin of it? There is nowhere else. If you steal in Mecca, if you commit adultery in Mecca, there is no place for you to go and wash the sin away. This is the place of repentance, this is the place that you will go to ask Allah to pardon you. The mistakes you commit here . . . This is the place you have to go to ask Allah to forgive you. This is the only place. If you sin here, where are you going to go again?

Hajiya Hauwa Adamu is one of the women leaders of the *Jama'atu Nasril Islam* (Society for the Support of Islam). She pointed out that the women members are divided into two groups: there is a *wa'azi* or preaching section and the *agaji* or assistance section. She is the director of the eastern *agaji* section, which stretches from Kano to Wudil, Birnin Kudu, and Gwaram. The volunteers administer first aid in case of accidents, send for food and water at large gatherings, and assist at births, being particularly trained to supervise the hygenic cutting of the umbilical cord. They are also the oldest of thirteen voluntary associations who work to help the pilgrimage. They keep an office in the Pilgrims Camp where pilgrims are accommodated before and after completing *haji*. Sick pilgrims are taken to hospital, their luggage reclaimed and their relations notified to collect them. Hajiya Hauwa went far in her Qur'anic school but did not finish. She later studied the *Dala'ilu* and *Risala* in Hausa in Roman script (*boko*) and completed up to class four of primary school at Gidan Makama before training for hospital work. Hajiya Hauwa is presently an employee of the Government Agency for Mass Education, where she teaches women hygiene, child care, and crafts. She noted that there are many other Islamic voluntary organizations in Kano which, no doubt, also have women members and leaders.

A thorough investigation should reveal many more women in this category who, through piety and dedication, devote a good portion of their spare time and energy to helping the society in some Islamic capacity.

Conclusion

What are the implications of female Islamic leadership roles in Kano for the larger society and for the future? The women in this study are all middle-aged.

Most of them have lived fairly traditional lives and acquired their education, at least initially, through traditional methods. Their lives are important within the context of the wider society in two ways. First, they demonstrate that in large, cosmopolitan areas that were affected by the Fulani jihad (with its respect for female scholars and mystics), women were able to develop leadership roles that were specifically Islamic in nature. Their involvement with the Islamic religion was preeminent in their lives, *not* marginal. Second, the responsible manner in which these women have handled themselves when they reached positions of leadership and authority has set an example for the thousands of other Muslim Kano women who have been their students, their mystical initiates, and their wards on pilgrimage. These women leaders served as positive role models whose example shows how to organize and strengthen religious activities.

One issue worth raising is how typical the women of this study are of other Kano women. For their time and generation, they are an elite, although not in the economic sense of the word. Most of them live modestly; none are rich. They are elite in the sense of being exceptional. They do not live very far away from one another. Research in other wards of the city famous for scholars and mystics like Madabo, Alfindiki, and Shatsari will doubtless produce more reports of outstanding women, some reaching back several generations in the same family. Another area that needs more investigation is the particular nature of the circumstances which enabled these women to devote their lives to scholarship, mysticism, or public service. Many of these women are divorced or widowed and have no children, few children, or grown children. Those who were active while they were wives and mothers seem to have had access to servants.

The lives of the women in this study are an important indication of possible future trends in Hausa society because they form a transitional bridge between the private and public spheres of activity. In Muslim Africa, women are increasingly emerging from the private sphere. Whereas the older women in this study were primarily educated at home, the younger ones attended government primary schools and two attended Bayero University, where they were in the same classes as male students. The women of this study are now organizers of activities for women that require their leaving the home in order to participate. Teaching in girls' schools, running Islamiyya schools for married women, initiating women into *ɗariƙa,* or coaching pilgrims, they provide a respectable environment in which men trust their wives and daughters outside the home. In recent history it has been the custom for women of child bearing age to avoid being seen in public in daylight hours. Today with the existence of Islamiyya and government schools, and of literacy, hygiene, and craft centers, the streets are full of women going to school. Some are driven by husbands, some go in taxis, and some walk, covered in their newly adopted, long, black cover garments called chador or *'abayah* (Ar.).

Although the West thinks of the chador as a symbol of female supression, in the Muslim world it may be interpreted as a symbol of women entering the public sphere. In earlier days, Kano men who could afford it kept their wives at home in purdah (*kulle*) or seclusion until after sunset. They gained prestige by adopting this expensive custom which they believed was an essential part of Islamic culture. Kano women were not veiled; they were secluded, excluded from markets, government offices, government schools, open streets, and nearly every possible salaried job. Kano women absorbed and perpetuated these values as well, and it was a source of family pride for a woman to be remembered by having passed through her husband's doorway twice: going in as a bride and coming out at her funeral. A woman might die at home after successful childbirth because her husband would not allow her to go for simple surgery to a hospital where she might have been attended by a male doctor or nurse. These practices are now eroding. Young and middle-aged married women now crowd the hospitals, adult literacy classes, Islamiyya schools, secondary schools, and universities. What is notable, even if some of these still meet at night, is that they meeet in large groups outside private homes. In a study of women and mystical orders in Senegal, Christian Coulon similarly notes that whereas previously women depended on their father's or husband's shaikh, they now belong to mystical orders on an independent basis (1988: 123). University mosques now have separate rooms for women. Typical of the new public presence of women are the female students of the Aminu Kano School for Islamic Legal Studies, who walk down the dual carriageway after classes in small groups, their '*abayah* blowing gracefully in the breeze.

Muslim women in Kano are not adopting the chador strictly for fashion or self-interest. It is also a political and economic statement. As part of the wider Muslim world, Kano women using the chador are making a statement of sympathy with some of the ideas of countries like Iran and Libya, Egypt and Saudi Arabia. Western secularism and multiparty democracy did not bring them the expected fruits of a house, car, and prosperity for every Kano family. Instead there was corruption, political violence, international debt, and economic crisis for which the West is blamed. The Islamization of the economy and the political system is the logical and final stage of decolonialization in the view of many Muslim Africans. Although not all Kano women have had the education to appreciate the details of international politics and economics, those who have are widely heard and seen as lecturers at universities, commissioners and permanent secretaries, television and radio broadcasters, and newspaper journalists. Adopting the chador does not mean that the Kano women expect to reduce their opportunities and rights. On the contrary, they are using religious arguments to advance their acceptance in many public spheres formerly closed to them. Coulon's study in Senegal also noted that certain reformist groups like the Union Culturelle Musulmane have specifically adopted policies on the promotion of

Muslim women (1988:118). Ironically, the economic crisis may actually help some feminist causes by discouraging husbands from taking more wives and encouraging husbands to let the ones they already have become educated and take up jobs.

We have seen that the religion of Islam is a central force—not a marginal one—in the lives of Kano women, Islam has not prevented women from occupying important leadership positions in Kano. More research will likely show that women Muslim leaders are a widespread urban phenomenon in Africa. How far this extends into the rural, agricultural, or nomadic setting is another field for future exploration. The long legacy of female literacy among Tuareg women would make this a logical place to start among nomadic peoples. Whereas the older women and women of previous generations exercised their leadership positions primarily in the private sphere, the modern, younger generation is bursting into the public sphere in all disciplines and sectors. Change in the perceived correct role for Muslim women is coming rapidly in Kano, supported by the trends of women in other Muslim countries.

Appendix

The works studied by women in this chapter are introductions to several fields of Islamic knowledge and include or touch on such areas as law (*fiƙihu*), the traditions of the Prophet (*hadisi*), biography (*sira*) and eulogy (*madahu*) of the Prophet, theology stressing the monotheism of Islam (*tauhidi*), and Arabic grammar (*nahawu*). These works take women several steps beyond Qur'anic school in a society where all children may begin, but where not all finish even the first reading of the Qur'an. From this start, some women went even further to study more advanced works; these include the books described below:

Ahalari (*Al-Mukhtasar al-'Alamat al-Akhdari fi Mathab al-Imam Malik*) by Abu Zaid Abdul Rahman ibn Muhammad al-Saghir al-Akhdari al-Maghribi al-Maliki is an introduction to Islamic law according to the Maliki law school, with emphasis on ritual, especially ablutions and prayers. It is about thirty pages long, a condensation of a larger work, and is often studied over a six-month period together with *Ashmawi*.

Arba'una Hadisan (*Arba'una Ahadith*) by Abu Zakariya Yahya b. Sharaf al-Din al-Nawawi has forty-two traditions of the Prophet on various topics. It was the custom for scholars to make collections of forty *hadith* which they considered particularly instructive, sometimes on particular topics such as belief or prayer.

Ashifa'i (*Kitab al-Shifa' fi Ta'rif Huquq al-Mustafa*) by al-Qadi Abdul Fadl Iyad ibn Musa al-Yaqubi al-Andalusi is an interpretive composition on the mission of the Prophet and its implications for Islamic law. It emphasizes the miracles performed by the Prophet, which distinguish his life from that of others.

Ashmawi (*Matn al-Ashmawi*) by Shaikh Abd al-Bari al-Ashmawi al-Rufa'i was the original work from which a sixty-page, locally used commentary by Shaikh Salih Abd al-Sami'i al-Abu al-Azhari was made. It is also concerned with the correct rituals of the religion according to Maliki interpretation.

Dala'ilu (*Dala'il al-Khairat wa Shawariq al-Anwar fi Dhikri al-Salat 'ala al-Nabi al-Mukhtar*) by Abu Abdallah Muhammad ibn Abd al-Rahman b. Abi Bakr Sulaiman al-Jazuli is a book of prose which praises the life of the Prophet.

Hayatul Islam (*Hayat al-Islam fi Sifat Allah wa Sifat Rasul Allah 'alaihi al-Salam*) by Shaikh Muhammad al-Dad al-Asindibsidi is a work describing the characteristics of Allah and the Prophet.

Ishriniyyat: Al-Wasa'il al-Mutaqabbala, commonly referred to as *Qasa'id al-Ishriniyyat fi Madh Saiyidna Muhammad*, is a joint work by Abu Zayd 'Abd al-Rahman b. Yakhlaftan b. Ahmad al-Fazazi and Abu Bakr ibn Muhib. The work is a mystical and allegorical poem praising the life of the Prophet.

Izziyya (*Al-Muqaddimat al-'Izziyyat lil Jama'at al-Azhariyyat*) by Abu al-Hassan 'Ali al-Maliki al-Shadhili is also a condensation of a larger work on the same topics of alms, ablutions, prayers, and other areas of Maliki ritual and law.

Kara'atu Irrashida (*Al-Qira'atu al-Rashidat*) (in four volumes) by Abdul Fattah Sabri Biq and 'Ali Umar Biq was for a long time the only work locally available for Nigerian students who wanted to study the Arabic language in a somewhat modern manner. Written by two Egyptians, the books included a collection of short stories that could be used for teaching Arabic grammar.

Kawa'idi, or in Arabic, *Qawa'id al-Salat*, is a pamphlet of about thirty pages by an unknown (and probably local) author. It concerns the principles of prayer. Other topics, such as the attributes of Allah and the meaning of "There is no god but Allah," have been added to the pamphlet.

Kurdabi (*Manzumat al-Qurtubi fi'l-'ibadat*) by Shaikh Yahya al-Qurtubi is a series of poems on the important rituals according to Maliki interpretation.

Nural-Absari (*Nur al-Absar fi Manaqib Ahl al-Bait al-Nabiyi al-Mukhtar*) by Shaikh Mu'umin Hassan Mu'umin al-Shabalanji is about the lives of the people in the Prophet's family.

Risala (*Al-Risala*) by Abu Muhammad Abdullah ibn Abi Zaid al-Qairawani is the longest and final work in the introductory series in law. The first half is on ritual; the second concerns aspects of law such as marriage, divorce, trade, inheritance, and murder. It is usually studied over a period of about eighteen months.

3 *Deborah Pellow*

From Accra to Kano: One Woman's Experience

In 1984 economic deterioration and other related forces induced Hajiya's husband, a trader, to relocate his expectant wife and their five children from Accra, Ghana, to Kano. This northern Nigerian city was foreign neither to Hajiya nor him: both are Hausa from families who hail from the Kano area; he has traveled frequently to Kano on business; she has periodically visited her father, a wealthy businessman who lives there; and their fourth child, at the age of three, was sent to Kano to stay with Hajiya's stepmother two years before the family's move. Their connectedness and familiarity with Kano has thus been considerable. Nonetheless, Hajiya complained bitterly about the move to Kano. "I was born Accra, married in Accra, bore children in Accra. In Accra, too, I did my business. . . . In Ghana I have everything; here I do not."

This chapter is based upon research carried out in Accra, Ghana, in 1979 and 1982. On both occasions, I was supported by a Syracuse University Senate Research grant and in 1982 additionally by a grant from the American Philosophical Society and the Appleby-Mosher Fund. The Kano material was collected during the summer of 1984, when I participated in the Advanced Hausa Language Seminar held at Bayero University, sponsored by Stanford University. I presented my ideas for this essay to the Women's Studies Faculty Seminar, Syracuse University, in October 1984, and the paper itself at the African Studies Association meeting, October 1984. I am grateful for the comments given on both occasions, as well as those by Roberta Ann Dunbar, Barbara Lewis, Ronald Cohen, Frank Salamone, and my two editors, Catherine Coles and Beverly Mack. I alone am responsible for any errors.

What initially appeared to me as an unfortunate personal situation is in fact considerably broader. The personal is reflective of the larger cultural realm; it is intertwined with a whole configuration of cultural elements—a configuration which differs from Accra to Kano.

In this essay, I explore the varying influences of the two social environments upon this woman from both the personal perspective—how she experiences them and talks about them—and the perspective of society and culture—the organization and structures that differentiate the two.

I begin with a description of her living situations, as that is what she brought to my attention. I take into consideration the social and spatial differences between her Accra home and the new one in Kano. Is it the lack of room, the absence of her belongings, the distance from female kin, that were unsettling her? I then take a step back and consider more generally issues of what it is to be Hausa, Muslim, and a woman in both Accra and Kano. Is it the prevailing Muslim ethos in Kano, the rule of seclusion, the inflexibility of roles that Hajiya disliked? Finally, I explicate the lack of overlap between the two living situations—the incongruencies of a cultural sort which are experienced and played out idiosyncratically.

The Nima Homefront

Alhaji owned his compound in Nima, a shabby section of Accra, infamous for its dirt and overall conditions of poverty. (He also owned a recently completed house in one of the newer Muslim areas, Darkuma, where he had planned to move his wife and children.) He and his family were very much a part of the *zongo* community: he whiled away free time in street corner conversation with male friends and neighbors. As the wife of the house owner (*uwar gida*), Hajiya had respected status in her compound and in the neighborhood as well.

Their Nima home was located at the end of an unpaved road so badly rutted that few chose to drive on it. The rusted carcasses of cars and trucks lay abandoned along the roadside. Their dwelling, however, was comfortable and well equipped. The family of six (the three-year-old child lived with Hajiya's stepmother) occupied one corner of the compound, which included three and a half rooms—a sitting room, a master bedroom, Alhaji's room, and a foyer where the children slept on mats. In her bedroom, Hajiya had her dowry (*kayan daki*), a wall-sized glassed cupboard full of porcelain tureens (see Cohen 1969; Schildkrout 1983). More of her "things for the room" (fancy dishware and iridescent pyrex bowls) graced the sitting room, alongside the refrigerator, a blender, pasta machines, a settee, an armchair, a coffee table, a television, and a stereo. In a corner of the room was a door to the shower, specially equipped with running water instead of the more usual bucketful of water. The second bedroom, Alhaji's room, contained a wardrobe for his clothing, a desk and chair, books, and a double bed. The remaining rooms were rented. Tenants included a Yoruba man and his Ewe wife, a Buzanga man, a Yoruba woman whose husband was in Yorubaland, Alhaji's sister and her Hausa husband, and an Asante woman whose Buzanga husband was living in Abidjan.

In the compound yard, all had access to a water tap. Around the back of the compound was a shower room for the tenants and a locked latrine for the use of some of the tenants.[1] Alhaji had built a pen there, which housed about twenty goats as well as some sheep and chickens.

Hajiya cooked in the courtyard on a kerosene stove. She had no kitchen, a situation typical of many in Accra. And like many, she kept her cooking utensils in a wooden cupboard which she locked at night.

In Accra, Hajiya was largely confined to the compound—her husband did not want her to be "roaming about." But, even among the Hausa, her confinement was unusual. Despite her appearance as a simple housewife, she did little of the household work alone. Marketing, food preparation, cleaning, clothes washing, and the like was accomplished with the aid of a young illiterate woman she had hired. Hajiya's business enterprises involved much of her time and energy and were particularly important to her. With the help of her young worker, she made spaghetti on a pasta machine and dried it over the sides of baskets in the compound yard. Her worker then took it to the main market to sell. In addition, Hajiya made "ice cream" from orange squash, which she froze in tomato paste tins and, along with penny candies and biscuits, sold from the doorway of the house. The money she earned was hers to spend as she pleased.

Back to the Nigerian Homeland

On his way home from a business trip abroad in late 1983, Alhaji stopped off in Nigeria. Ghana's land borders were closed, mobility was limited, business had ground to a halt. Determining that this was the time to relocate, he sent word to Hajiya to pack up what she could and fly with the children to Kano. Because she was pregnant when she left Accra and her mother could not attend to her, Hajiya's mother's sister accompanied her.

Alhaji also owns the house in Kano which he bought to relocate his wife and children. It is located in the neighborhood of Kurna, on a small, unpaved road off the Katsina Road, a busy four-lane highway about 7 kilometers from Sabon Gari, Kano's modern commercial center. The block does not look particularly well cared for—refuse floats in rivulets left by the rain and a large, broken-down lorry sits on its axles—and it is generally deserted save for small children

---

1. The latrine was kept locked, a not uncommon practice, because some in the compound refused to contribute to payment for the night-soil collector.

playing. The house is a traditional mud-walled structure. The compound is self-contained; only the family lives there. There is no running water; instead, water is stored in a large drum in the compound. There is electricity and an indoor kitchen where Hajiya stores all of her cooking utensils and ingredients and cooks on a wood-burning stove.

From the small compound yard, one can also enter the sitting room (which leads into the master bedroom and a windowless second bedroom) and a room occupied by Hajiya's brother. On the wall to the right of the kitchen is a blackboard, which Alhaji uses to tutor the children in arithmetic and English. The shower room, typical of this type of house, is an empty room with a hole leading to an outside gutter; adjacent to it is a latrine.

The house is minimally furnished since little was transported from Accra. The master bedroom has only a double bed with overhanging mosquito net and suitcases containing Alhaji's clothing. Although undecorated, the room is bright. The sitting room has a large pinkish mat on the floor (a large version of the plastic prayer mats). Against one wall on the floor is a double mattress; near the opposite wall sits a broken-down garden chair, with a portable cassette tape player nearby. A threadbare settee sits under the window, and opposite it a video cassette recorder. The second, smaller, windowless bedroom has a single bed and suitcases containing the clothing of Hajiya and the children. The latter sleep here and in the living room.

Hajiya is dissatisfied with her work situation. Upon departing Accra, she sold one and gave away another of her pasta machines. She brought the third along, but in Kano she has no access to flour. Without a refrigerator, she cannot make ice cream to sell. She no longer has a hired girl to help out. Her eldest daughter, fourteen years of age, does much of the cooking and child care, but when she is at school, Hajiya must do the housework herself. Her time is occupied, but in what she considers unproductive—and certainly not lucrative—labor.

Confirming Hausa folklore (Skinner 1969) and observations in the literature (M. F. Smith 1981), Hajiya describes the woman-man, wife-husband relationship among Hausa as one of distrust: "Men are not dependable—you may ask them for something which they have, but they'll refuse to help you out, because men say women want everything. [Thus] you need to work. Can't ask your husband for everything. That's why I like Ghana more."

Hajiya has no independent income in Kano. She is confined to the compound with the children, whose play often exceeds what can be comfortably accommodated there. In addition, she lacks the adult company that she enjoyed in the Accra house—not only a friendship with the Yoruba woman tenant but also the simple fact of contact and the respect that accrued to her as the *uwar gida*.

Moreover, to her mind, she is too old to have been uprooted. "You see why I don't want to be in Kano: since my father married my mother and bore me in Accra, and I had six children there. If I was a young girl like [her daughter]. . . ." On her mother's side, Hajiya's ties are to Ghana: her mother's mother's mother was a northerner (Gurunsi) who married a Kano man and lived in Accra. There, she gave birth to Hajiya's mother's mother. Taken by her father to a village near Kano (Yelwa), Hajiya's mother's mother married there to a Kano man and bore a daughter (Hajiya's mother). Accompanied by her husband, she went to Accra to see her mother (Hajiya's mother's mother's mother). Following imposition of the Aliens Ordinance of 1969 in Ghana,[2] Hajiya's mother's father moved back to Kano, divorced her mother and re-married; her mother's mother, however, stayed behind in Accra. Hajiya's father was born in Kano City (*birni*); he came to Accra to trade in kola, met Hajiya's mother, married her, and sired one child, Hajiya. He divorced the mother when Hajiya was small, but left the child with her mother. Hajiya was raised by her mother and maternal grandmother. Until she left Accra, they figured significantly in her social network.

Hajiya's father has always been generous with her. When she came to visit him for a few months a year earlier, knowing she had no access to money (she was away from her husband), he provided her with ample amounts of cash. Even after she and Alhaji had settled in Kano, while Alhaji was out of town for a protracted trading venture, her father learned that she lacked a refrigerator and ordered one for her. Hajiya's father's house is always open to her.

One month after relocating to Kano, Hajiya went into labor in the middle of the night. There was a curfew, from 1:00 A.M. until 5:00 A.M., enacted to cut down on armed robbery after the military takeover on December 31, 1983. Her husband was out of town, and when she began to hemorrhage, she was afraid to break the curfew and go to the hospital. Finally, her fourteen-year-old daughter went to Hajiya's mother's father's house for help, and Hajiya was taken to the hospital, where she was given two pints of blood ("I almost died"). Hajiya, her aunt, and the children moved to her father's house until her husband returned from Lagos. Her father's second wife, to whom he has been married for forty years, cares especially for her. She has kept in touch with Hajiya regularly over the years and now that Hajiya is in Kano, the older woman welcomes her visits. But in spite of the support and assistance of her father, Hajiya judges her personal situation regarding housing, belongings, family, friends, work, and domestic help to have been far more satisfactory in Accra than it is in Kano.

2. The Aliens Compliance Order of November 18, 1969, enacted to nationalize businesses and provide more occupational slots for Ghanaians, resulted in the departure of foreigners—other Africans (mainly Nigerians), Europeans, Lebanese, and Indians.

The Zongo in Accra

Mālam Idrissu Nenu, a Hausa, is credited with establishing Accra's first *zongo* (strangers' quarter) when he arrived from Katsina in the mid-nineteenth century as a Qur'anic teacher. He and his family lived among the indigenous Ga in Usshertown until he secured a piece of land from the Ga Manche (chief), Tackie Tawiah, at nearby Swalaba. This came to be known as *Zongon Malam,* in honor of the first Hausa house owner, and with the blurring of time, Zongo Lane. There Malam Nenu built a house.[3] On May 31, 1881, a document was witnessed and signed, formally awarding property rights to Malam Nenu.

Accra became a magnet for Hausa in the late nineteenth century.[4] Large numbers of kola nut traders were drawn to the city following the decline of Salaga Market in the north as the major trading center. The Hausa also came as military recruits in the Gold Coast Hausa Constabulary, established by the British in 1870. Many brought wives and families. Malam Nenu took them in and helped them to settle. Strapped for space, he was granted more land by the Ga elders for his people adjacent to his own house.

Although Accra's *zongo* had a later start than that of Kumase, the early development of each was tied to the settlement of migrants from traditionally centralized states outside of the Gold Coast (Schildkrout 1978c:67–77). The Hausa were joined by Yoruba, Fulani, and Kanuri, who were also Muslims. In 1891 Muslims numbered 8 percent of Accra's population (1,617 people) at a time when Christians constituted only 12 percent (Dretke 1968). By 1908, according to Alhaji Muhammad Ali, a prominent Hausa, Muslims occupied more than 3,000 huts.[5]

Thus with time the initially "pure" Hausa community (*sosai*) was diluted by settlers of other ethnicities, who, although they were primarily Muslim and northern in outlook,[6] followed some of their respectively distinctive customs. For example, the Hausa did not recognize the Yoruba as orthodox Muslims, since the sexual segregation insisted upon by the Hausa was not observed by the Yoruba. In fact, in matters of religion, the Hausa considered themselves

3. Interview with Nii Sampah Kojo Oshaihene of the Ga Jamestown Stool, April 29, 1982.

4. Material garnered from Adamu 1978, Crooks 1923, Dretke 1968, the Ghana National Archives (primarily the ADM 11/1502 and SNA 1986 series), and interviews with members of Accra's "first families of Islam," such as Malam Hamisu, Chief Amida Braimah, Chief Sha'aibu Bako, and Chief Ali Kadri English, and with Mr. Junius Geoffrey.

5. National Archives of Ghana, ADM 11/1502, July 9, 1908.

6. The southern community, the "hosts," are noteworthy for their Western orientation, stressing Western education and a typically southern Ghanaian cultural posture, in contradistinction to the northern community, composed of Nigerians, northern Ghanaians, Voltaics, and others, whose ethos is strongly influenced by Islam (Peil 1979).

superior to all the other Muslim tribal entities,[7] and they became models for the other stranger groups (Schildkrout 1978c:83).

Although the colonial government was cognizant of cultural differences within the *zongo*, it administered the population as a cultural entity, for example, designating one man to represent all local Muslims.[8] But feuds over secular and religious leadership erupted, and about 1912 Malam Nenu's son, Malam Bako, led a group of his countrymen in creating a Hausa enclave, Sabon Zongo (new strangers' quarter), where they could observe the customs associated with their ethnicity and religion as practiced in their homeland. Over time, however, it too became ethnically mixed.

Besides the original Accra Central (Zongo Lane–Okanshie) and its offshoot, Sabon Zongo, eight other *zongo* evolved. One of these was Nima, founded about 1950 by Alhaji Mai'yaki, a Kanuri whose father had come from Bornu to join the Gold Coast Hausa Constabulary and who is said to have been the first man to live in the area subsequently called Nima.[9]

In Accra's *zongo* generally, the Hausa are influential beyond their numbers. They provide the model for Muslim orthodoxy, for chiefly offices, for manner of dress; their language is the *lingua franca* for the "strangers." This has been true in Nima as well, even though there are a number of ethnic groups in residence there who are of substantial enough size that they are represented by their respective chiefs—including Fulani, Togolese Chamba and Kotokoli, Benin Zugu, and two separate Buzanga groups. The Hausa chief (*sarki*), in fact, is perceived by Sha'aibu Mai'yaki, the *sarkin zongo* (chief of the *zongo*), as superior in rank to the other chiefs.[10] This is particularly interesting since Sha'aibu is Kanuri, but Hausa has been a catch-all category since the early days of Accra's *zongo* (and Kumase's as well; see Schildkrout 1978c), and many have chosen to identify themselves as Hausa in light of the group's preeminence.

Like the other Muslim enclaves, Nima characteristically has been self-governing, regulating its own affairs as much as possible. Unlike the situation in Kano, however, these Muslim *zongo* are pockets within a primarily Christian, Western-oriented society. And Qur'anic law has been more weakly observed in Ghana than in northern Nigeria, where Islamic law was applied "under the extensive and elastic umbrella of 'native law and custom' " (Anderson 1970:77).

Nima exudes an Islamic character. Mosques, both grand and small, are scat-

7. Interview with Junius Geoffrey, former general secretary of the Ghana Muslim Mission, June 21, 1982.

8. National Archives of Ghana, ADM 11/1446, SNA 35/1926. See also Schildkrout 1970a, 1970b.

9. Interviews with Chief Sha'aibu Mai'yaki, January 28, 1982, and Alhaji Faruk, secretary to the Council of Muslim Chiefs, March 29, 1982.

10. Interview with Chief Sha'aibu Mai'yaki, January 28, 1982.

tered throughout. Each has its own *muezzin* (Ar. prayer leader), whose voice echoes through the air in daily calls to prayer. Many residents choose to attend their local mosque for Friday prayer rather than travel to the central mosque. Public ritual, such as the *salla* festival concluding Ramadan, is celebrated by Nima residents en masse.

To maintain the faith, Hausa, like other parents, send their children to Qur'anic school. Typically, children are sent to school (*makaranta*) once they have learned to talk and can be away from their mother—certainly by the age of five. At the center of their Islamic education is learning to recite the Qur'an by rote (see Hiskett 1975). In the early days of the *zongo*, Hausa girls and boys were educated separately. Today all Muslim children attend the same classes, although boys and girls are separately seated. Moreover, those who continue on in schools of higher Islamic learning are males. Some of the weekday *makaranta* teach English as well, because the Muslim teachers (*malamai*) fear that children will stop attending *makaranta* once they begin Western-type school. For example, the Kubatil Hadra school in Nima has an English-language teacher. Nima's Qur'anic schools have a total enrollment of 1,403 students, who are taught by 23 teachers. The ethnicity of teachers and students reflects the admixture characteristic of the *zongo*: in addition to Hausa (a minority—only 81 pupils and 2 teachers), there are Kotokoli, Chamba, Yoruba, Fulani, Zabrama, Buzanga, Mossi, and a variety of northern Ghanaian groups such as Dagomba, Wangara, Gurma, and Sisala. All of these ethnics and both sexes learn together.[11]

Hausa custom is itself practiced (again, as in Kano) with an Islamic tinge, including the naming ceremony (*suna*), the confinement of infant and mother for forty days, and the fostering of children, either to family in Accra or even to those living as far away as northern Nigeria. Public observances such as funerals and weddings include traditional drumming. Women earn money by trading in prepared food.

During the early part of the twentieth century, when the Hausa consciously set up their first community in Sabon Zongo, they built compounds according to socio-spatial conventions still found today in Kano (Pellow 1988). Male-female lines of division were well reinforced, based upon cultural precept and spatial norms (Pittin 1979a). The only people who freely entered and left the compound were resident males. Nonkin (tenants) generally did not live in these family houses. The women lived in the interior courtyard (*cikin gida*), which could only be entered through a series of entrance rooms (Moughtin 1964; Schwerdtfeger 1982). In addition to fulfilling their domestic responsibilities—taking care of children, cooking, seeing to their husbands' needs—the women worked from within the home. Maid-servants or children were

11. I collected this material on Nima while doing research in Accra in 1982.

their runners.[12] Women's economic ventures were very much a spin-off of their household personas; men were public persons whose lives were played out outside of the house.

The Larger Context: Living in Accra

Basic attitudes and commonly held values adhered to in Kano are diluted in Accra. First of all, Ghana in general and Accra in particular are not theocracies. Religious doctrine is not utilized to support social ideology. In southern Ghana polygyny has been traditionally practiced, men and women operating in separate domains. However, in Accra, where polygyny is still practiced but is by no means the norm, co-wives tend not to live in the same compound; they may even be situated in different parts of the city. Thus, female sodalities potentially present in the polygynous, co-resident family do not develop here. Nevertheless, in southern Ghana and Accra reverence for women has resulted in their traditionally wielding influence in the home and the public sector (Smock 1977a; Robertson 1984).

Indeed, in Accra women carry much cachet as economic powerhouses. For example, they monopolize market trade, and their association sets the regulations for operation of the markets (Robertson 1984). They also carry civic responsibilities: women are credited with helping Nkrumah win his battle for election as president of the First Republic. Women have been elected as parliamentarians, have served in government secretarial posts, and a member of Ghana's Supreme Court is a woman.

Second, the stringency of Kano's ethos regarding women's place simply does not hold. In Kano, where Qur'anic dictates prevail, women are expected to submit to male authority and to maintain the honor of the family; the seclusion of married women is prescribed, even among the lower classes and rural folk (Callaway 1987). Male-female segregation is mandated in the celebration of social events in the delineation of spatial domains occupied by the respective sexes. According to the *zongo* Hausa mentality, men and woman should, and do in the main, function in separate realms, but in Accra segregation tends to be vestigial or symbolic. It is particularly at traditional rites such as births, weddings, and funerals, that men and women play out their separateness. One regularly sees men gathered together in small groups by someone's doorway or under a tree, as in Kano, even though in Accra women are not kept in seclusion. They can be seen out in public at any time. Some wear a veil over the head. Most, however, drape the veil more casually over the shoulder, keeping it handy for prayer time.

---

12. See Hill 1969 and Schildkrout 1983 for an account of this "hidden trade" in Kano and environs.

In Accra, women can be seen out in public at any time. Some wear veils over their heads. Most, however, drape the veils more casually over their shoulders, keeping the veils handy for prayer times. Photo by D. Pellow.

There is no wife seclusion in the society at large, and many of the Muslim *zongo* residents, such as the Nigerian Yoruba or the northern Ghanaian Dagomba, do not include seclusion in their repertoire of customary practices. Thus it is not peculiar that seclusion of wives is the exception to the rule: according to the Nima chief, only one man in the community, a *malam*, keeps his wives in seclusion.

Today, space is at a terrific premium in the Accra *zongo,* and although the Hausa may dominate, they do not constitute a group apart as they once did. Tenancy in compounds is the norm. Thus, the modesty of women can be only somewhat controlled. Hajiya refers to her marriage in Accra as *auren tsare* (marriage with partial seclusion), which keeps her from "roaming about," but which cannot enforce absolute concealment from the unrelated men who rent rooms in the family compound. In general, not only are co-resident renters of different families, but they may even be of different ethnicities. Moreover, these "strangers" often marry one another.[13]

Both Nima and Kano women trade, but only the former sell in public. Certainly in Accra at large it is women who run the markets. In the main market, the only men who sell trade in meat (butchers), charcoal, and Islamic paraphernalia (books, hats, lavender scent, incense). Women sell in the Nima market as well.

Ghana has had a well-established public education system since before independence (Pellow and Chazan 1986:106–11). The Hausa, as well as other Muslims, have come to realize that, along with Qur'anic education, Western education is necessary. Moreover, parents have also consented to an expansion in education for girls. They are not expected to marry young (as young as thirteen or fourteen, as in Kano); they do go to school beyond the primary level; and it is not assumed that they will have to work from behind the compound wall and remain separated from the public domain. The girls' role models, both within the *zongo* and outside, support such changes.

In Accra women's participation in voluntary associations is legendary. Women belong to societies that are both traditional and modern in nature— hometown and ethnic, religious and secular, occupational and social. Some are sexually segregated, others are not. Within this context, there are five Muslim women's associations (Pellow 1987). Their membership draws from the various *zongo,* including Nima, Sabon Zongo, and Lagostown. They provide financial, moral, and emotional assistance to their fellow members. Ethnicity is neither a divisive nor a unifying feature, for it is overridden by the binding nature of the northern, Islamic ethos. It provides a legitimate outlet for women who, in the customary situation, would presumably be in purdah.

One of the associations, called *Zumunci,* the Hausa term for "clan feeling,"

13. See Pellow 1988 for the relationship between *zongo* housing and women's roles.

was established during the summer of 1969 to combine the prayer and advisory aspects of Islam with sociability (Pellow 1987). Although *Zumunci* is closely associated with baby outdoorings (the parties held on the seventh day after the baby's birth when he or she is named), meetings take place whenever there is a life event to be celebrated. Members contribute money (for which they are credited), and grants are occasioned by special circumstances, generally tied to rites of the life cycle such as birth or marriage. In addition to financial aid in times of great expenditure, members receive instruction and advice, primarily of a domestic nature. The ethnic diversity of the association has increased as the society has flourished. Its members include Hausa (at 31 percent the largest group), Buzanga, Yoruba, the indigenous Ga, and several other Ghanaian and non-Ghanaian ethnicities. The women lack Western education and are illiterate in English; if they are economically productive, it is in the area of trade. They regard themselves as good Muslims, and all subscribe to the primacy of marriage and childbearing.

Some of the Muslim women have another, perhaps less legitimate (in the eyes of the orthodox) outlet for activity and means of meeting with other women. This is as adepts of the spirit possession cult *bori*. There are *bori* troupes in several of the *zongo*. Like the associations, the *bori* troupes encompass many ethnicities—primarily Hausa, Fulani, Zabrama, and Adar—but in each *bori* troupe, one ethnicity predominates. For example, the *bori* troupe in Sabon Zongo is considered Hausa, whereas the one in Nima is Zabrama. The majority of the members in each are women. According to the Sabon Zongo *Magajiya bori* (head of the *bori* dancers), this is because "men do not catch the spirit like women." [14] Indeed, when a troupe gathers for a curing ceremony, one group in the *bori* pantheon always dances first; they are all women, and they are the ones most easily possessed. The various *bori* members come together primarily when there is a curing ceremony (for a new initiate who has contracted "*bori* sickness") and less frequently when invited to perform at a marriage or outdooring. All of the *bori* women also carry out the "normal" adult female roles of wife and mother. Traditionally, the Hausa chief has a *Magajiya bori* in his court. Currently, the only *sarki* in Accra who has acknowledged the symbolic usefulness of such an official is the chief of Sabon Zongo, and he appointed a new *magajiya* in 1982, following the death of her predecessor.

Like other Muslim women, Accra's Hausa women are expected to marry and to show their husbands respect. They should also gain the latters' permission on matters ranging from going out to setting themselves up in some economic

14. Interview with *Magajiya* Hadjo, June 26, 1979. It has been hypothesized that *bori* is a pre-Islamic institution (Tremearne 1914; Greenberg 1946), although some say exclusion from formal religious functions in Islam may explain why women are the primary adherents in the *bori* (M. G. Smith 1965b; Barkow 1972; Besmer 1983; Broustra 1967), the spirit possession cults of the interlacustrine cultures (Berger 1976) and East Africa's coastal Muslims (Strobel 1979:78–79).

Men do not catch the spirit like women do. A *bori* adept in Ghana. Photo by D. Pellow.

venture. But unlike women in Kano or in Ibadan's *zongo* (Cohen 1969), they are generally free to come and go, insofar as permission is *pro forma* and permission denied can be circumvented. They do not experience the sharp disjunction between the out-going life of the single girl and the highly regulated restrictiveness of the secluded married woman (M. G. Smith 1965b). Upon marriage, they are not removed from the milieu with which they are familiar; they can easily maintain their female ties. They still marry polygynously, and jealous relations often obtain, but polygynous families rarely cohabit in one compound, and the wives generally do not live among affines in an extended family household. Thus their whereabouts are not scrutinized by an overbearing mother-in-law or senior co-wife (Coles 1990a).

Divorce is still common, but people think it is less frequent than in Kano and other Hausa states. For one thing, women have more outlets and are thus less hemmed in. Furthermore, there is less pressure for a divorced woman to remarry (and then to provoke divorce). Pittin (1979b) contends that in Katsina, a city to the north of Kano, many women seek or provoke divorce rather than tolerate an unhappy marriage. In Accra at large the general ethos holds that women should marry in order to be accorded their proper place as adults (Pellow 1977); however, they need not *stay* married or remarry upon divorce (see Dinan 1983). In fact, in many cases the simple fact of having borne a child (acknowledged by a man, although without benefit of marriage) will suffice. Thus

Women are the ones most easily possessed in *bori*. Photo by D. Pellow.

women can lead lives as single women without breaching religious teaching—indeed, to a large extent with impunity.

Among Accra's Hausa, as among most southern Ghanaians, husband and wife continue to lead separate lives, but the separateness is far less formalized than among Kano residents. Spouses are less cut off from one another, and if a man wants to spend time with male friends, he is free to bring them to his home. Relationships with same-sex friends are still fundamentally important, and one area of husband-wife role segregation is manifest in spouses' respective membership in associations, which, as follows from the Islamic ethos, are sexually segregated.

Incongruencies Explained

On one level, this essay concerns one woman and her place in society. However, on another level, it concerns others in her situation, others who deal with her, who must also negotiate that society. It is about the constraints that society—in two contexts—places on its female members.

The circumstances of Hausa women in Accra and Kano are very different, because of variance in the general ethos guiding female behavior, differences in definitions of Muslim orthodoxy, and differing societal contexts of Hausa and Islam. In Kano the norms and values of the society at large (essentially those of Kano City) are coincident with those of the Hausa population, 99 percent of whom are Muslim. In Accra, the Hausa (about 98 percent Muslim) are first of all situated in a city which is neither Islamic nor Hausa—indeed, where there are many disjunctions with traditionally normative Muslim Hausa life-style. Second, in Accra the diaspora has diluted Muslim "Hausaness," so that even within the *zongo*, attitudes and practices are at variance with those of Kano. (Ibadan's *zongo* provides an interesting counterexample; Cohen 1969.) The variance between Kano and Accra fleshes out the bare bones of Hajiya's personal misery and provides a more profound, more universal explanation of its etiology.

The character of the different situations has a spatial and social component. In Kano the extended family household is the ideal, and any hindrance to the accommodation of kin is more likely to be due to a lack of sufficient space than to the use of that space for unrelated persons. In Accra *zongo* people own a share in the family house, but they may rent out their portion; thus compounds are mixed with regard to kinship and even ethnicity.

In Kano, marriage, ever an obligation of Hausa adulthood, has received affirmation at the state level.[15] Because women marry young, and married women

---

15. During the summer of 1984, Kano State government declared that any adult woman who remained unmarried must leave the province.

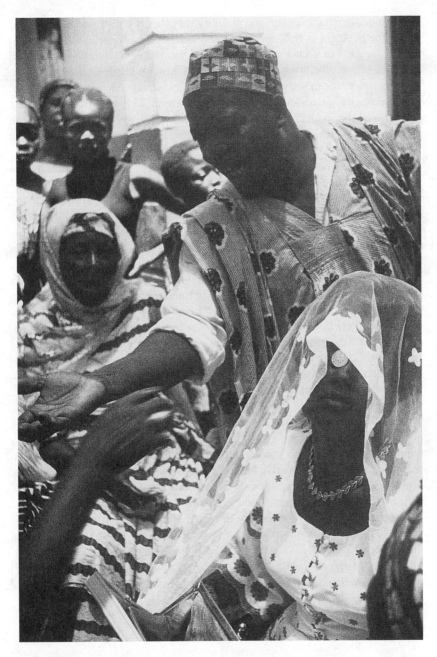

Like other Muslim women, Accra's Hausa women are expected to marry and to show their husbands respect. This photograph shows the master of ceremonies and the bride at a wedding in Accra. Photo by D. Pellow.

are secluded, their movement and mobility is explicitly constrained. The *zongo*
mentality in Accra is different. Here too marriage is important; however, it
occurs for girls at a later age. Modesty of women is encouraged; the Chief
Imam of Accra, officiating at a Sabon Zongo Hausa wedding, decried in his ser-
mon behavior that might attract men to the newly married woman. However,
the community possesses no power to contravene such behavior effectively.
Men resent the associational outings of their wives which make it difficult
to keep track of the women,[16] but the men in fact have no leverage against
their wives.

For example, the chief of the Accra Central *zongo,* Ali Kadri English, was
angry because he felt that his wife had "taken the law into her own hands—
anytime she feels like going out she goes. She puts the baby on her back and
she goes. I told her I don't want that kind of thing, but she's still doing that." [17]
But he also realized that he could do nothing about it since his mother sanctioned his wife's behavior—"You know, we can't go against the words of our
parents." [18]

Kano women, unlike Hausa women in Accra, are relatively invisible. In
Accra there is virtually no true seclusion. In Kano social norms prohibit women
from selling in the marketplace. The vast majority of traders at the main commercial market, *Kasuwar Sabon Gari*, are men; women selling there are generally either menopausal or southern Nigerians—both of whom are liberated
from purdah. Indeed, after marriage a woman need not work for money, as
her husband is expected to support her. This is not to say that women do *not*
work, but trading is constrained by an increase in school attendance among the
"runners."

Ghanaian women are not only encouraged to work or trade, it is incumbent
upon them to do so. Kano's comparison with Accra is striking, for in Accra
women are pivotal to the market and to the country's food distribution system. Providing access to such a basic resource as food, they wield considerable
power. Southern Ghanaian women have been raised to underwrite many of
their own needs, aside from those dictated by conjugal role reciprocity.[19]

In Mirria, a farming community in Niger, Hausa women are economically
active as processors of foodstuffs and as traders as well, not only selling from
their doorways but also in the small daily food market (Saunders 1980:67).
Of course, Mirria is essentially rural, and Accra and Kano are urban. The real
question is, how lax are Kano Muslims when in Accra? One would think that

16. Interview with Chief Ali Kadri English, head of the Accra Central *zongo* Hausa community,
February 21, 1982.

17. Ibid.

18. Ibid.

19. See Mikell (1986) for the role of rural southern Ghanaian women in food production and
its relation to their autonomy.

the presence of all of those strangers would make them insist upon even more female modesty. We know that Chief Ali Kadri English, who hails from Kano, can insist all he wants, but to no avail.

Like the Kano women, Hajiya herself did not sell in the Accra market, but her partial seclusion was unusual in the Accra *zongo* and also not in keeping with her personal models for female behavior: her mother, her sister, and other female kin sell in the market. Her husband described as "cruel" a local *malam* who kept his two wives in seclusion in a very small house. Yet it was also her husband who set her restrictive parameters, who limited her commercial activity to the home, in line with his notion of proper female behavior.

What does it mean for Hajiya to be at the conservative end of "appropriate" female behavior in Accra's *zongo*? Certainly her situation irritated her. At one point, while living in Nima, her husband did not speak to her for five weeks because she went to Lagostown one day to see a member of his family, and when he came home, she was not there. He said that she had no right to go out without asking him. But if she were to ask him, she said, he would say no. She complained that since her child's birth six months earlier, she had not seen her grandmother because she was not allowed to go out. "I'm not in *kulle* [seclusion] . . . [but] even *kulle* people let you go see family or friend." [20]

The marriage Hajiya made denied her the explicit freedom of other Accra *zongo* women. But, in Accra, she could still finesse it, even though she was feeling constrained, since neither Accra nor the *zongo* provided sanctions to enforce her husband's will. Moreover, her husband traveled a lot as a trader. Whenever he left town, she felt free to go where she pleased. When she went to visit her grandmother on such occasions and by late afternoon had not hurried home, the older woman would say, "Your husband must be away." [21] In Accra she had collaborators in subverting the oppressive rules, and a normative context to support her. There are institutions (such as *zumunci*) which enhance the public alternatives for women. In Kano such associational life is absent, and this in turn reinforces the domestication of women already presented by the stricter maintenance of seclusion.

Hajiya's life in Kano felt more oppressive to her in part because her husband traveled less, in part because of the context of seclusion, in part because she felt socially bereft and was in purdah. He did not even have to impose his rules since they were built into the cultural rule book. When he was away and she took advantage of the situation to go out regularly, a neighbor woman who stood outside grinding tomatoes teasingly told her that she would tell Alhaji of his wife's wanderings when he returned.

In this patrilineal, patriarchal culture, where the children of divorce nor-

20. Interviews with Hajiya April 15 and 18, 1982, in Accra.
21. Interview with Hajiya April 18, 1982.

mally go with the father, Hajiya remained with her mother and her mother's kin. Despite her father's presence, his willingness to help her, and the openness of his household to her, she does not feel connected—or not sufficiently connected to Kano: "Your father's family is not like your mother's family, is it?" she asks rhetorically. Thus the pull of kinship continually draws her to her former home.

In time, Hajiya's personal situation in Kano could change. Eventually her household goods, her "capital" in china, would be brought from Accra or replaced. Her distance from maternal kin could be accommodated, perhaps through fostering one or more of her children back to her grandmother or other female kin in Accra. Reciprocal visiting, like the six-month stay of her aunt in Kano, although different from informal daily contacts, is also possible.

However, in political and cultural terms, the Kano situation could worsen for Hajiya and other women. Not only are Alhaji's preferences for his wife's behavior reinforced by all social institutions, but the social climate is becoming more restrictive as Islamic fundamentalism has caught on. Kano's strict, sober, homogeneous atmosphere stands out in comparison to the outgoing, free-wheeling, heterogeneous milieu of Accra. The two competing explanations for Hajiya's unhappiness—the personal and the cultural—may thus be mutually reinforcing.

4 *Roberta Ann Dunbar*

Islamic Values, the State, and "the Development of Women": The Case of Niger

Political developments in the Republic of Niger over the last decade are transforming the role of Islam at both the mass and national levels. These changes together with the elaboration of a proposal for the restructuring of Nigerien political life that is now underway will influence the tone, substance, and implementation of development in that country. This essay is concerned with the consequences of that process for "the development of women," defined as public policies or economic, political, and social conditions which enable them to improve effectively the quality of their lives. A discussion of Niger's geographical and demographic context will precede the exploration of several themes that are fundamental to the way these changes will affect women. The first is Islam's historical influence on the status of women in Niger and the manner in which colonial policies altered it in the twentieth century. Second, the background and design of the Development Society, implemented in the 1970s, will provide the context for the restructuring of Niger's political culture that is envisioned by its leaders. The significance of the Development Society for women will be made more specific by a study of two of its institutions—

Research on which this chapter was based would not have been possible without the funding I received, which I acknowledge with thanks, from the Fulbright Islamic Civilization Research Program, and from the University of North Carolina at Chapel Hill Kenan leave and University Research Council grant programs.

the Association of Nigerien Women (*Association des Femmes du Niger*) and the Islamic Association of Niger (*Association Islamique du Niger*). As defined in government policy statements and the pages of the national press, their ideological objectives will be contrasted with the ambiguities that have sprung from their interaction so far. The conclusion will assess the promises and the constraints which the interaction of all these factors holds for the future of Nigerien women.

Profile for Development

Niger's geographical location situates it astride the Sahel. Over one half of the country receives less than two hundred millimeters of rainfall annually as demarcated by a line running from west to east just south of Agadez (Fuglestad 1983:8). Agriculture, in which the overwhelming majority of the population is engaged, is precarious under the best conditions; Niger has suffered at least three catastrophic droughts of several years' duration in the twentieth century and many of shorter periods as well (Baier 1980:30–34; Fuglestad 1983:7–9, 195). Thus, despite the numbers of people engaged in agriculture, its contribution to production in recent years (33 percent) varied little from that of industry (31 percent) and services (37 percent). Niger's Gross Domestic Product (GDP), $1.3 billion in 1984 (World Bank 1986:184), is significantly altered by the price of uranium, its principal attraction for foreign investment, which has declined in recent years (Legum 1984:B-529).

In comparison to many other countries of sub-Saharan Africa, Niger's population of six million is relatively homogeneous. Conservative estimates place the Muslim population at 85 percent (Weekes 1978: app. 1), and ethnic groups are few. The principal ones and their percentage of the population are Hausa (45–48 percent) and Zerma-Songhay (20 percent). Kanuri (or Beriberi) (6.8 percent) inhabit the southern third of the country. Others are Fulani (11–13 percent), Tuareg (10–12 percent), Tubu, Arabs in the East, and Gurmantche on the Burkina border (2–3 percent) (Fuglestad 1983:1, 4). Several of the indicators customarily used to compare levels of development as a whole and of women in particular are listed in table 4.1. These figures together with the ones cited above portray a statistical profile of a socioeconomic situation typical of low-income economies and that is in stark contrast to industrialized ones. Despite the problems with statistical data for third world countries, they remain our primary if primitive tool for comparison. Tools like the Physical Quality of Life Index (PQLI) (Liser 1982:201–36), which attempt to penetrate below the surface of economic growth (or decline) to assess how well the benefits of the economy are reaching the population, focus on life expectancy, literacy, and infant mortality. Niger's data on these (life expectancy 43, literacy 8 percent

Table 4.1. Socioeconomic Indicators for Niger in Comparison with Three Other Countries

Indicator	Niger	Senegal	Ivory Coast	Sweden
Population (millions, 1986)	6.6	6.8	10.7	8.4
GNP per capita ($ 1986)	260	420	730	13,160
Average annual GNP growth rate (1965–86; %)	−2.2	−0.6	1.2	1.6
Adult (15+ yrs.) illiteracy (1985; %)[a]	86.1	71.9	57.3	n.a.
Male	80.6	62.6	46.9	n.a.
Female	91.4	80.9	68.9	n.a.
Life expectancy at birth (1986; years)	44	47	52	77
Male	43	46	51	74
Female	46	49	54	80
Average annual population growth rate (1980–86; %)	3.0	3.0	4.2	0.1
Infant (under age 1) mortality rate (1986; per 1,000)	135	130	96	6
Total fertility rate (1984)	7.0	6.5	7.1	1.7
Number enrolled in primary school as % of age group (1985)	28	40	78	95
Male	36	66	92	97
Female	20	45	65	99
Number enrolled in secondary school as % of age group (1985)	6	13	20	83
Male	9	18	27	79
Female	3	9	12	88
Women age 15–19 married (%)[b]	81	n.a.	n.a.	n.a.
Married women of childbearing age using contraception (%)	n.a.	12	3	78

Source: Unless otherwise indicated, all figures are taken from *World Development Report*, 1988 (New York: Oxford University Press for the World Bank, 1988), pp. 222–23, 274–77, 280–81, 286–87. The comparison with Sweden was chosen to illustrate contrasting indicators from an industrialized country.

[a]UNESCO *Statistical Yearbook* (Paris: UNESCO, 1985), pp. 1/16–1/17.

[b]*A 1980 People Wallchart* (London: International Planned Parenthood Federation, 1980).

in 1976, and infant mortality 142 per thousand) demonstrate the precarious existence many Nigeriens have.

The percentages of school-age children in school (27 percent for elementary and 6 percent for secondary) represent great progress since independence when less than 3 percent were even in elementary school, but they are still modest. At the elementary level, the contrast between males (34 percent) and females (19 percent) is striking. There are many reasons to account for these statistics: Niger's Sahelian location and the consequent restrictions on agriculture paired with the dependence of the economy on agricultural and mineral resources are primary ones that have been intensified by the colonial experience and Niger's subsequent role in the international economy. Nevertheless, individuals involved with the development process on the ground while acknowledging these as important factors, also stress the resistance to change of attitudes and cultural values even though the society which these attitudes informed has long since given way to a new order. An example of this posture that addresses the situation of Muslim women in Niger is seen in the following quote and sets the stage for examining the historical influence of Islam on women in Niger:

While marriage, property, inheritance rights (especially in relation to real property), and succession rights continue to be interpreted or applied according to local practices and customary (Qur'anic) law, actions on behalf of women will collide with a stone wall. Paradoxically, it is the Nigerien social reality which is in advance of the constraining juridical structures. . . . There will be no positive action for Nigerien women until there has been a change in attitude and behavior on the part of men concerning the "status of women." (Fofana 1980:31–32)

Islam and Women in Niger

The dichotomy between ideology and reality suggested above provides the background to the contemporary issue of public policy and its objectives for women. Socialization and education, marriage, and the public roles permissable to women have all been influenced over time by the interaction of indigenous custom and Islamic teachings made manifest through the *shari'a*. In the twentieth century, Western norms and colonial policies have further altered both expectation and practice.

Socialization and Education

As children, girls are expected to cultivate the values recommended to them for adulthood. A pervasive ideal is modesty leading to deference in all areas of social intercourse and, beyond the age of seven, to a pattern of life segregated from that of men. Absence of this quality is a source of shame—*hawi* in Zerma, *kunya* in Hausa (see Janet Beik's discussion in this volume of *kunya* as a barrier to women actresses in Niger's popular theatre). The Zerma apparently did not practice female circumcision. Although the evidence is not consistent for other areas, historical allusions to it suggest that, for the Hausa anyway, it was not unknown (Diarra 1971:50–53, 55–68; M. F. Smith 1981:141–42; Hake 1972:54).[1]

1. Citations of Qur'anic verses are taken from *The Meaning of the Glorious Koran: An Explanatory Translation* by Mohammed Marmaduke Pickthall. Whether or not such values originated with Islamic contact, the Qur'an would support the substance of them (Surah 24:30–31; 33:59). Female circumcision was practiced in Arabia before and after Islam, but the Qur'an does not address the

The pattern of education for women in precolonial Nigerien societies is relatively unknown. There is no trace in Niger, as there still is among the Hausa-Fulani of Nigeria, of the *'Yan Taru*, a movement for the education of women inspired by the teachings of Usman dan Fodio in the early nineteenth century and implemented by his daughters Nana Asma'u and Maryam (Boyd 1984, 1989). At present, a girl will receive at most three or four years of Qur'anic instruction. Education in the Western format is viewed with open hostility. Fewer girls than boys attend school, and the percentage is negligible for the 12–17 age group (81 percent of the women are married by the age of nineteen) (International Planned Parenthood Federation 1980). Parents fear the unmarriageability of women who attend secondary school as a result of pressures the girls confront from male instructors. The morality of students attending an all-girls school in Zinder in the late 1970s, was frequently the subject of public derision as displayed in gossip and song (Arnould and Henderson 1982:36).

Marriage

To a great extent, Muslims in Niger have embraced both the qualitative ideology and the legal precepts of Islam governing marriage. Nevertheless, local customs do intrude, and in ways which affect the issues related to women with which we are concerned (Dunbar 1983). Marriage in Niger is a bonding of two families, a process involving prolonged discussions and exchanges of gifts; for some it may not even be acknowledged as definitive until the bride rejoins her husband's home after the weaning of a first child (Diarra 1971:171; Saunders 1978:222–39). First marriages are arranged, and although forced marriage occurs, the customary tradition that consent was necessary (if only to ensure the stability of the marriage) is widely acknowledged. Islamic law accords the wife a right to dower for her own use (which should be modest in amount); its exchange is one of the conditions for a valid marriage (Hinchcliffe 1975: 455–56). In Niger, however, the dowry is only a small part of the customary exchanges between families. These have been inflated by economic and social changes over the past one hundred years and efforts of both colonial and post-colonial governments have failed to stop the rising costs (Cys 1975:37; Dunbar 1983:10). In 1975 the Nigerien chief of state proclaimed a ceiling on marriage expenses of 50,000 CFA (about $200 at the exchange rate of the time). Although it is true that marriage customs in Niger generally support the expenditure of a significant portion of the bridewealth on goods the bride will carry to her new home, this is one instance where the realization of Islamic provisions would be a reform.

---

issue specifically. Other Islamic sources advise that only a woman should perform the operation and should do so in secret; the customary meal held at the time of a male circumcision should not be held in the case of a girl's (cited in Pesle 1946:104–5).

Once married, Islamic norms governing marriage are the ideal. The husband is the head of the household. He must maintain his wife with food, clothing, and lodging even if his wife is financially able to do so. If there is more than one wife, he must treat each equally (Surah 2:221, 228; 4:34). A wife is in charge of domestic responsibilities. She owes her husband obedience and he may inflict corporal punishment within specified limits if she is recalcitrant (Hinchcliffe 1975:457–59). Seclusion of women in marriage has had an uneven history in Niger: pre-Islamic customs recognized nothing of the kind and women enjoyed complete freedom of movement. By the end of the nineteenth century, wives of the chiefs, sultans, and the wealthy might have found themselves in seclusion, in part a result of the teachings of Shehu Usman ɗan Fodio, who favored it, along with the restricted movement of women (Ogunbiyi 1969: 45–50). The significant role of rural women in agricultural production precluded seclusion, although for the Hausa, *armen kubble* (secluded marriage) held (and still holds) high social status. When women's husbands are well enough off to hire laborers, women desire seclusion to escape from the rigors of farm work, and in some areas of rural Hausa, seclusion is on the rise (Saunders 1978:183–93).[2] For urban Hausa women, seclusion may be more widespread than is generally admitted, and where it exists, it tends to diminish the economic activities and therefore the revenues of wives (Arnould and Henderson 1982:33; Schildkrout 1983:106–26; Arnould 1984:130–62). A barrier much more widespread than seclusion and one that has import for adult education of women is the rigorously enforced principle that wives must have their husband's permission to leave the house.

Polygyny is practiced where economically feasible by urban and rural people alike and, as we shall see below, is a hotly debated topic in the capital city. The Qur'an (Surah 4:3) recommended marriage to more than one wife only if the husband could afford the responsibilities he thereby incurred. But the other verse (Surah 4:129) which has served as the basis for outlawing it in some Muslim countries like Tunisia, and which stresses the real impossibility of equal treatment of wives, is never voiced. Economics and male "freedom" lie at the heart of the matter. While tension between wives in polygynous marriages is recognized (the Hausa term for co-wife is *kishiya,* "jealous one"), rural women still find real support from the institution for help in the intensive labor of their domestic chores and other economic activities.

The separation of marital property recognized by Islam is reinforced in Niger by the customs of the different ethnic groups. Women are engaged in a wide range of revenue-producing activities such as agriculture and gardening, house trade, and commerce. Although women do agricultural work on the family

2. When Saunders was in Mirria, however, only 8 percent of the wives in the town were in seclusion.

held farms, Zerma and Hausa husbands tend to allocate their wives a private plot whose fruits the wives control. Islamic law on inheritance has modified Nigerien customs in that women do inherit from their husbands. In the past, this was restricted to movable property, dwellings, and the products of farms, with the land a woman inherited continuing to be exploited by her male relatives (Veillard 1939; Archives National du Niger 1936; M. G. Smith 1965a:249, 271–72; Thomson 1975:246). Women may acquire parcels of land in urban areas and in some regions where male migration has altered land tenure (like the Maradi Valley), and women are now cultivating lands acquired by inheritance (Arnould and Henderson 1982:27, 29). James Thomson has argued that the separation of property within the family poses a drag on the accumulation of domestic capital for development purposes (1975:165). But women are reluctant to invest their capital in communal ventures. First of all, even goods they acquire on their own like seeds or young animals may be appropriated by their husbands (Arnould and Henderson 1982:30–31). Second, they feel under some pressure to keep their property disaggregated because of the likelihood of divorce.

Brief marriages and frequent divorce are characteristic of the peoples of southern Niger (Saunders 1978:264, 269; Ide n.d.) and have been so for a long time. It has been said that for women, first marriage is little more than a rite of passage to adulthood. Repudiation, decried as one of the major discriminations Islam visits upon women, is also common. But in Niger (as in northern Nigeria) repudiation is frequently instigated by women, most often by returning to their paternal home or that of another male relative or guardian. The reason for this is that a repudiated wife does not have to return the bridewealth (Pittin 1979b) as she does if she is the one who seeks a divorce (Surah 2:229–30). Women may seek a judicial divorce on specified grounds which are more numerous as allowed by the Nigerien courts than those acknowledged under Maliki law. A woman is free to remarry after the customary delay of three months (*idda*) or, if pregnant, after the birth of her child. There is no alimony granted in Muslim law and the courts rarely award a wife damages in divorce actions.

Custom rather than Islamic law governs child custody: in some areas the children are turned over to the father's family as soon as they are weaned; in others, they remain with the mother until the age of seven. Child support may be awarded the mother by the court, sometimes retroactively. Paternity represents one final point relevant to discussions about prospects for women. Islamic law does not recognize the right of an unwed mother or her child to sue a progenitor for paternity, and claims for paternity by a married woman may be made only under certain conditions (Dunbar 1983:34–38, 25–26). This issue has become one of great concern, especially in the urban areas where the number of unwed mothers is on the rise.

Political and Public Life

In the past, Zerma and Hausa pre-Islamic societies accorded women a greater
public role than is permissable today; some carried out critical functions in the
spiritual life of the community or held important political, administrative, and
judicial functions. These offices were retained by the nascent Islamic kingdoms
of the nineteenth century (Dunbar 1970:139), but were suppressed by colonial
officials who relied on the male hierarchy to govern.

Two pre-Islamic institutions which have survived, *karuwanci* and *bori*, offered significant roles for women. As practiced in the Ader region of Niger (and
discussed elsewhere in this volume by Nicole Echard), *bori* has been conven-
tionally understood as an institution that offers women in this hierarchical society an opportunity to step out of that hierarchy. As Echard shows, the reality
of *bori* may be different from the ideology: despite the public coming together
of men and women, in the context of *bori* ritual in Ader patriarchy persists in
the allocation of more important and innovative spirits to the male practitioners
than to the women devotees. *Karuwanci* is of interest because of its transformation in the modern era. The term *karuwanci* stems from old Hausa custom
but is today practiced by Fulani and Tuareg women as well. Often translated
as "prostitution," it more accurately refers to the state, often temporary, when
a divorced woman lives away from her own family in a compound under the
supervision of an older woman called the *Magajiya* (*magada*, pl.) until such
time as she chooses to remarry. In such a state she is known as a *karuwa* (pl.
karuwai). Although the women do offer sexual services, their attraction to the
life *karuwanci* is the greater opportunities it affords (than does marriage) for
broader social contact and for knowledge of and participation in public affairs.
Today, each village in southern Niger or each quarter of a large town is likely to
have a community of *karuwai* and a *Magajiya*. *Karuwai* were actively involved
in party politics in Niger during the nationalist era, and since independence,
have often been the ones on the local level quickest to take up various adult
education programs as participants and teachers. Janet Beik, in her article on
Hausa popular theatre in this volume, discusses the new opportunities women
have to participate in this genre, and also notes the variant opinions of theatrical directors about the suitability of young girls or independent women as
actresses. Even though these *karuwai* are not regarded as outcasts to the extent that prostitutes are in Western society, their situation is marginal, and their
association with programs of the state directed to women accounts in part for
the ambivalence of more conventional women toward them (Piault 1971:110–
12; Saunders 1978:255; Arnould and Henderson 1982:39; see also Pittin 1983:
291–302). Nevertheless, the state and its agencies such as the *Association des
Femmes du Niger* (AFN) are the most likely sources at present of technology,
capital, and (possibly) moral support for women seeking to establish greater

control over their own lives. The history of the AFN, discussed below in the context of the Development Society, illuminates the potential benefits, as well as the challenges, of transforming an elite organization sponsored by the state into one beneficial to the masses whose participation they seek.

The Development Society

A territory within the Federation of French West Africa during the colonial period, Niger became independent in 1960. Its first government was led by Hamani Diori and the *Parti Progressiste Nigérien* until 1974, when a coup d'état during the height of a period of extreme drought brought to power Colonel Seyni Kountché. Kountché ruled until his death in November 1987, supported by the Supreme Military Council (*Conseil Militaire Suprême*) and assisted by the bureaucracies of several ministries from the pre-coup days.

In 1979 the government launched an ambitious project called the Development Society (*Société de Développement*). Its ultimate goal was to provide a framework for the participation of Nigerien citizens in their own government (although the relationship of the Development Society to the military remains shadowy), which would operate according to the principles of a National Charter. That Colonel (then Brigadier Colonel) Kountché hoped this project would provide institutions uniquely suited to Niger is apparent in his statements along the way. As early as 1976, he declared, "We are Nigeriens, aspiring to conceive life for Nigeriens, [created] by Nigeriens, for Nigeriens" (Lanne 1983). By decree of October 29, 1979, he established a National Commission for the Establishment of the Development Society (*Commission nationale de la mise-en-place de la Societé de Développement*) which began its work in March 1980. Beginning in February 1982, the infrastructure of the Development Society, called Development Councils, was established at various levels throughout the country. With the National Council in place by August 1983, the chief of state proceeded to the installation of the National Charter Commission (*Commission de Reflexion sur la Charte Nationale*) by Decree 84-01/PCMS/CN, January 11, 1984. The National Charter Commission elaborated a draft document which was circulated throughout the country, revised, and submitted to the Supreme Military Council, and Brigadier Colonel Kountché. It was adopted by the Nigerien government May 11, 1987, and was overwhelmingly confirmed in a national referendum on June 14 of that year.[3]

The pyramidal structure of the Development Councils is elaborate, as is the composition of each council. At the lowest levels are the village, urban *quar-*

3. Lanne 1983; *Le Sahel*, January 10, 1984, p. 3, and January 27, 1984; *Sahel Hebdo*, January 16, 1984, p. 7; *Africa Research Bulletin* 24, June 1, 1987, pp. 8504–5, and July 15, 1987, p. 8531.

tier, or nomadic group councils (6–16 members) which send representatives to the local councils at the canton level (20–30 members). The succeeding levels are the subregional councils (12–30 members at the *arrondissement* administrative level), the regional councils (16–30 members at *département* level), and finally the National Council. The founding commission decided to base the Development Society upon two local institutions: the *samariya,* a traditional Hausa group for youths now composed of young adults who are the prime movers of local self-help; and the rural cooperatives, farmers organized through village structures called mutual groups. One half of the members of the Development Councils at each level consists of members from these two groups; the remaining half's members are selected from among ten other socioprofessional associations, also organized along hierarchical lines. Among these are the Association of Nigerien Women (*Association des Femmes du Niger*) and the Islamic Association of Niger (*Association Islamique du Niger*). The objectives and activities of these organizations provide particular insights into the potential for women contained within the Development Society (Wall 1982: 9–11; Lanne 1983:42; *Le Sahel,* May 30, 1984, pp. 4–5, 8).

The Association of Nigerien Women

In 1956 the first women's organization, the *Association des Femmes,* was founded in Niamey under the leadership of the town's four *magada.* It was superseded in 1958 by the more inclusive *Union des Femmes du Niger,* whose objectives were to promote the education and mobilization of women. This group's activities were largely restricted to the capital city, where the influential women members of the educated elite that witnessed Niger's transition to independence, were represented by the honorary presidency of Aissa Diori, the wife of Niger's only civilian president, Hamani Diori. Madame Diori was killed at the time of the coup d'état in 1974; intensely disliked because of her great personal wealth, it is widely believed that she was an intended victim of the uprising (*Sahel Hebdo,* May 30, 1977, p. 17; Decalo 1979:38, 90, 230).

Brigadier Colonel Seyni Kountché authorized the idea of a renewed women's association in September 1975, at a mass meeting of the women of Niamey at the *Maison des Jeunes.* On that occasion he said that "complete integration of the Nigerien woman in the national effort for development, her complete emancipation, and her full contribution to the equilibrium of our society" was imperative for economic reasons more than for those of political mobilization. In concluding these and other remarks on the limitation of ceremonial "excesses" (e.g., expenses for marriage and baptism), he challenged the women to lend their support to the *Conseil Militaire Suprême* in the "restoration of order in our society" (*Sahel Hebdo,* December 12, 1975, pp. 36–37).

The *Association des Femmes du Niger* (AFN) was founded on September 21, 1975, following upon the *Ordonnance* No. 75-11 of March 13, 1975. Its governing statute establishes the congress as its major decision-making body (article 7). The congress elects a central executive bureau charged with the administration of the organization. Mme. Fatoumata Diallo was elected the first president of the association and was still serving in that capacity in 1982. Mme. Aissata Mounkaila is the secretary-general (*Matan Niger* 1980:no. 1/7).

By the time of the First Congress, May 23–27, 1977, much had already been accomplished: national and regional bureaus were either established or underway; an organizational document had been devised; a development seminar had been sponsored to define some specific projects and begin the search for funding; and members of the national bureau had participated in several international conferences. The resolutions of the First Congress set forth objectives of the founding statute and proposals, which have remained guidelines for the organization's work. These included objectives concerning both general institutional change as well as specific recommendations affecting social and economic benefits for women. A greater role for women in decision making at all levels, the creation of an administrative office charged with the problems of women, and the early implementation of a family code were advocated. The government was asked to create a variety of women's centers providing support for women and girls in both urban and rural areas. Greater involvement of women in the elaboration of agriculture and pastoral development projects was to be sought and several specific recommendations were made for creating cooperatives attentive to the needs of women, the extension of credit and financial facilities to women merchants as well as to men, the provision of family subventions for children of women civil servants, and the multiplication of grinding mills. Among the educational objectives were the multiplication of schools at all levels, reduction of the numbers of dropouts among women, and the development of sex and contraceptive information in schools and adult education classes (*Sahel Hebdo*, May 20, 1977, pp. 7–8). The leaders of the organization planned to use the radio clubs of Niger, public debates, and the publication of a magazine for Nigerien women as the primary means (beyond staff and membership) to present the desires and perspectives of the AFN to the public (*Sahel Hebdo*, May 30, 1977, pp. 16–17). Although consciousness-raising was an important part of their efforts to reach women, the leadership was often at pains to stress that complementarity, not antagonism, was the role they envisioned for relationships between women and men (*Sahel Hebdo*, June 6, 1977, p. 24).

Colonel Seyni Kountché's speech before the First Congress provided grounds for optimism that the government was going to attend to women's concerns. In addition to promising an end to discrimination against women's employment in the civil service (*Fonction Publique*), the chief of state sympathized with women's having had their fill of repudiation, intemperate divorces, and discrimination in matters of inheritance. He promised that the state was trying to provide them with "the security at home that [they] await and to which [they] have a right." However, he also commended diligence, patience, and self-discipline as the proper virtues for women to strive for in the process of seeking social transformation:

The task is all the more difficult in that you must conciliate our past, its historical and moral values, its immovable requirements. For to move ahead is not to deny one's past; to make progress is not to cut off all the values and realities upon which rests our patrimony. You must search for evolution but not mutation, adaptation rather than blind and brutal transplantation. Be open to new values, but refute all alienation. (*Sahel Hebdo* May 30, 1977, pp. 6–7)

The Second and Third Congresses, which stressed the "Participation of Rural and Urban Nigerien Women in the Development Process" and "Literacy, Training, and Work of Nigerien Women" were held in May 1979 and August 1982. Their resolutions, reports, and statements of objectives indicate the continued expansion of the organization's bureaus throughout the country, the development of more specific water, gardening, and self-help projects, and the gradual implementation of women's centers—primarily in the western and central parts of the country. Of continuing concern, however, was the failure to achieve a family code, popular resistance to extending literacy and education, and the reluctance of local civil servants to cooperate with AFN in their projects (*Matan Niger* 1980: no. 1; *Sahel Hebdo*, September 6, 1982, pp. 22–27).

Articles and documents in the Ministry of Information's weekly news magazine, *Sahel Hebdo*, and the daily paper, *Le Sahel*, trace the evolution of the AFN's activities, and illuminate some of the perspectives and challenges facing Nigerien citizens. Since these are government organs, it is assumed that the subjects followed and the opinions voiced reflect a measure of the government's position on these issues.[4] Public attitudes and general developments with respect to polygyny and the family code will be summarized here before proceeding to an evaluation of the AFN's progress and a look at some of the factors inhibiting its work.

Polygyny

The AFN has supported widespread debate on this subject in the context of the roles of men and women. One of these, held in late 1976, solicited discussion from workers in a continuing education center of NIGELEC (the national electric company). Proponents of polygyny argued that Islam commends it

4. *Sahel Hebdo* for late 1975, 1976, 1977 (six months), 1978, 1982 (three months), and 1984 (six months) were examined for data on women, the family code, and elaboration of the Development Society.

(some went so far as to say it *commands* it) and ensures that women can have a "moral" and responsible life without having to become prostitutes. The latter opinion is a frequently expressed view of city dwellers who believe that women far outnumber men. Others who favored abolition or restriction of polygyny cited it as a source of tension in the home, as the cause of hardship for children of frequent divorce, and as a cause of neglect of children in urban areas where economic resources are often strained in providing for two or more house-holds. Another objection was the link in the minds of some with repudiation, especially in the rural areas where, it was asserted, men frequently divorced their wives at the end of the harvest season (when their agricultural labor was no longer necessary) or took on a second wife only to abandon the first. The AFN has not called for the suppression of polygamy; rather, its position is that while polygamy may not be in the best interests of women, it is better that it wither away (as they believe it will "despite religion") by virtue of choice and response to economic conditions.[5]

The Family Code

The discussion of the NIGELEC employees was lively when it addressed the prospects of the family code. Both men and women were enthusiastic and agreed that it should include provisions for consent of both parties; the prohibition of race and caste barriers; minimum age at marriage of seventeen for girls and twenty-one for boys; and a minimal bridewealth (10,000–15,000 CFA). There was also general agreement that divorce should be made more difficult to achieve and that the "delay" period before remarriage be required for men as well as for women. In addition, women discussants sought grounds for divorce equal to men, especially with regard to adultery; access to child support and custody; and an option for monogamy and community property at the time of first marriage. In the heat of the debates, men complained about the "materialism" of women, but women replied that men chose to observe only those aspects of tradition amenable to them without taking into account their wives. This plea for consistency was reiterated later that year by a female clerk at the *Palais de Justice* in Niamey who stated that in the absence of a family code, Niger ought to at least apply Qur'anic law in matters of custody rather than granting men custody only to have the children turned over to a stepmother (*Sahel Hebdo*, January 12, 1976, p. 28).

Work on the family code was one of the principal activities of the AFN during its first year. A commission was formed to undertake research and to sensitize women about the idea of a code. The results of their investigations were presented to another high-level commission which had been established by the

5. *Sahel Hebdo*, June 6, 1977, p. 24; January 12, 1976; November 22, 1976; December 6, 1976, pp. 29–30; December 18, 1976; September 6, 1976.

government to develop a draft document. Although by December 1976 the outlines of the document were just beginning to emerge, likely provisions would cover inheritance, marriage, problems of women and children, and matrimonial relations (*Sahel Hebdo*, December 18, 1976, pp. 45–46). The code was given a high priority by the AFN the following year as well: it was the focus of considerable attention at the First Congress and appeared in that meeting's resolutions (*Sahel Hebdo*, May 16 and 23, 1977). Work on the code was complicated by the diverse ethnic traditions to be taken into account and the need to command the cooperation of various offices and officials at the ministerial and local levels.

By 1982 the leaders of the AFN found that progress on the code was blocked (*Sahel Hebdo*, April 15, 1977; September 6, 1982, p. 22). Although neither the chronology nor the precise circumstances are clear, the failure of the code project was probably the result of insufficient attention on the part of the principals at work on it in Niamey to solicit the participation of local officials, especially the *préfets* of the *départements* (Garba n.d.). At some point the chief of state suspended all work on the code; it languished until 1989, when work was resumed under a new regime (*Sahel Dimanche*, December 15, 1989, pp. 12–13).

Critiques and Problems

The most frequent cause of the slow progress of mobilization of Nigerien women for the association's activities was the indifference—sometimes the hostility—of segments of the population. Despite good organization and leadership, the AFN encountered high absenteeism of women at local functions, often attributed to the refusal of men to grant permission to their secluded wives to attend. Achieving bureaucratic cooperation and the extreme burdens that programs placed on the AFN's leaders, few in number and already pulled in many directions, led the organization to request that some individuals be attached to a ministry to concentrate on women's affairs (a Woman's Office was established within the Ministry of Youth, Sport and Culture in 1980) (*Sahel Hebdo*, August 3, 1978, p. 53; December 18, 1978, p. 64; interview with Maiga Hamsou, February 24, 1982).

The *Sahel Hebdo* articles also reflect contradictory messages about the pace and manner of change and the AFN's role in it. In particular, the theme of avoiding social trauma, a likely result of moving too fast, occurs again and again. Women were not to allow their desire for social reorganization to provoke social disequilibrium: "Don't organize, educate," was the admonishment on this theme (*Sahel Hebdo*, June 7, 1976, p. 29; March 7, 1977). The AFN may also have been diverted from their central pursuits by succumbing to the plethora of social demands placed on the small group of leaders. Writing in 1982, a male "supporter" of the organization said that the AFN did not have to "struggle against men, but against retrograde social structures. . . . [The leaders need] to leave behind its folkloric side: tam-tams, spectacles . . . in order to concretely and efficiently pursue the struggle with which they had been charged . . . the full emancipation of women" (*Sahel Hebdo*, September 6, 1982, pp. 2, 20). The judgment is harsh, but the problems are real.

Press reports about the AFN during the first six months of 1984 were relatively few in comparison to previous years; and the coverage was as much of ceremonial, diplomatic, and official activities as of development or mobilization projects. The second annual women's week activities in Niamey included tree plantings, cooking competitions, a football match (to attract the interest of men!), a cultural evening, craft displays, and a beautiful baby contest. Madame Diallo, who had become a member of the National Charter Commission, accompanied the head of state on an official visit to China. Construction on a new AFN center had begun in Zinder; domestic-housekeeping materials were donated to another of the AFN regional centers. The AFN and the Islamic Association were slated to cooperate on a publicity campaign for the start-up of a Maternal Child Health and Family Planning Center in Niamey.[6]

The AFN's accomplishments are remarkable given the multiple fronts on which it has had to operate. While co-optation in the ceremonial round may be a problem, there are more critical ones such as the small number of trained women available to do the work, budgetary cutbacks, and the cultural barriers to education and mobilization discussed earlier. That the organization has sustained the momentum it has is admirable. But a factor of ultimate importance is how the government will choose to support or diminish the success of this organization it founded. The direction of government policy in this choice will be influenced by other developments. The Islamic Association of Niger and its supporters both within and without the country are prime examples.

The Islamic Association of Niger (AIN)

Information about this important constituent organization within the Development Society is scarcer than that on the AFN. It was founded in 1974, and, like the AFN, has branches at the level of the *département, arrondissement,* and *sous-arrondissement.* In 1978 the AIN was characterized in the following way: "Apolitical and religious, its goal is to encourage respect for the precepts of the Qur'an, the basis of Muslim tradition; to extend it, to unite Muslims of the two sexes, and to work for the creation and development of libraries (*Sahel Hebdo*, August 5, 1978, pp. 50–51).

The chief body of the AIN is its national assembly which elects the members

6. *Sahel Hebdo*, March 12, 1984, p. 3, and May 14, 1984, pp. 14–15; *Le Sahel*, March 9–11, 1984, pp. 1–2; January 4, 1984, p. 3; March 21, 1984, p. 1; April 2, 1984, p. 5; May 10, 1984.

of the executive board. The directorate tours the country, aiming to establish sections in all the departments and county seats. The organization has perceived itself to be operating against the legacy of the civilian government which had concerned itself little with the Muslim religion. It also seeks to eliminate "marabouts cognac"—characterized as scarcely literate teachers whose dishonesty was enough to confuse the gullible. In its early days, the AIN worked to eliminate excessive fees levied by the marabouts on ceremonial occasions and to suppress the automatic 10 percent estate fee. Similarly, the AIN encouraged the public to substitute the sacrifice of sheep for that of bulls at ceremonies in an attempt to diminish their cost.

In a personal interview, an official of the directorate emphasized education at both the formal and mass levels, and local improvement projects as the primary thrusts of the AIN's program of activities. Improvement projects, undertaken in close cooperation with the *Samariya*, typically consist of the cultivation of gardens, and the construction of sports fields and hostels for unemployed young men. The education program is implemented on many fronts and commands local, national, and—significantly—international support. There are daily religious broadcasts on the radio and television with special programs offered on Thursday evenings (the eve of the Friday congregational prayer). Religious studies (*animations de points de vue d'Islam*) are offered in thousands of schools, including a Qur'anic preschool in Zinder. Across the country there are fifty-five *franco-arabe* elementary schools and *Colleges d'Enseignement Generales* (the CEGs are lower secondary schools) that exist in Zinder and Niamey. The capstone of the AIN's efforts to extend Islamic education is the Université Islamique de Say, one of two Islamic universities established in sub-Saharan Africa (the other is in Kampala) with substantial support of the Organization of the Islamic Conference (interview with M. Al-Khassam, April 4, 1982). The Islamic University of West Africa at Say opened in January 1987 (*Europa Year Book 1988* 2:2005). Its faculties, which are open to students from other countries as well as Niger, will eventually include schools of Arabic Language and Islamic Studies, polytechnical studies, sciences, and medicine; in addition, a university hospital center will be constructed to supplement the school of medicine. The student enrollment when all the schools are operational is expected to be about 10,000 (*Le Sahel*, June 13, 1984, pp. 1, 3).

In the early 1980s, press reports of AIN events suggested that the government laid considerable responsibility upon the organization to rid Nigerien Islam of fanatacism and to further the integration of Islamic ideals into the ideology of the Development Society. Thus, in March 1984, a senior official of the Ministry of the Interior in the opening address before the Fourth Congress of the Association commended his audience to "action, justice, and vigilance." By providing a model based on the precepts of the Qur'an the members of the association would be furthering a universal code able to create a society of justice: "The *shari'a*, a factor in the confidence, solidarity, stability and national unity, ought to be faithfully interpreted and to be the object of a healthy, general and rigorous application in all daily activities." The close association between a just society and security was of paramount concern: "Security is the *sine qua non* of development and is everyone's affair." The equation between security and authenticity of Islam was further underscored by the local *préfet* in his speech to the group (*Le Sahel*, March 29, 1984, p. 5, and April 2, 1984, p. 5).[7]

The evidence is too scant to assess the long-range influence of the *Association Islamique du Niger* with respect to the *Association des Femmes du Niger* or to the "development" of women in the larger context of Nigerien society. But examination of two developments—one internal and the other external—suggests preliminary indications of future directions. The first is that so far there appears to be no role for women in the Islamic Association. In 1982 there were no women members, although the possibility of "women's sections" being developed in the future was not precluded by officials of the association. Cooperation between the AIN and the AFN is frequently anticipated in press reports, but if it has occurred, it has received no publicity, and general impressions confirm that there is none.

Second, the extent of international interest in and support of the Islamic Association of Niger, the location of the Islamic University at Say and Niger's financial commitment to it, and statements by government officials suggest that the military regime has committed itself at the very least to a pro-Islamic policy with important international and domestic consequences. Up until 1980, Libya is alleged to have been a major source of funding for the Islamic Association. Libya's regional ambitions, as signified by the proposal for the United Muslim States of the Sahel, the situation in Chad, and its probable involvement in the internal affairs of Niger in 1981, led to a break in diplomatic relations between the two countries. These were restored in 1982, but it also seems likely that the frequent emphasis upon security in the speeches of officials is directed at Libya (Nicolas 1981:213).

If bilateral ties with Libya remain cautious, the same cannot be said for Niger's participation in the Organization of the Islamic Conference, or the "Islamic Conference," founded in 1969.[8] Primarily concerned with the politi-

7. The April 2 issue identified further topics discussed at the meeting and present in the final communique as being education, customs, diffusion of religious works, and Islamic justice.

8. Founded in Rabat, with headquarters in Djedda, the Islamic Conference is composed of forty-two member states, sixteen of which are from sub-Saharan Africa: Cameroun, Guinea, the Comoros, Djibouti, Gabon, Gambia, Guinea–Bissau, Burkina Faso, Mauritania, Mali, Niger, Uganda, Senegal, Somalia, Sudan, and Chad. It is significant to note that Nigeria is not a member although it attends meetings as an observer, yet countries like Gabon, Cameroun, and Burkina with small Muslim minorities are full-fledged members. Its primary objectives are to work for the renaissance of the Muslim world, cooperation among member states, preservation of the Islamic

cal tensions of the Middle East, the Islamic Conference, through policies formulated at four major international conferences, has also made a substantial commitment to economic and educational development in Africa. In 1981 the capital of the Islamic Development Bank was expanded to $3 billion. At the Taef meeting that same year, the majority of the sums designated for projects was assigned to Sahelian states (Nicolas 1981:126–28; *Sahel Hebdo*, January 23, 1984, p. 8). The location of the Islamic University in Niger, funded by some $60 million from the Islamic Conference, and the extensive coverage given to the Nigerien chief of state's participation in the Casablanca meeting in 1984 point to the fact that the Islamic Conference is a source of sympathetic allies and assistance—both technological and ideological—as Niger progresses through the stages of implementing the Development Society and the National Charter. Furthermore, during the first session of the Commission for the National Charter in January 1984, Islamic models were prominent among those featured in addresses by invited lecturers including one on the Algerian Charter and another on Islam and Development.[9]

The association with Muslim states and their programs offers an ideology useful for domestic concerns as well. Islam helps to unify otherwise different people. In the face of what many Africans believe to have been the corrupting and destructive influences of Western culture and colonialism, it offers an alternative moral order that is closer to their own because of the historic ties. Local Muslim associations provide a vehicle for the state to advocate the continuity of religion and yet exert control over older foci of authority by bringing them under its wing (Nicolas 1981:126–40, 145, 150–51, 242–50).

But what are the consequences of this pro-Islamic evolution for women in the societies involved? And how does this evolution interact with the efforts of the AFN or with the status of women as conceived in the fusion of Islam and custom that exists in Niger?

Conclusions

Perhaps the only generalization that can be made is that Islam's effect upon women in Niger today is not monolithic. The evolution of Islam's interaction with indigenous custom brought about changes in women's status even before the transformations of the colonial period. The essays of Beik, Echard, and Stephens elsewhere in this volume enrich our understanding of the com-

---

patrimony, support for the Palestinian cause, and the liberation of Jerusalem (Nicolas 1981:126–27).

9. Presented by the Algerian ambassador to Sweden, M. Hamdani Smael, and Dr. Abdel Gelil Abdou Chalabi of El Azhar University respectively. The third address presented by a Nigerian was entitled "What Development Models for Africa?" (*Le Sahel*, January 27–29, 1984, p. 3).

plex interplay between ideology and reality, pre-Islamic customs and Islamic identity. Colonial authority introduced new ideals, but, more crucial to the argument presented here, it also inaugurated patterns of social and economic relations that affected family life in substantive ways. Recent efforts by the government of Niger to restructure political culture have reinforced Islamic values as a means to establish a national identity at once more authentic and less dependent upon Western norms. The consequences of these new directions for women, as seen in the activities of the two component associations of the Development Society, are not uniform: they offer the potential for both promise and constraint.

The fusion of Islam and pre-Islamic custom in Niger has been profound. As Islam was adopted, interpersonal conduct and freedom of action were modified for women in the direction of deference and obedience, restrictions of actions, and low public profile. In marriage women gained formal rights to protection, maintenance, and inheritance, at the cost of the greater complementarity between men and women of the pre-Islamic patterns. Land and the labor to work it over time (as manifested by children)—the bedrock of the old lineage structure—were more resistant to intrusive ideas than other custom. If the association of Islam with wealth, commerce, and new economic opportunities was more attractive for city than for rural dwellers, it became the pervasive ideal in the precolonial and colonial periods except where exploitation occurred at the hands of Muslim rulers.

The psychological and economic dependence of married women that resulted from this ideal had its costs which are even more striking today. When times are hard, women become more insistent upon their material claims, and if thrown onto their own devices, are ill-equipped to cope. Men struggle to meet their demands, but faced with many forces they cannot control, exert even greater force on what they can—their wives.

The nation state, as seen in the example of Niger, seeks to provide an ideological and an institutional framework for directing and at the same time controlling the process of social and economic change. The *Association des Femmes du Niger* and the *Association Islamique du Niger* are innovations on both the levels of ideology and institution. The AFN aims to improve facilities for women, to reverse their prior neglect in the exchange of technology and services, and to bring women into the civic process. Its experience shows that it will be easier to accomplish the first two goals (if given adequate resources) than the third. Until education and training of women are no longer equated with corruption, and until women's voices are not muted by fears of insecurity and social change, the AFN leadership's ability to sustain its drive will be limited.

This is where the apparent evolution of the government's ideology has high-risk, high-gain potential for women. The high-risk lies in the fact that the priority for women's concerns may diminish; with respect to the project for a family code in Niger one could say it already has. Moreover, the models for an Islamic society it is examining, if Algeria is an example, do not augur well for the maintenance of a visible concern for the increased participation of women in molding the direction of society (Minces 1978:158–71, esp. 168–69).[10] The high gain lies in the potential that the educational expansion and reform envisioned by the Islamic Association, which benefit from far greater resources than Niger could afford alone, will be open to women. The ability of the state and of the participants in the AFN and the AIN to resolve the competing interests represented in these two institutions will be critical in determining whether the as yet unfulfilled expectations of cooperation between them will expire or be made real.

Epilogue

In the hours before President Kountché's death from a cerebral hemorrhage in November 1987, the Supreme Military Council designated Colonel Ali Saïbou, Army Chief of Staff, as interim head of state. Colonel Saïbou announced plans for the establishment of a constitutional committee in December 1987 (*Europa Year Book 1988* 2:2004), and later that month in a government reshuffle, created a new Secretariat of State for Public Health and Social Welfare in charge of social welfare and women's affairs to whose leadership he named a woman, Mrs. Moumouni Aissata (*Africa Research Bulletin* 24 (December 1987): 8693–94). In January 1988, Colonel Saïbou appointed two other women to senior posts, one of whom was Madam Bazeye Salifou, named to the appeal court (*Africa Research Bulletin* 25 (February 1988): 8756). Later in the year, the president officially reconstituted the National Development Council. The NDC, composed of 150 military and civilian advisers elected for three years, will act as a constituent assembly to draw up the Constitution of the Second Republic (*Africa Research Bulletin* 25 (August 1988): 8947). A single political party, the National Movement for the Developing Society, was created August 2, 1988 (*Africa Research Bulletin* 25 (September 1988): 8973), and President Saïbou announced in December a timetable for Niger's return to constitutional rule toward the end of 1989. Press reports indicate that the National Development Council will review the draft constitution and present it for a national referendum, possibly in December. Presidential and parliamentary

---

10. The core of Mince's argument is that, despite the profound role of Algerian women in the war of liberation from colonial rule and despite initial recognition of that in legislation of the early years of independence, Algerian women have witnessed a deterioration in their position and a reversal of some of their steps forward as identification with the wider Islamic world has come to play a larger role in the ideology of the Algerian government. See also "Le Code algérien de la famille" by Hélène Vandevelde in *Maghreb Machrek* 107, 1985:52–64.

elections will follow. Details of the electoral process remain shadowy: President Saïbou has stated that there will be competition for elective positions, but the military will also be represented in any new legislative assembly (*Africa Research Bulletin* 25 (December 1988): 9075).

The appointment of women to high office and the steady progress toward a restoration of constitutional rule are positive signs that the present government intends to pursue President Kountché's objectives on the domestic front. The significance of these developments for the issues considered above are likely to become clearer in the coming months.

Hausa-Fulani Women: The State of the Struggle

The history of Nigerian women's struggle to improve their situation is similar to that of their counterparts in other areas of the world. As is true everywhere, they have been more successful in certain fields than in others. In northern Nigeria particularly, sociocultural factors associated with Islam have had considerable effect on women's literacy rates, political awareness, and world view, resulting in significant differences between the lives of these women and their sisters in the south. Educational opportunities are central to women's situations in Nigeria. Western education was introduced to Nigeria through Christian missionary activities, which were focused on the non-Muslim south. Thus the largest concentration of mission schools and Western-educated elites grew up in the southern part of the country. The north, however, was influenced by Arab North Africa. Islam was introduced through the trans-Saharan trade, along with an educational system quite distinct from that of the West. Because Islam pervades every aspect of life, it has had a greater effect on its adherents in northern Nigeria than any other single factor. As several other studies show, Islam in northern Nigeria affects women's spatial freedom, and therefore access to education and politics, more profoundly than in the south. Despite these sociocultural differences, however, the condition of and problems faced by women throughout Nigeria have much in common.

Although the 1979 Nigerian constitution forbade discrimination on the basis of sex, it has been difficult for women to achieve equality with men because

Bilkisu Yusuf at work. Photo by B. Mack.

of resistance by those in power. For instance, during the Second Republic the Speaker of the House of Representatives, Benjamin Cha'aha, was asked in an interview why female legislators were excluded from appointment as committee chairpersons. He responded that women were unsuited for such appointment: "If women were picked to head any of the thirty-four committees, men would refuse to serve under them. . . . Such committees would die natural deaths" (*Sunday Guardian*, July 31, 1983, p. 5). The Speaker of the House, representing his colleagues, blatantly discriminated against women, expressing a viewpoint that clearly violated section 39 of the constitution and articles 2 and 21 of the universal declaration of human rights.

Voter registration surveys of 1983 showed that women constituted over 50 percent of the country's population, 40 percent of its total labor force, and 52 percent of the agricultural labor force. Despite the significance of these numbers, 50.4 percent of urban Nigerian women and 78 percent of rural women are illiterate, and only 0.7 percent of the federal legislature is female (Awosika 1981:86; *Sunday Guardian*, July 31, 1983, p. 5; WIN 1985a).

Hausa-Fulani Women

Constituting a majority of the population, women in Nigeria remain underrepresented, poorly educated, and victims of superstition. This is especially true for the Hausa-Fulani women of Kano, a major urban center in the north, where it is considered unwise to invest in female education because girls are married so young. It is assumed by many that educating girls does not provide the family with added income because wives usually are not allowed to work outside the home.

This neglect of women's education is not a new phenomenon. In the north the custom predates the early-twentieth-century campaign of reform (*jihadi*) led by Shehu Usman ɗan Fodio, when superstition was rife and the status of women was synonymous with degradation and deprivation. His daughter Nana Asma'u's example as an educator notwithstanding, minimal literacy skills and religious tenets were taught to women—just enough to allow them to say their obligatory prayers. When religion has been taught to women, Islamic injunctions on women's rights nevertheless have been distorted by local traditions to favor men. In some cases local customs have been confused with Islamic law because of ignorance. At other times, where Islamic law clearly favors women, some men—even some Islamic law scholars—deliberately interpret laws to deprive women of their legal rights.

Most Hausa-Fulani Muslim women lack formal education. It is no exaggeration to say that until recently their role has been no more than that of subordinate to men, illustrating Felditch's statement that "in all but a very few societies, instrumental roles which include political and economic leadership are played by the husband/father while expressive roles are played by the wife/mother" (quoted in 'Abd al' Ati 1982:54). This attitude runs through all aspects of women's lives in Nigeria and is manifested most strikingly in the north among the Hausa-Fulani. There are relatively few middle-ranking Hausa-Fulani women professionals, and female administrators are fewer still in the decision-making organs of government, both at the state and federal levels.

The deplorable situation of Muslim Hausa-Fulani women as subjects of men has been in effect for ages. Nevertheless, it is a condition which has no relevance to, much less justification in, Islam. The subjugation of women, in fact, is in opposition to Islamic principles and injunctions. Thus in the early nineteenth century, the religious reformer, Shehu Usman ɗan Fodio, had cause to warn Hausa-Fulani Muslim women:

Oh Muslim women, do not listen to the words of the misguided ones who seek to lead you astray by ordering you to obey your husband instead of telling you to obey Allah and his messenger. They tell you a woman's happiness lies in obeying her husband. This is no more than a camouflage to make you satisfy their needs. They impose on you duties which neither Allah nor his messenger impose on you. They make you cook, wash clothes, and do other things which they desire while they fail to teach you what Allah and his apostle have prescribed for you. Neither Allah nor his apostle charges you with such duties. ('Dan Fodio 1981)

The reformer's warning is still relevant for the Hausa-Fulani community, where traditions like the rigid imposition of wife seclusion—the confinement of women in their houses during the day, when they could be attending school—are still widely practiced as part of Hausa interpretations of Islam. Islam attaches a great deal of significance to learning; the Prophet Mohammed urged Muslims to seek knowledge even if it took them as far as China. Failing to educate individuals under one's care is not only advised against but is a violation of the tenets of Islam. The Shehu himself advocated the education of women:

All the female members of Usman dan Fodio's family (wives, daughters, etc.) were learned. They all left a tradition of scholarship behind them. Nana Asma'u was reported to have written fifty-five original works on her own. If translations are included, the number rises to sixty-two. She wrote on a wide range of topics: history, theology, philosophy, and medicine. (Kabir 1985)

Adult Education

Many women are now reclaiming their rights under Islam. There has been an upsurge of women's adult education activities focusing on both Western and Islamic education. Kano City had only one women's primary education center in 1980. By 1984, through programs set up by Kano State's Agency for Mass Education, there were nine in the city and over a dozen more in surrounding rural areas. These centers hold day or evening classes in literacy, numeracy, child care, nutrition, income-generation projects, and Islamic religious knowledge. Attendance is free, but women must find transportation to the centers, and taxi fare is high. After a full day's domestic work, women are tired; nevertheless, many attend classes as often as six times a week, often carrying an infant along with them. Perhaps most difficult is the stipulation that women may attend these classes only with the permission of their husbands: the agency does not want to be responsible for conflict between partners. For this reason, the establishment of evening classes has been crucial to the success of the project. When husbands realize their wives can attend school without disrupting the domestic schedule and without violating sociocultural mores, they are usually willing to give permission. Thus even secluded women who drop out of school to marry at adolescence can now attend school without violating their traditional obligation to remain secluded during the daytime. The adult literacy campaign—another Kano State–sponsored education scheme—has also proved to be extremely popular; approximately 40 percent of Kano's women benefit from its classes, which are held at primary schools and the local university after regular classes have finished for the day.

Women's enrollment in Kano State's Agency for Mass Education Women's

Centers has increased dramatically since its inception, attesting to the success
of its culturally appropriate approach to educating secluded Muslim women.
The number of women students increased 27 percent between the program's
first and second year and another 44 percent in its third year. The program is
carried out by 34 permanent and 131 part-time staff members.

Although adult education has existed in the area for decades, the present
boom can be traced directly to the People's Redemption Party's (PRP) commitment to education and raising the status of women (PRP 1978:5). When
the party came to power in 1979, it borrowed a leaf from its predecessor, the
NEPU party. The late Mallam Aminu Kano, leader of both parties, was remarkable for promoting women's education. Even during the repressive period
of the 1950s, Aminu Kano, together with radical members of NEPU, urged
northern women "to escape the state of total subjugation" in which Hausa-
Fulani women found themselves and to react against centuries-old concepts of
respect, deference, modesty, and their "proper place." Again in 1979, under
the PRP banner, Aminu Kano campaigned to ensure that "women were granted
the right to move freely about their compounds, extending the vote to them, as
had been done in Southern Nigeria, and giving them the all-important right to
education" (Feinstein 1973:179).

In addition to its focus on mass literacy centers, the Agency for Mass Education also organized a program geared toward training women to earn an
income. Programs with a similar plan are also strategically operated from the
houses of accepted community leaders, and women in seclusion who cannot
attend classes in the agency's center may participate in this scheme.

Islamic Schools

Alongside the successful Agency for Mass Education classes, various Islamic
organizations have developed a wide range of courses directed at raising the
standard of women's Islamic education. Islamic schools, located throughout
Kano City and in other Nigerian cities with large Muslim populations, are of
utmost importance in reaching a broad range of women. They count among
their students women in seclusion, career women, and students from institutes
of higher education. Their aim is not only to impart Islamic knowledge and to
enlighten Muslim women about their rights and obligations but also to eradicate
superstition emanating from traditional cultural beliefs.

If all these schools can achieve the goals they have set for themselves, Nigerian society could soon have a crop of women educated in both Western and
Islamic fields. Currently it is the dearth of just such a group of educated women
that has hampered progress among Hausa-Fulani women in developing active
leaders. In a society where men distort Islamic injunctions to suit themselves,
the acquisition of Islamic knowledge, apart from being necessary for the per-

Islamic schools are of utmost importance in reaching a broad range of women. Photo by B. Yusuf.

fection of one's faith, becomes indispensable for articulating one's claims and demands. Thus women who have the relevant knowledge would be in a position to cite the Qur'an and the *Hadith* to defend their positions on political and religious issues of the day without risk of being labeled outcasts or disbelievers.

Women's Associations

Among the female graduates of both Western and Islamic schools are activists whose enthusiasm has led to the establishment of a variety of women's organizations in Nigeria. Dating from the late 1950s, when the National Council of Women's Societies (NCWS) originated, at least some Nigerian women have participated in social and community endeavors. Lately, however, greater numbers of women have become more active in asserting their rights in both the national economy and Nigeria's several distinct religious communities. The auspicious acronym WIN denotes the organization Women in Nigeria, which focuses on the rights and opportunities of all women, regardless of ethnic group, class, or religious affiliation. Another organization has addressed the religious issue, uniting Muslim women in the Muslim Sisters Organization (MSO), from which grew the Federation of Muslim Women's Associations in Nigeria, or FOMWAN.

Perhaps the earliest of Nigeria's women's organizations was established toward the end of the colonial period, two years prior to independence from Britain. Founded in Ibadan in 1958, the National Council of Women's Societies of Nigeria (NCWS) reflects in large part the service orientation of women's groups of the same period in the West. It is a nonpolitical, nonreligious, and nongovernmental organization created to join together all voluntary women's groups in the country. Under the auspices of the NCWS umbrella organization, women's groups operate with a variety of different aims. Some, like the Soroptimist Club of Lagos, are primarily social groups; Jamiyyar Matan Arewa (Northern Women's Community Work Group) organizes women for health care, nutrition, and hands-on mutual aid; and the Young Women's Christian Association (YWCA) operates to promote Christian ethics. Membership in NCWS is also open to individuals. Its aims are:

— to promote the welfare and economic and social progress of women, laying special emphasis on education and training;
— to awaken and encourage in women the realization of their responsibility to the community;
— to secure guarantees that women are given every opportunity to play their part as fully responsible members of the community;
— to encourage the affiliation of all women's nonpolitical organizations in Nigeria; and
— to foster cooperation with other national and international bodies with similar aims.

More recently, several other, more activist women's groups have claimed increasing membership.

WIN was launched in 1982 at a seminar organized by the Sociology Department of Ahmadu Bello University (ABU) in Zaria, Nigeria. This meeting of academics, social activists, and artists throughout the country provided a forum for the examination of women's situations in contemporary Nigeria. Part of the motivation for founding WIN stemmed from the conviction that previous women's organizations in Nigeria had been elitist in both ideal and objective, dominated by the 5 percent of Nigerian women who supported and represented the status quo. WIN's founders felt that such organizations were unable to address issues of interest to any but the economic elite and therefore failed to meet—or even to recognize—in particular, the needs of rural women.

All the WIN conferences have advocated positive change for Nigerian women and have been attended by men and women practicing in a wide range of careers. Opening the 1983 conference, ABU's Dr. Dalhatu Muhammad stated, "No nation can be said to be developed or civilized if its menfolk relegate its womenfolk to the background. . . . Such nations must be condemned as primitive." This comment by a devout Muslim man seemed to acknowledge

Under the auspices of the NCWS umbrella organization, women's groups operate with a variety of different aims to organize women for health care, nutrition, and hands-on mutual aid. Photo by B. Yusuf.

tacitly the widespread image of the Muslim husband as an oppressor of women. Indeed, the theme of the second conference—"Women and the Family"—provided the context for discussions of the domestic oppression of women. At this meeting the practice of forced early marriage was condemned. Pregnancy at too young an age may result in death during childbirth; it may also cause internal rupture of the bladder and rectum (vesico vaginal fistula; *Newswatch*, April 17, 1989, pp. 36–37). In the latter case, the condition is often worsened through treatment by some midwives, whose unsuccessful surgery leaves a young girl with permanent internal damage. Thus she becomes "undesirable" to her husband, who promptly divorces her, leaving her suited only for a life of prostitution.

Among other domestic issues debated was the universal problem of women's double workload, in which unpaid housework and childcare are accomplished in addition to wage labor such as farm trade or food processing for profit. In. Nigeria the double workload means that many women toil for sixteen hours a day or more, depleting their energy and damaging their health.

Participants stressed that no solution to these problems was possible without radical social change and the complete elimination of all forms of human exploitation. Furthermore, representatives of both Islam and Christianity emphasized that the oppressive treatment of women was condoned by neither religion. A Muslim scholar commented on the rights of women under Muslim law:

The uniqueness of women as far as Islam is concerned permeates the entire life of the woman. She has in the first place to seek her own salvation on her own. Indeed, she owes herself a personal, individual responsibility to do so. She has a legal existence of her own and thus she acquires and retains her own property; she inherits from others, and others inherit from her. She disposes of her wealth and benefits from it as she likes and retains her individuality and personality as a right.

Such commentary indicates that Islam not only accepts a woman's active pursuit of her individual rights but fosters it.

The second WIN conference closed with concrete suggestions for change. In the economic field, participants advocated the improvement of women's opportunities to earn a living. Women, it was stressed, should have access to land, wage labor, and other social resources on the same basis as men. With regard to health, women must take control of their own physical welfare, refusing to stay with men who mistreat them and actively participating in decisions concerning the number and spacing of children in the family. Also advocated was the need to improve women's legal status by enforcing equal rights among both sexes, as guaranteed by the country's constitution. These include the right to inherit land, to gain custody of children upon divorce, and equality in marriage agreements. Considering that education is a basic necessity for the advancement of any society, the participants recommended that women should be assured access to education equal to that of men. For the younger generation, boys and girls should have equal access to education of comparable quality. By providing such constructive criticism of our society and suggestions for the correction of gross inequalities between men and women, WIN is moving women's organizations away from the myopic view of society that has characterized them heretofore.

Concerned about their status as Muslim women, secondary and university women throughout the country organized the Muslim Sisters Organization (MSO) as early as 1965. Because women remained active even after graduation from the school through which they joined, the MSO grew steadily, establishing branches throughout the country. Eventually MSO membership was able to coordinate activities that led to the formation of FOMWAN.

As MSO membership grew, and especially since about 1980, educated Muslim women throughout the country had been considering the establishment of a national Islamic women's organization through which to increase their religious knowledge and enhance their practice of Islam. Some had already formed smaller Islamic study groups; others had organized classes for uneducated women; still others had established Islamic nurseries and primary schools. Nevertheless, these groups remained isolated from one another and thus were unable to benefit from mutual support and inspiration. Furthermore, many women had no access to any of these groups. Thus there developed the need for a central focus that could unite existing groups and establish new groups in areas where they were needed.

Also needed was a representative voice at the state and national levels to express the views and concerns of the country's Muslim women. Such concerns were often in conflict with the views expressed by women in other nondenominational organizations and contrary to the teachings of the Qur'an and Sunnah. Muslim women felt that certain issues, such as *shari'a* legal rights and women's access to religious education, could be addressed satisfactorily only by working within the Muslim community, in cooperation with their male counterparts. Therefore women united under the banner of Islam to demand their religious rights, influence national policy, and condemn state and federal decisions they felt to be detrimental to their well-being and progress.

In 1985 two international MSO conferences brought these concerns to light. The first, drawing over five hundred delegates from Nigeria and abroad, was held in Kano in April. In August a similar conference was held in Ilorin. These two meetings provided platforms for the discussion of Muslim women's concerns, witnessed the condemnation of the NCWS, and resulted in the establishment of FOMWAN as an umbrella organization for Nigeria's Muslim women's groups, whose aim was to assist Muslim women in living according to the tenets of Islam, as expressed in the Qur'an and the Sunnah.

The group's condemnation of NCWS occurred over an issue that exemplifies the divergent religious foci of the two groups. The NCWS had put forth a proposal aimed at reducing the country's divorce rate and protecting divorced women. The proposal stated that any man who intended to terminate a marriage that had lasted for ten years should also be ready to relinquish half of his assets to the wife he intended to divorce. This was based on the supposition that the wife must have contributed both financially and otherwise to the family's wealth during the ten-year period. Where divorce was inevitable, it was reasoned, the wife should be entitled to her share, which is "half the wealth accumulated by the family."

On the surface this proposal looked neat, but a closer look revealed loopholes that needed to be eliminated prior to its becoming a law. These faults were outlined during the conference of Muslim women. First, the proposal did not address the real issue of rising divorce rates in Nigeria. A man can still divorce his wife after nine years and eleven months—just under ten years' time—and thus avoid the intended action of the law on a technicality. Second, there was implicit in the proposal an assumption that the threat of parting with half his wealth would force a man to back down and decide to remain with a wife against his will. A third problem involved the designation of who would determine what amount constituted half the man's wealth and the question of whether unbiased parties could be found. Fourth, and perhaps most offensive to Muslim women, was the assumption that a man had only one wife: the proposal did not allow for the situation of his having up to four wives, most of whom had lived with him for ten or more years. If half a Muslim man's assets were awarded to one divorced wife (assuming the woman would ever receive the amount), it would result in adverse effects for the children and wives who remained in the family (Yusuf 1985a).

With this proposal the NCWS members unknowingly ventured beyond a minimal platform and risked alienating a large number of potential allies among Muslim women. The shortcomings of the NCWS proposal demonstrated a disregard for the multiplicity of cultures that exist in Nigeria. Organizations with poor representation and inadequate information are bound to display these traits in their approach to policy formulation. In many other instances, faulty generalizations have been made about issues having a direct bearing on Muslim women. Solutions to women's problems devised by such organizations have often proven irrelevant for Muslim women.

The Federation of Muslim Women therefore recognized the urgent need to end long-standing disregard for the concerns of the average Muslim woman in the formulation and implementation of national policy. The federation's main objectives are threefold: (1) to promote cooperation and common action among the Muslim women's groups in Nigeria, (2) to encourage and coordinate development of Islamic education and awareness among women, and (3) to enable Muslim women to express their views on national issues. The federation took women's struggle a step further by moving from generalities to specifics. In its first communiqué, the federation made known its views on topical issues by demanding the establishment of Islamic (*shari'a*) courts, condemning infringement of the rights of Muslim women at work, and calling on the government to reject the IMF loan which was then under negotiation (FOMWAN 1985).

One of FOMWAN's first actions called for the establishment of *shari'a* courts in every Nigerian state. In the north, a Grand Kadi presides over all *shari'a* courts, where issues relating to Muslim personal law are handled. But in the south, where a large Muslim population exists without the benefit of *shari'a* courts, Muslims' legal complaints are judged at customary or magistrate courts instead of being dealt with according to Muslim law.

Another of FOMWAN's objectives is to empower Muslim women to make a positive influence on national matters, both religious and secular, with a view to guarding the interests of Islam. Echoing the concerns of WIN members, FOMWAN's International Seminar, held in Lagos July 24–27, 1986, had as its theme "Family and Society." The session dealt with issues ranging from family planning to education and domestic economics. FOMWAN members expressed concern over the practice of marrying off preadolescent girls and ap-

Prizes presented to graduates at a FOMWAN affiliate school. Photo by B. Yusuf.

pealed to religious leaders to discourage such a trend. The deplorable state of the nation's economy was another topic of concern, as participants noted that materialism, mismanagement, and dishonesty were the true sources of Nigeria's downward economic spiral, rather than a dearth of resources. FOMWAN members advocated that the government tackle such national problems at their root by inculcating moral education in senior secondary schools and establishing interest-free Islamic banks. Participants also urged the government to ensure that the rich were adequately taxed for the benefit of the poor, reflecting the Muslim obligation to contribute to charity.

As part of its effort to provide Muslim women a forum for the discussion of social problems, the conference deliberated on the fiery issue of family planning. Muslim jurists and scholars who were also health experts freely expressed their views, following which FOMWAN noted in its communiqué that "family planning which is permissible in Islam" should be geared toward spacing, rather than limiting, childbirth. Furthermore, such planning, FOMWAN noted, should only be practiced with the full agreement of both spouses. The conference approved methods involving sexual relations during the safe period or use of the condom and the diaphragm. Birth control methods such as oral contraceptives, intrauterine devices, injections, castration, sterilization, and abortion were not approved. Family planning is a topic most Muslim scholars avoid, but FOMWAN, perhaps because it is a women's organization, chose to make a public statement on the sensitive topic, risking the alienation of conservative Muslim scholars.

Under FOMWAN's promotion of education and social development programs, classes and institutions have been established for women's Islamic education and literacy, while two MSO nurseries have been established at ABU's main campus in Zaria. It is hoped that such nursery schools will develop the practice of *tarbiyaa*, the proper socialization of Muslim children.

To succeed in their struggle will require good judgment, careful scholarship, and even-handed motivation to provide an articulate response to issues that arise. Some Muslim scholars and some traditionalists have expressed fears that the Muslim woman's Islamic identity will be eroded and that they will suffer the same moral disintegration and degradation as their counterparts in the West, but the emergence of FOMWAN has allayed these fears. Its members, while working through Islamic principles, appear to have silenced any attempt by saboteurs and opposition groups at tagging them as just another Western-style liberation movement.

The history of women's liberation movements in the West has raised suspicions about feminist movements elsewhere. Some of these women's organizations have been accused of breeding pervasive traits like lesbianism[1] and "abstracting the individuals from all concrete and collective bonds, pitting the individuals against institutions, relativizing and trivializing the family" (Murad 1984:45). Muslim women, however, view FOMWAN as a way to reclaim their self-esteem, which has been vastly damaged by stereotypic traditional and cultural values and negative Western influences.[2] In their communiqué, the members condemned pornography, the promotion of prostitution, and the proliferation of breweries. In this regard FOMWAN has distinguished itself from other women's organizations, first, because it incorporates a wide spectrum of viewpoints, and second, because it has a core of intellectual leadership which has a deep understanding of Islam and Western knowledge and is very much aware of the sociopolitical context.

FOMWAN has remained distinct because it hopes to develop the full personality of Muslim women as a model for other women, based on the belief that true Islam makes adequate provision for women.[3] The federation recognizes the need to enforce Muslim women's rights through the *shari'a* courts

1. For details of lesbian feminist movements, see Germaine Greer, *The Female Eunuch* (Paladin, 1971).

2. The *Punch*, a national daily, carries nude pictures of white women on p. 3 every day.

3. The rights of women under the *shari'a* are numerous, including the right to own and dispose of property; to inherit; to conduct legal transactions; to vote and be voted for; the right to be housed, fed, and maintained by her husband; the right to pursue education and to participate fully in all fields of human development. For details, see Yusuf 1985 and Lemu 1986.

Hajiya Ogunkin of Ogun State College delivers her address at the FOMWAN conference in Kano, February 12, 1989. Photo by B. Yusuf.

and put an end to a situation where Qur'anic verses are misinterpreted by ignorant scholars to legitimize the oppression and humiliation of women. Like its counterparts in the Muslim world, the federation's move toward religion "was neither traditional nor Western, the two previous choices obvious for women, but Islamic. In accepting this alternative, the women saw themselves neither as reactionary nor as compromising themselves culturally. They were instead asserting their own identity and strength by allying themselves with what they saw as an enlightened interpretation of Islam." [4]

The Breakthrough

The significance of the emergence of FOMWAN cannot be overemphasized: it is a breakthrough in the struggle for the uplifting of women. Its importance lies in the exposition of basic sociopolitical and educational problems in Nigeria, in the formulation of a methodology for the solution of these problems, and in making the society appreciate that the modern Muslim mind is as inventive as it is devoutly religious.

4. For similar movements, see Nashat 1983:111.

At a FOMWAN conference in 1989. Photo by B. Yusuf.

Hajiya Muslima Kamalin and Hajiya Adiya Fahm at the FOMWAN conference, February 12, 1989. Photo by B. Yusuf.

The federation is a crucial link between the government and the governed because it serves as an important spawning ground for Muslim activists who are presenting articulate demands to policy makers. There are some encouraging signs that policy makers now realize that the inclusion of women in policy making is critical. Increasingly, women's organizations are becoming havens for younger and more progressive minds rather than refuges for the unquestioning and gullible. The northern part of the country has awakened to the reality that Muslim women's rights, and the organizations that demand them, can no longer be suppressed.

Society has put this recognition into practice by giving practical support to emancipatory struggles launched by women's organizations sincerely devoted to the task. Progressive men in Kano City have responded by establishing and funding schools that serve the educational and vocational needs of women. This in turn encourages more Muslim women to attend Islamic schools, Agency for Mass Education classes, and even to consider taking up a career. Some learned and dedicated women have established their own schools, which cater exclusively to women,[5] and the staff and students of such schools are all women.

It is clear that FOMWAN has endeavored to establish an educational system that is based on Islam yet answers the needs of modern society. The federation—and indeed, society itself—has realized that it must respond to its environment because education, regardless of whether it is Western or Islamic, must bear the seal of its social and intellectual context. In the future, the federation will be appreciated by those who seek an objective assessment of the role of Muslim women in contemporary Nigeria. If the federation succeeds in the tasks it has set for itself, its existence will lead to a steady unfolding of information and observations that will answer most of the questions society will ask. However, the task of reexamining the judicial, educational, political, and economic systems of a secular state like Nigeria cannot fall exclusively on the shoulders of the FOMWAN. Other Muslim and non-Muslim organizations and governmental bodies must also be willing to carry part of the burden.

Appendix: Communication of the International Islamic Conference on Women

IN THE NAME OF ALLAH THE BENEFICENT, THE MERCIFUL

At the International Islamic Conference on Women, Organized by the Muslim Sisters' Organisation of Nigeria, held at the Government Girls' College Dala, Kano, from 4th–8th April 1985, we the members, participants, and organizers of the conference hereby issue this communiqué:

---

5. Prominent among these are Rabi Wali, Hassana Sufi, and Malama Mariya.

We are grateful to Allah the Most High for making it possible for the conference to be convened and for helping it to its conclusive end.

We have observed with grave concern the inadequate education of Muslim women which explains the deplorable conditions they face today. In view of the fact that the Qur'an and Sunna of the Holy Prophet Muhammad, Peace of God be upon him, have expressly made the search for knowledge incumbent on every Muslim, man or woman. We are therefore calling on all Muslims, parents and husbands alike and Muslim women in particular, to mount a serious extensive education campaign to efface this cancerous worm that inhibits the true understanding of Islam and its principles and, by extension, an inhibition to the Islamic process.

We condemn in its entirety the attitudes of some parents whereby marriage, even in Muslim communities, has been made a commercial enterprise, thereby making it very difficult for honest young men and women to get married and thus paving the way for corruption and prostitution. We also condemn tribal considerations in Muslim marriages, believing that any marriage contracted on considerations other than Islam is doomed to fail.

Without any reservation, we condemn in totality the flirtation of the Nigerian Ulama (Muslim religious leaders) with every successive regime that comes to power in this country. This attitude has therefore deprived them of the role of the custodians of the religion of Islam, thus making them part of the oppressors who wickedly exploit the deprived masses of this country. We therefore call upon them to take up their responsibility to protect the oppressed by forbidding what is wrong and enjoining what is right. They should speak against any form of injustice no matter who is concerned.

We have noted that women's liberation movements, with their history traced to Western countries, have no relevance in Muslim communities, as Allah has granted Muslim women all the rights they need, be they political, legal, economic, or social. However, we are not happy over the attitudes of Muslim men who ignore Islamic injunctions with respect to women's rights. We therefore call on both Muslim men and women to join hands together to allow women to exercise the rights Islam has granted them, as contained in the Qur'an and Sunna, in order to save the society from looking elsewhere for salvation.

PART 2. THE POWER OF WOMEN

6 *Beverly Mack*

Royal Wives in Kano

Structurally the Kano palace is a microcosm of the traditional walled city of Kano. Just as Kano's Old City historically was protected by a high wall with access only through gates set at intervals, so too the palace community of several thousand people is surrounded by a wall enclosing its myriad chambers, courtyards, stables, and gardens. Metaphorically the palace community constitutes the ideal Hausa-Fulani household—albeit on an extraordinarily large scale—for it includes the emir's four wives, numerous concubines, and various other attendants. More than any other household, the palace enjoys a sanctity that has allowed it to guard its traditions through several centuries. Thus the royal community remains a bastion of Hausa-Fulani society and is often regarded as the culture's "model home." It seems appropriate, therefore, to consider the roles of royal wives in the Kano palace as they exemplify the ideal roles of traditional Hausa-Fulani women throughout northern Nigeria.

The palace has long been regarded as the seat of traditional authority in a region where religion has for centuries been the foundation of the area's political life. Royal women's roles necessarily reflect both a religious and a sociopolitical ideal in the traditional Hausa-Fulani Muslim context (Paden 1973). In this respect royal women may be considered exemplars of Hausa-Fulani womanhood. At the same time, however, the wealth of the royal household guarantees that royal women are unique in their privilege and security: they enjoy far greater access than the average Hausa-Fulani woman to material goods as well as exposure to the West through various media. Such "covert" exposure to the West naturally involves a potential for conflicting aspirations among these women, yet they do not give up their marriages to take on the roles of women they see portrayed in American serials or Indian dramas. Even so, royal wives are not unaware of options they have relinquished in accepting their current positions.

According to legend, royal women once led armies and ruled much of Hausaland, but now they are strictly secluded according to the Hausa-Fulani practice called *auren kulle*.[1] This Hausa term, often translated literally as a marriage in which women are "locked away," is more accurately interpreted as a restriction and protection from the outside world, which is what the practice actually involves. Ideally, *kulle* is a privilege enjoyed only by those who can afford servants. Certainly "seclusion implies leisure, with no fetching of wood and water from a distance and no farm work, and this allows the women to pursue their own crafts and petty trade, the proceeds of which are their personal property" (M. G. Smith 1955:50).

The purported roles of royal Hausa-Fulani women have changed dramatically over several centuries. Their legendary power and authority appear to have diminished almost completely. In this chapter I discuss perceptions of royal women currently held by others as well as the perceptions royal women have of themselves. In the latter, legendary, traditional, and Western role models are selected by royal women in their efforts to define their own contemporary situations within the royal context. This study focuses on royal wives' rights and obligations, the extent of their authority, and the degree to which they influence the powerful men to whom they are related.

Royal Women in History

In northern Nigeria, historical traditions include accounts of queens and women warriors of the sixteenth century who are still remembered for their feats.[2] The queens of ancient Zazzau and Daura are legendary and remain popular in contemporary times. Part of their legacy includes titles that are still in use in the royal courts of Zaria, Daura, Katsina, and Kano—honorifics that testify to the public power women once held. Although women's public roles have disappeared in the social upheaval of both the Shehu's jihad and Western colonialization, the titles that remain in use suggest women's covert, private power of influence with the men who govern.

1. Also known as *tsari*. This and all subsequent Hausa terms may be found in Abraham 1962.

2. Whether these female warrior-leaders are mythical or real matters less than their continued popularity in contemporary historical accounts. Indeed, as David Henige has suggested, their mythical nature may be a more significant comment on women's roles than their actual existence (personal communication, May 14, 1987).

The queens of ancient Zazzau (Zaria) are perhaps the most renowned women warrior-rulers of Hausaland. A woman named Bakwa Turunku, the twenty-second chief of Zazzau, is said to have ruled between 1536 and 1566 (Dikko 1982:10). She had two daughters, Amina and Zaria (when Zazzau was moved a few miles to the north, the new town was named for the latter; Dikko 1982: 2–3). At sixteen, Amina acquired the title *Magajiya* (Inheritor), a state title traditionally held by a ruler's sister or daughter. Along with the title, Amina assumed dominion over forty female slaves and eventually took over the chieftaincy, becoming the *Sarauniya* (Queen) in 1576 (Dikko 1982:1–10). Her sister Zaria collaborated with her, conquering the surrounding territory on Amina's behalf. According to the *Kano Chronicle*, their cooperation was effective, and Amina's reign was innovative and long:

Zaria, under Queen Amina, conquered all the towns as far as Kwararafa and Nupe. Every town paid tribute to her. The Sarki of Nupe sent forty eunuchs and ten thousand kolas to her. She first had eunuchs and kolas in Hausaland. In her time the whole of the products of the west were brought to Hausaland. Her conquest extended over thirty-four years. (*Kano Chronicle*, quoted in Palmer 1928:109)

Even when women ceased to rule directly in Zazzau, their titles and political influence endured. Prior to the nineteenth century, the title *Magajiya* was traditionally bestowed upon a ruler's eldest daughter; if he had no daughter, it passed to his sister or aunt. Zaria's *Magajiya* was responsible for all internal arrangements of the palace community and had the right to attend sessions in which the emir held court (Dikko 1982:12, 24). *Mardanmi,* the title traditionally held by a ruler's second-eldest daughter, carried no fief, but it was a position of great power, for it gave her the right to speak with the emir independently even of the *Magajiya,* who was otherwise present during conferences. This title remained in use until the late nineteenth century when it was last held by Ai, daughter of Emir Musa (1804–21) (Dikko 1982:17). *The Chronicle of Abuja* notes that in Zazzau the women's titles of *Sarauniya* and *Iya* were in use long before the nineteenth-century Fulani jihad:

The Sarauniya . . . was usually the daughter of an Emir, and looked after women of the household during the absence of the Emir. She was in charge of the arrangements at the marriage of the girl children; and with the Iya she prepared the food for the feasts given by the Emir at the Middle Fast. . . . The Iya . . . was usually a wife of the Emir's father but not necessarily the Emir's mother. She arranged marriages for the Emir's concubines when he died. (Hassan and Na'ibi 1962:73)

In Zaria the title of *Iya* was traditionally given to a ruler's mother or, in the event of her death, to the ruler's paternal aunt or eldest sister (Dikko 1982:12). The *Iya*'s main function was to intercede between the ruler and his lesser chiefs (Dikko 1982:15). In his study of Zazzau, M. G. Smith noted the *Sarauniya*'s political influence. He observed that "neither the [male] heir presumptive nor the [head of the lineage] is reported to have controlled fiefs, although the king's eldest daughter, the *Sarauniya,* is said to have done so" (M. G. Smith 1960: 53). Like the *Sarauniya,* the *Iya* was also said to have been a fief-holder in Zazzau; in each case, the position gained for its holder significant economic power (M. G. Smith 1960:53; Dikko 1982:15).

Daura's ancient history also records a long line of queens, described in both Arabic and Hausa indigenous texts. One version explains that Daura, the queen, was succeeded by eight more queens, "each described as *Magajiya,* beginning with Gamata and ending with Shawata" (M. G. Smith 1978:56). Although the legendary line of female rulers gave way to an "immigrant hero" and agnatic, rather than matrilineal descent, the legend of women rulers was fixed in "the constitutional doctrine that the *Magajiya* could countermand the orders of the chief and might, if necessary, act to depose him. . . . There can never be a chief in Daura without a *Magajiya.* The state of Daura remains incomplete without the *Magajiya*" (M. G. Smith 1978:57). Another title, *Mai Daki,* has long been used in Daura to distinguish a wife or daughter favored by the ruler (Hajiya Abba Bayero, personal communication, 1979).

Katsina, an emirate whose history dates at least to the thirteenth century, also has a legacy of influential women. The town's name and the title of *Iya,* as used in other royal courts, are both said to have originated when the town's ruler, Korau (c. 1260) named it after his eldest sister, Katsina. Korau's wife was eager to be comparably honored, so he gave her the title *Iya,* with its attendant authority.[3] The *Iya*'s primary role was to act as an intermediary between the ruler and his lesser chiefs, and she also arranged marriages for the widows of former rulers (Dikko 1982:15). The title *Sarauniya* was used in Katsina for a ruler's eldest daughter, whose obligations were to attend to all royal daughters with regard to marriage, to take responsibility for other royal wives whenever they were away from the palace, and to assist the *Iya* in feast preparations (Dikko 1982:15).

Although women were not ruling Kano in the fifteenth and sixteenth centuries, as they were in Zazzau, they were nevertheless influential in the royal court. Kano's ruler, Rumfa (1463–99), is renowned for several innovations in the royal court, among them the establishment of the title *Mai Babban Daki*) that attaches to the title. There the *Mai Babban Daki* was attended by her own servants and retainers. Although the title carries no fief, it identifies a woman who is respected and revered. Evidently Rumfa's successor, Abdullahi (1499–1509) benefited from the influence of his grandmother Hauwa (Auwa), who

---

3. Dikko (1982) explains an alternative origin of the term: a pre-jihad ruler had two wives, each of whom bore a son. The elder, his heir, died just one month before his father, and the first wife mourned her son's loss. The new emir comforted her by saying, "*Iya ki hakura*" ("You must withstand") and then gave her the title *Iya* (p. 14).

prevented Abdullahi's overthrow: "[on Abdullahi's (1499–1509) way home from war] . . . he found that Dagachi was preparing to revolt, and that the Madaki [Maidaki] Auwa alone had prevented serious trouble, as her influence was very great in Kano" (Palmer 1928:112). This well-respected woman was also celebrated in praise songs:

> Mother! Kano is your country.
> Mother! Kano is your town.
> Old lady with the swaggering gait,
> Old lady of royal blood,
> Guarded by men-at-arms.
>   (Palmer 1928:113)

When Kisoki succeeded Abdullahi as Kano's leader (1509–65), he shared the power and responsibility of his position with female relatives: "Kisoki ruled the town with his mother, *Iya* Lamis, and his grandmother, *Madaki* [*Mai Babban Daki*] Auwa, and Guli, the brother of *Madaki* Auwa" (Palmer 1928: 113). After this time, the title of *Mai Babban Daki* appears to have declined in popularity; it remained vacant until it was revived by Emir Abbas (1903–19), who conferred it on his mother, also named Hauwa, at the start of the colonial period (Smith n.d.: ch. 7, p. 19).

Throughout history, changing balances of power among the Hausa-Fulani have been reflected in the disappearance of many traditional titles and their later reappearance or the addition of new ones as needed. Currently, few women's titles remain. Today in Katsina the titles of *Madaki* and *Iya* are still used as honorifics, but in Kano they have long been defunct, and royal Kano wives have no official titles. In contemporary times, Katsina alone is unusual among Hausa-Fulani royal courts for bestowing titles on royal wives. Theirs are the only remaining women's titles of importance in Katsina. Three titles—*Mai Lalle, Mai Wurare,* and *Mai Mashariya*—predate the colonial era, although their use is not recorded as far back as ancient times (Alhaji Ado Bayero, personal communication 1980; Hajiya Abba Bayero, personal communication 1982; Dikko 1982:24). A fourth title, *Mai Daki,* came into use during the 1930s. Since then, it has been used to designate the favorite of the emir's four wives (Mack 1988:76).

The overt power once associated with women's titles no longer obtains, and it is likely that the loss of female public power was directly connected with the growing influence of Islam in Hausaland. Even before Queen Amina's reign and Zaria's feats, Islam had begun to take hold among the aristocracy in Kano, becoming firmly established there by the mid-fifteenth century, when Rumfa is said to have begun the practice of wife seclusion within his royal court (Palmer 1928:76). Gradually women were ousted from positions of administrative control and public power; M. G. Smith notes that in pre-jihad Zazzau, despite their having held titles, "the *Sarauniya* and the *Iya,* being women, were ineligible for succession" (M. G. Smith 1960:60).

Seclusion was practiced almost exclusively among the court elite until some time after the Shehu's nineteenth-century jihad; travelers' accounts from the nineteenth century indicate that only royal women and devout scholars' wives were secluded, while other women moved freely about town (Barth 1857; Clapperton 1829 (1966); Robinson 1896). Nevertheless, it was in the court, at the highest social stratum, where women most often held titled positions and where seclusion was co-opted to political effect as an outward expression of religious devotion in the aftermath of the jihad; it functioned as an indication of allegiance to the new ruling elite.[4] Following the jihad, the word *Fulani* itself became an honorific for an emir's daughter or wife, indicating ethnic affiliation with the new ruling class (Alhaji Ado Bayero 1982, personal communication). But the new title involved no power, only class affiliation, and titles that had previously carried fiefs were explicitly taken away from women after the jihad. The second Fulani emir of Zaria, Yanmusa (1821–34), changed the woman's title of *Iya*—and all other women's titles—to a man's title. The last women to hold the titles of *Iya* and *Magajiya* in Zaria were the daughters of Yanmusa's predecessor, Malam Musa Atu (1804–21) (Dikko 1982:16–17).

Thus, during the centuries in which Islam gained its foothold in Hausaland, women's names gradually disappeared from historical accounts. Queens and women warriors also vanished under increasing Islamic influence, which, in northern Nigeria, carried with it the practice of wife seclusion. Although the influence of Islam on women's roles began during the fifteenth century, it has had its most profound effect since the nineteenth-century jihad, which spread the practice of wife seclusion dramatically, extending it eventually to rural areas.[5] The jihad profoundly revised and restricted women's public roles over the century that followed and was reinforced by subsequent British colonial influence, with its Victorian impressions of womanhood. Thus, in the nineteenth and twentieth centuries, Hausa-Fulani women lost whatever political standing they had once held, and their social roles changed profoundly.

Rights and Obligations of Royal Women Today

Royal wives in contemporary Hausaland are subject to many of the rights and obligations prescribed for other Hausa-Fulani women by Islam. In addition,

---

4. Seclusion was not advocated by the Shehu himself but by several of his followers, to whose pressure he eventually acquiesced (see Boyd and Last 1985).

5. Polly Hill reports that the "unusual severity of Muslim wife-seclusion in [rural] Dorayi . . . has developed quite recently"; there were no girls in the local primary school, and the marriage age for girls had fallen to nine or ten (1977:84).

however, they enjoy rights and experience obligations exclusive to their status as royal wives. The strict seclusion that these women observe is reflected in the spatial arrangement of their living quarters. Similarly, their special status is evident in their material wealth, gift obligations, comportment, childcare responsibilities, and income-generating pursuits.

Shelter

The Kano palace spatial situation reflects common Hausa household structure, with co-wives' compounds arranged around a central courtyard. Because the palace's central courtyard is considered too "public" an area for their free movement, however, royal wives are restricted to their own quarters. Only on rare occasions—such as for childbirth at the local clinic, to visit the emir in his quarters, to visit a new royal wife, or to make the pilgrimage (*haji*) to Mecca— may they leave their compounds, and then only with the emir's permission and with a suitable female escort.[6]

Although royal wives may not go into the courtyard, they often observe special processions or daily activities that take place there from behind a curtain in their own individual compound. If a wife's quarters share an adjoining wall with windows into another wife's compound, the two may visit in this way, but they may never be seen in the "public" space of the common courtyard, secluded from the city though it is. Thus royal wives do not usually interact with one another as do wives in town. They see only the women who come to visit in their own apartments and the emir himself, who visits them regularly. Such restriction on the wives' interaction guarantees the autonomy of each wife in her compound and secures her authority over the people who frequent it. The price of such autonomy and authority, however, is a woman's freedom of movement.

The palace's central courtyard is the territory of other palace women and is often bustling with activity. The emir's reception room is located at one end and the concubines' quarters are in close proximity to it, so the central courtyard constitutes the heart of the palace. It is the terminus for the annual *salla* procession on horseback and a gathering place for women musicians performing on special occasions.[7] With the rare exception of a palace worker or a male messenger scurrying through, the central courtyard belongs overwhelmingly

6. The practice of taking royal wives to Mecca for the *haji* is relatively recent, having begun during Sarkin Kano Alhaji Abdullahi Bayero's reign (1926–53) (Hajiya Abba Bayero, personal communication, May 16, 1982).

7. The custom of leading the *salla* procession into the courtyard was instituted by His Royal Highness Alhaji Sanusi, who reigned from 1954 to 1963. He felt it unfair that his wives and children had no opportunity to view the lavish public procession, so he brought it inside to them. Women musicians are discussed at greater length in Mack 1981.

to the palace women who live around it—the royal concubines, royal slaves, widows of former emirs, and women of the town seeking shelter.[8] All these women have sleeping quarters on the perimeter of the common courtyard, and they congregate there throughout the day for leisure or work.

Royal wives' apartments consist of spacious compounds with several rooms and courtyards; usually there is also open space for small vegetable gardens. The area is necessarily generous—very often the size of an entire middle-class Kano home—because it must provide living quarters for children, concubines, servants-slaves, and various other individuals who are attached to the royal wife. Thus, while a royal wife may be restricted in her movements around the palace, she is by no means in solitary confinement: a continual stream of women and children make the wives' quarters one of the busiest areas of the palace.

Architectural change is common: women are not "placed" in a former emir's wife's compound, but create their own space in conference with their husband. In the Kano palace, major reconstruction has been undertaken for each of the emir's wives to transform areas into living quarters for them. When an emir takes a new bride, he orders the reconstruction of her apartment compound and sees that the redecoration is carried out in accordance with her preferences. Moughtin describes the role that women play in the redecoration process:

Although in Hausaland the building and decoration of houses is the work of men, each wife decorates the inside of her own rooms. The various pots, pans and dishes that form her dowry are used by the wife and her female relatives to decorate the new house. After the marriage has taken place, the dowry is carried ceremoniously to the wife's new home, where it is plastered piece by piece into the walls of the hut, the whole composition making colourful patterns of shining brass bowls mixed with modern, enamelled tin plates. (1986:138)

In addition, these spacious compounds are usually equipped with modern conveniences like electricity and running water.[9]

A royal wife's compound is distinctly her own, separate from those of the other royal wives and separate from those of the concubines. Because she has command over the concubines and servants attached to her area, the space itself defines the area of her most immediate authority. It does not, however, define the limits of her authority, which are determined by many factors beyond her particular rank among the co-wives, as is discussed below.

8. Sir Rex Niven (1982:128) cites a former emir's complaint that he was responsible for "more than a hundred old women—all they could do was eat, the Emir said—willed to him by various deceased men who had little or no personal connections with the ruler." The fact of responsibility toward the destitute who appeal to the emir has been confirmed by both the current emir, Alhaji Ado Bayero, and several of his wives. The attitude, however, has been more generous.

9. Electricity and water supplies in the palace are as erratic as elsewhere in the city, where a rapidly increasing population puts too heavy a burden on facilities to prevent frequent breakdown.

Hausa wives bring to their marriage homes a dowry consisting, among other things, of many dozens of enamelled pots of different sizes. Photo by B. Mack.

Gifts and Material Wealth

Hausa wives bring to their marriage homes a dowry consisting, among other things, of many dozens of enamelled pots of different sizes. Among the more affluent, and certainly among the emir's wives, these pots are larger than average and often are made of brass rather than enamel. A royal wife might also inherit from her guardians gold jewelry, lengths of expensive cloth, or other heirlooms. In addition, to decorate her quarters a woman brings supplies (*kaya*) such as an iron poster-bed decorated in bright colors and covered with embroidered throw pillows, collections of small gilt knickknacks and toiletries, and stacks of yardage for traditional wrappers and head ties. These are supplied by the bride's family (usually by her mother) or by the prospective husband prior to the marriage ceremony; in either case, the items are hers to keep, sell, or pass on to her own daughters when they marry. Contemporary royal brides often bring items such as video machines, radios, and tape recorders. If there is a divorce, the wife's possessions are hers to take when she leaves the palace.

At various celebratory times throughout the year, a wife receives new outfits of clothing from her husband. The emir, like all devout Hausa men, fulfills his socioreligious obligations to his wives by giving them all beautiful lengths of cloth and other valuable gifts. His concubines and female servants-slaves are treated comparably, so he is likely to give the same item to all the women in the palace. Depending on the value of these items—whether toiletries, jewelry, or clothing—these gifts may be worn, saved, sold, or passed on as a gift to someone else. On special occasions, lengths of the same cloth are given to everyone. Wearing such an outfit signifies membership in an elite club and constitutes an act of community among the women of the palace, whatever their rank. The gifts of clothing and jewelry received from the emir may be sold or put aside to increase the dowry a woman accumulates for her daughters, and in this way the emir's obligatory gifts increase the assets and disposable income of wives and concubines in the palace.

Food and Etiquette

It is the Hausa husband's responsibility to supply provisions for food preparation in the home. This is also true in the palace, although the emir obviously has servants to do the buying and distribution for him. Some food is grown within the palace compound, some is grown on the royal farms on the outskirts of Kano, and some is purchased outright from merchants. In return for receiving provisions from her husband, a Hausa wife is expected to prepare the family meals, a task shared among co-wives according to a rotating schedule. Similar arrangements now obtain in the palace, but it was not always so. Traditionally, the entire palace community was fed from a central kitchen run by women slaves and concubines in the women's quarters, but as the task grew to impossible proportions, women began preparing food only for those for whom they were directly responsible. A royal wife now prepares meals for her own household and possibly for the emir, but she need not cook unless she wishes to, since there are always servants available to do the cooking for her.

Freed from domestic chores, a royal wife may spend her time preparing snacks for sale within her compound, which enjoys the constant traffic of children from other parts of the palace looking for playmates. Because she often has access to technology that others do not—refrigerators, cotton candy machines, popcorn poppers—the snacks she prepares may be more exotic than the usual fare, and if she sends little girls out to hawk them around the palace, she can be assured of good sales. This is just one way in which a royal wife, like other urban Hausa women, earns her own income.

Most important in terms of food preparation, however, is the royal wife's obligation to cater to the steady stream of visitors she receives; part of being a gracious hostess requires maintaining a constant supply of food—both meals and small snacks—for those who come to visit her. In exchange for some domestic obligations, the royal wife assumes the burden of constantly being "on call" for visitors. This obligation is especially heavy during the annual month-long fasting period of Ramadan and the celebrations that follow (*salla*). Throughout the year royal wives receive visitors, some of whom are local and some foreign. It is the latter who continue to visit royal wives during the fasting period, insensitive to their hunger, thirst, and fatigue. Not only will she feed them while observing a strict fast, but when the fast is broken, a royal wife will also provide delectable and elaborate meals for her family members, prepared during the heat of the day when her hunger and thirst are most extreme. Even if she does not cook the meals herself, she is responsible for overseeing them. In terms of preparing food for fast-breaking and *salla* celebrations, the royal wife's obligation is as difficult as the average wife's, and she too must play the role of gracious hostess without complaint.

Childcare

Part of a Hausa Muslim wife's domestic obligation involves the responsibility for molding her children as proper Muslims. This is especially true for royal wives, whose sons are prospective emirs and whose daughters will be married to influential men. In addition, a royal wife bears responsibility for the proper upbringing of the children of concubines who live in her compound, since they are also royal children, with the potential to ascend to the throne and to marry into powerful families. They share equal status with the children of royal wives.

A royal wife's compound may be home at any given time to between five and ten children who range in age from infant to adolescent. A girl raised in such a royal setting remembers the harem as "a fantastic place, [where] there was always something interesting to do; there were about forty children and we organized plays among ourselves and our mothers came to watch" (Trevor

Among the more affluent Hausa, the dowry pots are larger than average, and often are made of brass. Photo by D. Pellow.

The harem is "a fantastic place [where] there was always something interesting to do." Palace girls watch the *salla* procession in Kano. Photo by B. Mack.

1975a:260). Perhaps because of seclusion, royal wives seem to be unusually involved with the personal and educational development of their children. They are responsible for teaching their children the rigors of praying five times a day, sending them to the palace's Western primary school in the morning and Qur'anic classes in the afternoon, arbitrating childhood squabbles while imbuing behavior appropriate to their status, and monitoring their interest in activities outside the palace. A royal wife must also monitor the manner in and extent to which royal children interact with their contemporaries among the palace slave populace: royal and slave boys may be especially close friends during their early years, only to grow apart as their paths begin to diverge in adolescence.[10]

Fostering among the Hausa allows a woman to raise a child when she has none of her own. Later in life that child will return the care, providing for the foster mother in her old age. Royal children are often cared for by nannies or

10. There appears to be less occasion for royal girls to spend time with slave-status or servant girls, perhaps because the movements of the latter around the *cikin gida* area of the palace are more restricted by their own domestic obligations than are the movements of their brothers. Also, because they are married earlier than boys, girls move away from their birth homes at adolescence, whereas boys often remain longer with their parents. Slave-status families attached to the royal family live in the back of the palace near the stables.

A young Hausa bride with children of the compound. Photo by B. Mack.

foster mothers between the period of weaning and primary school attendance. Children may sleep in their nannies' quarters for naps and at night or alternate between the nanny and their mother's compound. The nanny is responsible for providing new clothes for the child during the annual *salla* celebrations and attending to its welfare as thoroughly as its mother would, although the biological mother usually pays for new clothes and any other expenses incurred in the course of such care.

Sometimes royal children past the age of being cared for by a nanny choose to join the household of another royal wife for a while, spending all their time there instead of in their mother's compound. Underlying such behavior is the sense of relatedness that pervades the royal household: it is a large single family community, and although family relations are not always sublime, the familial connection is clear. It may also be the case that a new royal wife is considerably closer to a daughter's age than to her co-wives' ages, and in such a case she and the daughter are girlfriends to one another.

It is never too soon to begin a child's religious education, and the child's mother takes primary responsibility for inculcating Muslim behavior. In the years just past weaning, a child begins to be considered an active Muslim, reciting prayers five times daily and fasting as many days as possible during Ramadan. Mothers announce with pride that "Amina (or Rasheed) fasted two days this year," meaning that the youngster observed the dawn-to-dusk fast for two of the thirty days of Ramadan. Children take great pride in this public announcement of their advance toward Muslim adulthood.

Secondary school for both male and female royal children usually involves attendance at boarding schools outside the palace, yet adolescent boys and girls can spend more time together in the palace than in other urban homes, congregating in the women's quarters during vacation periods. For this reason, royal wives have an unusual amount of influence over their children. There are two reasons why this situation differs from the norm: (1) affluence affords a greater investment in education, so that girls—even though promised in marriage at an early age—can often delay the move to their marriage homes while they continue their educations, and (2) boys spend more time in their mothers' compounds than do those in the average household because of the palace community's size. They often have friends, half-brothers, or cousins of their own age with whom to talk.

For adolescents the palace is a desirable place: it is both the most elite household and the most politically active community in the city. For young boys and girls it is an interesting locus of power and privilege. Thus it is common to find adolescent boys and girls spending time in the royal wives' chambers, talking about current events, school functions, and items of social interest; joking, gossiping, and flirting with one another; viewing videos or listening to music tapes.[11] They are interested in the foreigners who come to visit the royal wives and listen in on the conversations, many of which are in English and concern outsiders' views on topics of social and political interest. The education youngsters receive in the royal community itself may be as important as the classes they attend. It is in these situations that the royal wife's role as educator, arbiter, and resident historian are crucial to children's intellectual and social development, especially since children have very little direct contact with their father, the emir, beyond adolescence.

Personal Trade and Income

Unlike her urban counterpart, the royal wife does not have to earn money for her children's school fees, since these are paid by the emir. However, a royal wife is responsible for the major portion, if not all, of the trousseau (*kayan daki*) for girls in her charge. In addition to her own daughters, this may include nieces she has raised, the daughters of concubines attached to the royal wife, or girls who have been abandoned and taken into the palace. The trousseau includes large and expensive items such as a metal bed frame and mattress, several dozen brass or enamel pots, several dozen lengths of cloth, and gold jewelry, as well as smaller items such as soaps, perfumes, gold-painted knickknacks, and head ties. The trousseau becomes the wealth of the girl being married, and may cost several hundred to several thousand dollars, depending on the girl's status and the status of the man she marries. Thus a woman's personal income is crucial to the fulfillment of social obligations to her daughters and those in her care.

Many studies have demonstrated the facility with which nonroyal women pursue their own income-generating occupations while remaining secluded (M. G. Smith 1955; Hill 1969; Simmons 1975; Saunders 1979; Schildkrout 1983; Coles, this volume). Mahdi Adamu states that "[Hausa women] have full personal control and responsibility over their capital resources and equipment, and are not disadvantaged in their economic pursuits by the system of seclusion or purdah (Hausa *kulle*). During their spare time they are under no obligation to assist their husbands in their work, and if they do they can claim payment" (1978:7). This is even more applicable to royal women, who have greater access to capital to start a business, more space in which to pursue it, and more contact with potential customers, despite their greater degree of seclusion. The women from town who visit the royal wives, patronage of the palace personnel, and access to customers outside the palace via their children all provide royal wives with a great deal of opportunity to engage in lucrative trade.

---

11. The custom of avoidance is maintained, the wife not addressing her eldest by the child's proper name and, for the most part, not addressing him or her directly. This does not preclude communication between them altogether, but it does give it a somewhat awkward nature.

A Hausa widow, who is no longer bound by seclusion, has greater liberty to pursue income-generating endeavors than a married woman (see Schildkrout 1986:131–52 and Coles, this volume). This is equally true for widowed royal women, although they are less likely than other women to move about in public. While the divorce rate among royal wives is not as high as that for other Hausa women, the great difference in age between husband and wife and a reluctance among Hausa women to remarry after they pass their childbearing years mean that chances are high that a wife will outlive her husband. She is expected to be financially independent when he dies, which is important to her social independence in later years. Just as a Hausa woman in her childbearing years without a trade is an anomaly, so too an old Hausa woman without her own financial resources is an object of pity.

Power and Authority of Royal Women

Among nonroyal women, power and authority accrue to those past childbearing years (Coles 1990a) as their wealth increases and their increasing maturity commands respect. Power has been defined as the "right to make a particular decision and to command obedience" (M. G. Smith 1960:19) and authority as "legitimized and recognized power" (Sanday 1981:190). Since, as Sanday points out, ethnographers have had little to say about female power in the public domain, the assumption is often drawn that women secluded from the public domain have neither power nor authority, just influence. However, the community of the family is the context in which Hausa-Fulani wives exercise their power and authority over members of their households—children and whatever servants they might have. A woman's power and authority may increase in direct proportion to her control of material wealth and the number of people over whom she has jurisdiction.

Royal wives have greater opportunity to exercise power than most Hausa-Fulani women because they have greater access to wealth and authority over the many women of the palace community. But not all royal wives enjoy the same amount of authority. The senior wife is the most revered and usually the closest in age to, and most influential with, the emir; therefore, she is assumed to wield the greatest authority. The youngest wife (*amariya*)—especially if she is the youngest of four wives—may be closer in age to the royal daughters than co-wives. Often she is shy and hesitant about involvement in domestic affairs until she grows into her role, perhaps after the birth of her first child. Second and third wives are usually between the extremes in age and authority represented by the senior (first) and youngest (fourth) wives. They can be the most active of the four wives, restrained neither by high nor newly established rank. Each of the royal wives is a role model to the next in line, just as all four royal wives are exemplars of Hausa womanhood for other women in the palace and town. A royal wife's power is inherent in the authority she holds over others, male and female, both inside and beyond the palace. The concubines and female slaves who constitute the major portion of this community of women live together in the heart of the palace and are responsible for the daily operation of the palace, preparing food, and raising children.[12] Their tasks are directed by the royal wives, each of whom directs the women in her vicinity and oversees activities. Often a royal wife is called upon to settle interpretations of the Qur'an or to arbitrate conflicts among concubines and servants. Although she is confined to her own compound, news always reaches her, and individuals can easily be summoned for reprimand. It is the mandate of the royal wife to maintain a peaceful, productive environment in the palace community.

In addition to the women of the palace community, royal wives also have contact with town women who seek education and advice. Royal wives teach adult women literacy and Islamic knowledge in informal classes, held as the season's schedule permits. Occasionally a woman from the palace or from town will appeal to a royal wife for advice in marital or family matters. In these cases, because the royal wife acts on behalf of the emir, she is able to intercede for those who come to her with problems. If a woman from town complains about her treatment at home or about an inheritance decision, for example, a royal wife can suggest a course of action for the woman, such as an appeal to the local *shari'a* court. If the situation is urgent, the royal wife might act as liaison, appealing to the emir on behalf of the plaintiff. When it is beyond her authority to act, she can usually predict with accuracy the emir's decision and give advice accordingly.

It is a royal wife's background that enables her to anticipate the emir's judgment and underlines another basis for her importance to the emir (and thus her authority in the palace community). Each royal wife constitutes a political alliance for the emir, a formal bond with another emirate or sultanate. Whether she is the daughter of a concubine, a royal retainer, or another emir, the woman who becomes a royal wife has been raised in a royal community. She is therefore schooled in appropriate protocol, royal obligations, and has an instinctive sense of the parameters of her own power. Furthermore, although her background does not guarantee familiarity with strategic issues, it is often the case that the woman chosen as a royal wife is politically informed. Her influence with her husband is significant, albeit nearly undocumented in history.

Part of the mythology concerning wife seclusion is that it precludes intellectual communication between husband and wife, much less allowing the wife to influence her husband. Although such interaction has rarely been recorded

12. Slavery has been illegal in Nigeria since early in the twentieth century; however, people of slave descent continue to identify themselves as slaves. In the palace, some royal slaves hold positions of privilege and importance (M. G. Smith 1960). Only women of slave descent are eligible to become concubines of the royal family.

in historical cases, wives of political leaders often influence their husbands in Hausaland. Perhaps the first account noted in recent times involves the Shehu Usman dan Fodio, leader of the jihad for reformed Islam. The Shehu encouraged women's active involvement in the promotion of reformed Islam, and his daughters are still revered as Islamic poets, scholars, and teachers. One of them, Mariam, was a royal wife in Kano prior to the British conquest. As a wife of Emir Ibrahim Dabo (1818–46), she carried on work as a poet and scholar. Renowned as an intellectual, she was capable of discussing religious and political issues with the emir. Furthermore, this was her second marriage, one to which she came with a mind of her own.[13] Mariam's influence in the Kano Emirate was not restricted to her husband's reign but included that of Muhammad Bello (1883–92): "She was not the Emir's [Ibrahim's] first wife, nor was the dynasty descended from her. Nevertheless, Mariam in later life was looked on as an arbiter in Kano affairs. . . . The Emir of Kano, Muhammad Bello (1883–92), wrote to Mariam about the current wave of emigrants, and her advice is contained in her al-Wathiqa ila Amir Kano" (Boyd and Last 1985:294–95).

Even after many of the formal roles of royal women had disappeared, such women were still powerful. One of the few accounts of women's influential role in politics is M. G. Smith's description of the turmoil surrounding Aliyu's appointment as emir of Kano, c. 1893. The struggle for power between Aliyu and Sultan Abdu was resolved in great part through the intervention of Aliyu's mother, Saudatu. Upon learning of objections to his assumption of the throne, "Aliyu's mother, the daughter of Sultan Aliyu Babba, Saudatu, intervened at the ex-Ciroma Musa's divisive threats to overrule him by appealing to the assembled rebels not to set Yusufu's *wasiyya* [plea] aside" (Smith n.d.: ch. 6, p. 28). When Sultan Abdu's response was negative, a conflict developed between his vizier (*Waziri*), representing Abdu, and Saudatu, representing Aliyu:

Saudatu had aligned herself behind her son's assumption of leadership and responsibility for the revolt. Moreover, Saudatu was also a cross-cousin and affine of the Vizier Buhari. . . . Nonetheless, despite her failure to persuade the Vizier or Sultan Abdu that the rebels' cause was just, Saudatu was influential in securing the sympathy of her kinsmen descended from Caliphs Mamman Bello and Aliyu Babba for Aliyu and his people. . . . Aliyu was finally installed after the forceful intervention of his mother Saudatu. (Smith n.d.: ch. 6, pp. 28–29, 40)

Not only was Saudatu instrumental in securing the throne for her son, but the bad blood created in the process led to warfare: upon quarreling with Saudatu,

---

13. Boyd and Last (1985) note that Mariam was born in 1810 and widowed in Kano at the age of thirty-six. Mariam's first marriage produced two children. If she were first married at the onset of puberty or shortly thereafter, according to custom, she was probably at least twenty at the time of her marriage to Ibrahim Dabo.

the Waziri is said to have incited Damagaram to invade Kano, thus starting the Damagaram-Kano war of 1895–99 (Malam Adamu na Ma'aji, *Tarikh Kano,* cited in Smith n.d.: ch. 6, n. 39). However, women were as instrumental in preventing wars as in starting them. In 1894, when Sultan Abdu Danyen Kasko of Sokoto wanted to march against Kano, he was dissuaded by a kinswoman (Smith n.d.: ch. 6, p. 93).

During the colonial period, royal wives had interesting opportunities to intervene for their husbands through conversations with other royal wives. Hajiya Maidaki, a Kano woman who became a royal wife in Katsina, was not only her husband's confidante, but also accompanied him on trips to Kaduna, where she met with Lady Lugard and other colonial wives while the men conferred. When such meetings were held in her own home, the Katsina palace, she willingly offered her opinion on issues and discussed politics with anyone who visited her private quarters (see Mack 1988).

The assumption that royal wives influence emirs is evident in a colonial officer's remark in 1924. Haruna (the *Magatakarda,* an influential servant of the emir of Katsina) had embezzled Native Treasury funds. Eager to be rid of him, the officer observed, "The Magatakarda and Waziri probably have more influence with the Emir than anyone except the Magajiya, his [Haruna's] wife, and Haruna's sister and his concubine Malka" (Hull 1968:196–97). In 1931, when Emir Dikko of Katsina asked that Haruna be appointed to his council and his request was denied, the colonial division entry reported, "Nevertheless, Haruna continued to keep abreast of Native Authority affairs and to influence the Emir from time to time through his wife, who was Dikko's eldest sister" (Hull 1968:225).

In the Kano palace now, the emir visits his wives regularly in their compounds, where they discuss family business, current politics, and international issues. He solicits and respects his wives' opinions, confers with them on the educational progress of their children, and supports their efforts to promote education—both secular and Qur'anic—among those who frequent their compounds. The extent to which he is moved by his wives' attitudes cannot be measured, but the fact of his continued, active interest testifies to their influence with him.

Conclusion

Each royal wife recognizes that she is a role model for her daughters and the other women around her; she must fulfill her role with propriety and religious devotion. Like most Hausa wives, the royal wife's daily life is separate from that of her husband, but she, perhaps more than any other Hausa woman, has a social obligation to coordinate her life with his. She is expected to understand the emir's position on issues and to uphold traditional mores connected with her role as his representative in the palace.

Being in seclusion means neither being cut off from the world—for the world comes inside to her—nor being unable to influence it. A Hausa woman can uphold tradition by respecting her secluded status during childbearing years and still behave like a modern woman. As Jean Trevor, a Western secondary school teacher of Hausa girls in the 1960s, noted in observing her female students years later:

[In] the homes where educated aristocratic first wives were in purdah, these [women] seemed at first to be behaving traditionally, but as I got to know them better I saw that in the new way they organized the other women folk, took an interest in outside affairs they heard of on the radio, encouraged their own children at school, and were regarded as of equal status by their husbands, they were not; they were fulfilling their feminine role in a way which was acceptable to traditional men, but with tact, and were working the old system in their way (Trevor 1975a:263).

The roles of royal women in Hausaland have changed profoundly over the past several centuries. Women no longer lead armies or hold public political office. Instead, they have assumed domestic responsibilities and obligations within the private realm of seclusion. Some of them express a desire to function in the public world, pursuing the careers they see in videotapes of Western movies, yet at the same time, they recognize that the role they fulfill is a privileged and important one. Although royal wives appear in neither the daily news nor in historical accounts, they do contribute to current events and historical change in many undocumented ways, primarily by acting as a socializing agent to their children and as advisor-confidante to their husband, a man of significant social and political influence. Furthermore, they pursue independent trade activities for their own economic security. The fact of their being strictly secluded does indeed preclude their being involved in public activities, but it does not prevent their active involvement within that secluded world of women.

7 *Allan Christelow*

Women and the Law in Early-Twentieth-Century Kano

One day in the dry season of 1913–14, a man named Salim came before the Emir of Kano's judicial council with a special request. He reported to the council:

My mother Yamu was angry with me, so I was afraid, and I come to you so that I will not disobey my master. For it is known that the lot of those who go against their master is hell. I come to arrange a conciliation between her and myself and my four brothers, Abdu, Ishaq, Idris, and Musa, because they are the cause of our disagreement. . . . The Emir sent the *Kilishi*[1] to his mother to ask if she would pardon him. She agreed and said that she forgives him and pardons him. Then she said she was reconciled with him and his brothers on an equal basis, by the command of Allah. The *Kilishi* comes back with this (news) to the Emir. (99C)[2]

Research for this paper was carried out in 1982, while the author was a lecturer in the Department of History at Bayero University, Kano, Nigeria. Special thanks are due to Mr. John Lavers of the Department of History and Dr. Sani Zahredeen of the Islamic Studies Department for their help and encouragement. Any shortcomings in this paper are of course entirely my own. The register used for this study is in the Kano Native Authority Series at the National Archives, Kaduna, to whose director and staff I also extend my thanks.

1. The *kilishi* is the palace official whose duty it is to spread out the Emir's carpet. A slave eunuch, he was also the official sent to interview women living in seclusion concerning legal matters.

2. The numbering for cases is my own. The numbers refer to pages. Cases on a given page are assigned consecutive letters (A, B, C, . . .). Many of the ones referred to here will appear

A woman in early-twentieth-century Kano *could* hold her sons in awe—even to the point where they would beg the emir to send a palace official to entreat her forgiveness. She *could* achieve a degree of authority and power, and thus command obedience and respect. What the social historian would like to know, however, is under what terms, and by what means did a woman have access to power and authority? And in what respects was her access limited? Likewise, in what respects was she subject to the authority of others? And in what ways was that authority mitigated?

The ultimate arbiter of these questions was the emir's judicial council, the records of which provide an essential source for the historical study of women in Kano. The present study is drawn from a small sample of these records, from 1913 to 1914, involving some 2,000 cases. Of these, some 200 involved women, a fairly small sample, but one which enables us to sketch the most important legal problems encountered by women at the time, and to set the foundations for a more in-depth study.

The judicial council during this time was composed of Emir Abbas; the Waziri Muhammadu Gidado, who was his chief legal adviser; the chief Muslim judge (*alKali*) of Kano; the principal religious official of Kano's mosque (Ar. *imam*); the administrator of the community treasury (*ma'aji*); and several); prominent Islamic scholars of the city. Its membership was thus a combination of royal officials and independent religious leaders all of whom had training in Islamic law. The council applied a mixture of Islamic law, local custom, and, in certain matters, measures imposed at the behest of the British authorities.

The distinction between the jurisdiction of the emir's judicial council and the *alKali* court never had a hard and fast definition. In rough terms, the *alKali* dealt with those cases involving relationships between people, based on either contract or kinship. Especially for the rural *alKali*, the vast bulk of his work involved cases of divorce.[3] The *alKali* of Kano City was also involved in a large number of commercial cases.[4] The emir's judicial council was concerned with matters of violence, questions of taxation and administration, and cases involving property rights, whether over land, livestock, trade goods, or slaves. Women appeared more frequently before the *alKali*'s courts than before the judicial council, usually in routine matters, especially as they passed through the eternally revolving doors of divorce and marriage. It was the emir's judicial

---

in selection of translated cases which I am preparing, *Thus Ruled Emir 'Abbas*, to be published by Michigan State University Press. Dates are not given here, because they do not have a bearing on the analysis.

3. Divorce requested by the wife (*khul'*) entailed the return of the *sadag* (bridewealth) to the husband, and *ushiri* (H. a fee of 10 percent) was levied on this transaction. *AlKalai*'s record books include accounts of their revenue and demonstrate clearly the lucrative nature of divorce for the judicial administration.

4. This is based on my sampling of the *alKalai*'s record books at the Kano Area Court archives.

council, however, which laid down the fundamental parameters of women's access to, subjugation by, or protection from power. This study considers three areas of law of particular concern in attempting to outline those parameters: slavery, inheritance, and acts of violence. These are the three areas in which cases involving women arise most frequently in the records and the ones which have the greatest bearing on the question of women's access to and protection from power. An underlying assumption of the argument presented here is that effective social power in early-twentieth-century Kano involved much more than the formal legal freedom granted to an individual. Having effective power required that one be able to preside over one's own household and have the right to own and manage all forms of property, above all land and houses. One category of women, widows, had a good opportunity to achieve such power, since they often held real estate they had inherited or which they controlled as a trust for their children. It will be argued that slaves were of particular importance to women managing their own households. Furthermore, the prospects of a secure existence after the husband's death were diminished by the presence of another wife or wives, or of concubines. The highly charged conflicts which arose from plural conjugal relationships emerge in questions of violence—though, to be sure, this was not the only source of violence.

A second underlying assumption to this study is that the emir's judicial council did not simply apply the law in mechanical fashion, but at least in certain areas, made deliberate choices of social policy. It would be a mistake to see this choice as being between policies that favored or opposed the rights of women; rather the central concern of the council appears to have been to defend the social and economic continuity (or, in neo-Marxian terms, "reproduction") of the household against usurpers seeking to extend their own land holdings. Women household heads were particularly vulnerable to the usurpation efforts of village authorities or their husband's brothers. That the emir and his council defended their rights did not make them champions of women's rights, but champions of household continuity. Women could be both positively and adversely affected by the application of this principle.

Women and Slavery

Slavery had a bearing on Kano women's access to power in two ways. Most obviously, many women *were* slaves. As was often the case in African society, probably a great many more of the slaves in Kano were female than male.[5] But

5. The vast majority of slave cases in the register involved women. This may be in part because a good many of the male slaves had either deserted their masters or redeemed themselves. It may also reflect the type of cases which came up most frequently, such as conflicts over the status and custody of children. For the wider African picture, see Robertson and Klein 1983 and Miers and Roberts 1988.

women were often slaveowners, a position which gave them economic power as well as control over reproductive power outside of marriage, since according to Islamic law the children of a slave woman belonged to her owner. Slave ownership allowed a woman to preside over an economically viable domestic unit, something which she could not do as the subordinate partner in marriage except in the absence of her husband (a not infrequent occurrence among this people of inveterate traders). In Kano, as elsewhere in Africa, the end of slavery had a particularly important impact on women, both slaves and slave owners (Miers and Roberts 1988).

The years with which we are concerned, 1913–14, are crucial to the study of slavery in Kano. In 1901 the British had abolished slave raiding and slave trading, and they also proclaimed that those born after that date were to be free. In the first few years after the British conquest of Kano in 1903, it was a moot point whether or not a slave mother's toddlers were free. But by 1912 the children born in *zaman turawa* (the white man's time) were coming to the age where they could perform economically useful work, or could be married, and their status became a subject worthy of argument. Also in 1912, the railroad from Lagos reached Kano, setting off far-reaching economic changes. While acknowledging the importance of such changes, one needs to bear in mind that there were bases in Islamic law, completely independent of British decrees, upon which a woman could lodge a claim to freedom. If she had been a Muslim at the time of her capture and enslavement, she had the right to claim freedom. Also, a concubine who had born her master a child was legally free upon his death. And a woman, just as a man, could be redeemed. The most straightforward type of case was that in which a woman came to the emir's judicial council to claim her freedom (77D, 96E, 106A). Sometimes such women were recent victims of kidnapping. In other cases they had been captured and enslaved during the chronic troubles which afflicted the area around Kano in the late nineteenth century—the civil war of 1894, known in Kano as the Basasa, and the raids from Damagaram, an independent Hausa state to the north of Kano, or from Ningi, the hill region to the south. Individual women traveled to Kano to claim their freedom from as far away as Wadai, in the eastern part of present-day Chad (in this case a woman with two daughters) (7A); and from Asbin, in the center of Niger (72D). The critical point is that in order to make good a claim to freedom, women generally had to substantiate their free status by proving filiation to a free Muslim, which meant producing male relatives who were free Muslims. Without freeborn male kin willing to testify for her, a woman could not easily prove her free status before the emir's judicial council, and so might be vulnerable to reenslavement.

In a situation where women had been slaves at the time of capture, the legal situation was more ambiguous. In two such cases, the council offered the woman the choice between returning to her old master and staying with the new one. Both chose the latter (28C, 187C), one of them explaining her choice with the remark "he (her current master) has never frightened me." However, a slave woman returning to Kano after a protracted absence might not have any real choice but to return to the house of her former master (74B).

The problem which faced a woman seeking to lay a legal claim to freedom—namely the need for a domestic unit in which she could live as a free woman—also faced women who sought redemption by the payment of a sum of money to their masters. Under British policy, a master was in theory obliged to accept his or her slave's demand for redemption, a policy that the British saw as facilitating gradual emancipation. What the British authorities did not realize, or perhaps chose not to bring to the attention of their superiors, was that redemption of women slaves usually involved an unrelated man rather than the slave paying for her own redemption. In eleven out of seventeen cases where redemption is involved, this is true.

The significance of third party redemption of female slaves can be seen from specific cases which provide clues to the motives of redeemers. In one case, a woman gave birth to a son in her redeemer's household only 53 days after being redeemed. The former owner's son then successfully claimed custody of the child, who was legally recognized as his brother. Since the redeemer and the former master had in all probability been aware of the woman's condition at the time of the transaction, the expectation of acquiring a child was probably the principal motive for the redeemer, who may have been unable to father a child himself (98C). Whatever his problem, the solution he chose for it was legally flawed, and we should not assume that there was a heavy traffic in expectant slave women.

What may well have been the most common motive for third party redeemers was revealed in the council's judgment in a case where anonymous "people" claimed that a recently redeemed woman was already of free status. The council seemingly brushed this argument aside, and ruled that the redeemer still had the right of *wala* or patronship over her (7E), which meant that the redeemer had the right to give the woman away in marriage, receiving in return the economic and social benefits which accrue to one who offers a bride.[6]

The legal considerations behind this require explanation. A master could give a slave woman in marriage to another slave, but in the colonial era this arrangement would have been mutually unsatisfactory: for the slave husband, because the master still had the right to his wife's labor; for the slave owner, because British policy deprived him of the right to the children's labor. A master might take a slave woman as his concubine, but in the colonial era a master had rather tenuous control over a concubine. Concubines came to the judicial coun-

6. Most marriages involved the payment of bridewealth, but there was a type of marriage known as *sadaka* in which the bride was given away, usually to a religious scholar.

cil demanding dissolution of the relationship with their master. When asked for a reason, they offered precisely the same one given by wives asking for divorce before the *alkali*—"I don't like him." Emir Abbas was clearly uncertain about such cases and referred them to the local British colonial officer who in one instance granted the concubine's request, in another denied it (17B, 44D).

The judicial council further weakened the master's rights by its ruling in a case which involved a slave woman who had become pregnant by her master and had miscarried. She left him and found a prospective husband, and the council forced her master to consent to the marriage, but it did not require the husband to pay for her redemption (73F). The miscarriage, under Islamic law, had given her the status of *umm walad* (literally, "mother of a child"), which meant that she could not be sold or inherited, nor, by extension, redeemed. The council did not pronounce her to be free. Yet the combination of Islamic law—which denied the master the right to exploit the labor of an *umm walad* (al-Qayrawani 1945:226)—British antislavery policy—which denied the master the right to the labor of his slave's children—and the council's refusal to allow him control over her marriage choice made her effectively free.

Given these legal shadows hanging over traditional concubinage it becomes clearer why a master might allow, indeed solicit a young slave woman's redemption by a man who would marry her himself, or, using his right of guardianship (*wala*), give her in marriage to another man. Paul Lovejoy (1988) argues that such redemption-marriages were merely a disguised form of concubinage. However, on the basis of the considerations given above, it can be suggested that in the new colonial setting marriage was in fact important in assuring a woman's subordination. A concubine might, under some circumstances, go her own way leaving her master with nothing. A redeemed wife at least had the same financial obstacle as all wives if she asked for divorce—she would have to return to her husband the marriage payment (Ar. *sadaq*). It may well be that redeemed wives were considered to be of lower status than free wives, and had less effective power because of lack of support from their own families. But they were not concubines in the traditional legal sense.

Concubinage continued in Kano and remained a device exploited mainly by rich and powerful men. It seems likely that the women who were redeemed and then married would not, in the normal course of events in precolonial Kano, have become concubines, but would have been married to their fellow slaves. The British policy of emancipating children born after 1901 undermined the basis for such marriages, except in cases where the master-slave relationship was easily transformed into one of patron-clientship, which does not seem to have been the case in Kano emirate. Redemption-marriage thus can be seen as a legal strategy of slave owners to minimize the negative effects of child emancipation.

If it is correct to assume that redemption of a slave woman while she was still young was the optimal course for a master in the early colonial period, one could conclude that masters would be more eager to conclude a deal than were prospective redeemers. Such a hypothesis would help to explain why masters were willing to accept partial payment and a promise to pay the remainder in installments (33G), and why one redeemer came to the council complaining that malicious rumormongers in Kura were spreading the word that he had paid a paltry 7,000 cowries to redeem a slave woman when he claimed to have paid 200,000 (23B).[7]

To add a further twist to the matter, there are two cases of slave owners refusing redemption of a slave woman and then setting her free (44D, 90E). According to British antislavery ordinances, an offer of redemption could not be refused. In the case of manumission, female slaves were given a choice of where to go. If they had no family outside the master's household, they usually stayed there, taking on a fictive kinship role within the household (Mary Smith 1981). It is not clear from the records, however, whether a former master who manumitted his or her slave had the right of patronship over her.

Considerations of slave ownership were different for women than for men, and, for reasons to be discussed in the section on inheritance, these considerations were probably especially important for widows. If a man wished to expand his household at this time, he could easily do so up to a point by marrying or taking concubines and fathering children. A woman could, in principle, marry, but she would no longer be head of the household if she did so. The desire to run her own household may have prompted the typical widow not to remarry, and unlike a divorcée, who was dependent on one of her male kin and an encumbrance on his household, a widow might not have been under strong pressure to remarry. In any event, a single woman could only expand her household by having a slave who bore children, and she might be able to maintain the viability of her household as an economic unit only by retaining her slaves.

It is these factors which underlie the frequent disputes one finds involving the right of control over children between women slave owners and their slave girls (Ar. *amma*) (26D, 36C, 161B, 170H, 194A) who claimed freedom for those children who had been born in *zaman turawa*. Male slave owners also got into such quarrels, but since they often had numerous children of their own and could take on more wives or concubines, their *amma*'s children were probably not as essential or irreplaceable as they were for a single woman's household.

A particularly interesting case (65E) involves a woman named Gabasu who freed her *amma*, perhaps, as with the male owners mentioned above, as a strategy to foil redemption. A local office holder, Sarkin Gabara, went off and

7. The records under study do not offer sufficient data to compare redemption prices or bride-wealth for redeemed slave women and free women, but the *alkali*'s record books should provide abundant data on these matters (unfortunately these records begin ca. 1920).

"hid with her." An indication of the importance of this case was that Emir Abbas severely rebuked Sarkin Gabara, and then returned the former slave girl to the custody of Gabasu.

While female slaves might provide their mistress with practical services as well as the benefits of progeny, male slaves could also perform important roles. Harun of Gugir took up the cause of his widowed mistress and her orphaned son (the status of orphan [Ar. *yatim*] being reckoned by the loss of one's father) when the village head of Gugir attempted to seize a plot of their land. The emir consistently and strongly defended the property rights of widows—as he did in this case. In Hausa Muslim society, farm work is typically a male occupation, and male slaves would have been essential for women landowners, since rental of land was not common at the time.[8]

Inheritance and Women's Property Rights

The rules of inheritance are one of the most highly developed and distinctive aspects of Islamic law. Strict mathematical formulas provide for inheritance division in every conceivable situation. Both wives and daughters have inheritance rights under Islamic law, though a daughter may inherit only half of what a son does, and a wife, or wives, inherit one-eighth of the estate if there are children, one-fourth if there are none (Esposito 1982). These provisions, which have a fragmenting effect on accumulated wealth, can be evaded if the inheritance is not divided or if parties with potential claims do not invoke them. In Kano there was a financial incentive not to divide the inheritance—or at least not to divide it before the courts—since a fee of one-tenth (*ushiri*) was levied on inheritance divisions. In several recorded cases, women came by their property not through formal division of an estate but as trustees for their children of their late husband's estate, so "inheritance" as used here does not imply a formal inheritance division executed by the *alƙali*.

Women's inheritance questions usually came before the judicial council when a widow sought to defend her land rights against greedy local officials or her husband's male relatives. Less frequently they involved property inherited by a married woman from her father, which her husband claimed from her male kin on her behalf (143I). The emir's judicial council handled all of these cases—or at least recorded them—in summary fashion, without concern for the fine points of Islamic law.

In dealing with widows, the principal concern was whether or not the woman had children. If she did, her land rights would be defended against all challengers. There were numerous cases where village heads or local titleholders

8. *Rahn* (pawning) of land was a very common practice, *'aar* (loan) apparently less so. The records show that *rahn* especially was a risky practice, since it was often impossible to distinguish from outright sale.

attempted to appropriate a woman's land, and in each case the woman's rights were confirmed by the council. In one case a village head was told to remove his house from a woman's property (21F). These cases were also quite frequent for men, however, and there is no distinction between the treatment of men and women. One could also argue that the fact that land usurpation cases were so common indicates that there were probably many instances where it was carried out successfully, even though Emir Abbas stood staunchly against the practice.

A number of inheritance-related cases involved conflicts between a widow and her late husband's brother. Sometimes the husband's brother had a role as supervisor of the widow's and orphans' affairs: in such cases the council warned the brother to confine himself to a strictly supervisory role (168A). However, supervision by the brother was merely an option. In one case a widow's husband's brother was able to expel her from his household, while she retained ownership of her late husband's land (167B).

There were significant qualifications placed on a widow's control over property inherited from her husband when she had young children and was, in effect, acting to administer their inheritance. The emir ruled, in a case involving agricultural land, that a widow-trustee could not sell, pawn, loan, or donate to a third party any of the land concerned (28C). In one case where a woman did sell a piece of land, her son complained, and the sale was ruled invalid (192G). Another case involved an inheritance of six cows: the widow and her late husband's brother were both warned that "if the wealth is spoiled, we will order you both to return [to the emir's judicial council] and we will rebuke you both" (168A). The importance of this prohibition is lent weight by the fact that women never appear in the scores of disputes over land pawning (Ar. *rahn*) in the records. There are, however, two cases which mention widows buying land (115G, 123B) that was ultimately inherited by their sons.

There is no direct indicator in the legal records as to whether widows were encouraged or prevented from remarrying. The emir did rule that a previously married woman (Ar. *thayyiba*) could marry whomever she loved (31E) and thus could not be forced into marriage by her male relatives. Since a divorcée would not normally have substantial resources of her own, she would be under pressure to remarry, whereas a widow, who might well have resources which she owned or at least controlled, might be loath to run the risk of letting a new husband achieve control. Thus a widow not only had the legal right *not* to remarry, but she might also have had the means to survive comfortably outside of marriage—or, in a sense, within the framework of a marriage where the partner was absent (Schildkrout 1986).

The rights of women without children were diminished. When a childless woman was challenged by her late husband's brother, she was obliged to divide the property with him. In one case a woman whose husband had set out to trade in Lagos thirty years previously was obliged to split the land with his brother (111H), although until that point, she had been allowed to hold the property in trust while her husband remained the legal owner. In another case, a widow who was so challenged claimed the land on the basis of donation (*hiba*) rather than inheritance, but Emir Abbas nevertheless ordered division (112C).

The council's defense of widows' property rights was closely connected to its consistent defense of orphans' rights. One such case involved a brother, Barau, and his sister, Gambu, who inherited land from their father. When Gambu died, she left her land to her son, and then her son died, leaving it to his own young son. Barau attempted to seize the land of his sister's grandson, but was prevented from doing so by the council (109B).

What practical reasons did the emir have for so consistently upholding the property rights of orphans and widows, aside from the important consideration that this was enjoined by the Qur'an? One consideration may have been to assure their economic integration into the society as controllers of property, to prevent them from falling into destitution, or to prevent their being forced into a situation in which they would be, so to speak, second-class members of a distant kinsman's household. (One might of course argue that this is the motive behind the Qur'anic injunctions.) But, especially when considering widows, there was also a question of spiritual integration, since widows and divorcées were commonly adepts of the *bori* spirit possession cult, a role often combined with courtesanship or prostitution.

The *bori* cult had been strongly condemned as un-Islamic by the leaders of the Sokoto jihad in the early nineteenth century, and this condemnation was retained in principle by their successors. In practice, Emir Abbas seems to have been lenient toward practitioners of *bori*. Hassana and Hadija of Madabo ward "did something which the Emir of Kano had forbidden as *bid'a*" (a blameworthy practice in the eyes of Islamic law). They were imprisoned for one day, and then they repented and were released (41F). The people of Goron Doma quarter reported that Inna was carrying on prohibited practices. She was imprisoned for two days, then released (18G).

The records also give a few glimpses of the circumstances in which the spirits whose behavior is thought to be controlled through the *bori* rituals (Ar. *jinn*) chose to attack. They suggest, moreover, that the emir and his council subscribed to the reality of *jinn*. A widow named Habiba, from Garko town, came to Kano market with a suckling girl on her back. She went around the market, was struck by *jinn*, and left the infant on the ground. When the child's guardian (*wali*)—in this case the child's paternal uncle—heard about this, he came to the emir, asking for help from him. The emir had Habiba and her daughter brought from the market and put them into the hands of the child's uncle (60C). This case seems to underscore the tensions between widows and husbands' brothers, since the latter bore a burden of responsibility but could not benefit from their brother's inheritance in the event that there were children. The case may also suggest a possible link between the *bori* cult and prostitution—namely that widowhood or divorce precipitated spiritual crises, such as the one described above, which might lead a woman into the *bori* cult at the same time as her unmarried status and need for resources led to prostitution. Having substantial resources of her own and being able to perpetuate her husband's household could leave a woman less susceptible to spiritual crisis or economic need.

Violence

A society's rules of inheritance both reflect and shape the network of alliances and tensions within its kinship structures (Goody et al. 1976). The tensions are sometimes precipitated in acts of violence. For a Kano woman, the prospect of a comfortable inheritance for herself and her children were reduced dramatically by the presence of another wife or a concubine. Wives were limited to one-eighth (or one-fourth in the absence of children) of the inheritance, regardless of whether there was one wife or four. Although concubines had no legal inheritance rights, they could produce legitimate children who would diminish other children's shares.

The emir's judicial council could usually do little to prevent or punish the domestic violence which resulted from these tensions. The following case offers a dramatic illustration of this:

There came to us [the judicial council] Sarki Maiaduwa of whom it is said he killed his wife Hafsa. We ask who was her *wali al-dam* [executor of a blood feud—the person who had the right to exact compensation or revenge for her murder], and he mentioned to us Sarkin Yaki Ibrahim, her uncle. We called him, and her mother Hajja, and her father's paternal cousin, Muhammad. We asked Ibrahim about what had taken place. He said that her husband Maiaduwa struck her, and she died after six days. We asked did you see the blow? He said no. We asked her mother. She said that her husband struck her. She came to her (mother) crying, and her mother asked why. She said that her husband had taken her bed and given it to his concubine, and she did not agree to this. Then he struck her with his hands on her neck and side and chest. She went back to her husband's house one night, then she came back to her mother's. [Her mother] asked why she had returned, and she said that the blows on her neck and side hurt her. She died six days later. Maiaduwa denied the stories of the blows and quarrel. He said that she had been ill from an attack of *jinn* (Ar. *mass al-jinn*) for twenty-four days at his house. We asked the mother for witnesses, and none were found who saw the blow or heard it. [It is noted that] Maiaduwa did not originally report the attack of *jinn*, but said that she had been violently ill.

The mother then withdrew the complaint, and Maiaduwa was exonerated. Then the mother said:

When she came back, Hafsa told her, by Allah and the Prophet, do not complain against her husband Maiaduwa, leave him be. Allah will judge between us on the day of reckoning (Ar. *yawm al-qiyama*). So she (the mother) did not tell anyone and did not inform the *wali al-dam*. (54A)

In this case there was an alternative to insisting on witnesses to the act of murder. If the judicial council felt that it had grounds for grave presumption (Ar. *lawth*) of the husband's guilt, Ibrahim and Muhammad would have been allowed to take the oath of compurgation (Ar. *yamin al-qasama*) and thereby gain the right to blood payment. Clearly it was with this expectation that they appeared in court. The council did permit this oath in a number of cases, notably in instances where food thieves had been killed by granary owners (Christelow, forthcoming). Permitting the *yamin al-qasama* seems to have been as much a political as a legal judgment. Emir Abbas evidently felt on stronger political ground in condemning the killer of a food thief in time of famine than a husband who had killed his wife.

The involvement of a concubine in this case may reflect a growing incidence of concubinage, a conclusion which would follow from Lovejoy's study (1988). But it may indicate the growing status and power of traditional concubines who, since they were no longer tightly bound to their master by law, may have been able to command new favor. Traditional concubines were most commonly found in the homes of the elite. The wives of the elite, like Hafsa, typically faced greater pressure than those of commoners to avoid divorce, since their marriages involved high stakes in terms of marriage payments and political alliances. Hafsa herself seems to have been pressured to return to her husband despite obvious evidence of his brutality.

The fact that Hafsa's uncle was a titleholder indicates that this case involved a prominent Kano family.[9] In other cases involving commoners the more typical response of the husband who had killed his wife was to flee (34G, 66C). This was even the response of a man who killed his wife's lover when he caught him with her in a cassava storehouse (8B).

In some cases, domestic tensions led to violence between co-wives (38I), and in one case a son seems to have felt animosity toward his mother's co-wife, whom he shot and killed with an arrow, claiming that he had mistaken her for a thief. He fled, but returned after three years, and paid the blood money (*diyya*) of 100,000 cowries (68C).

Women also ran a risk of assault by strangers. The path to the well was a typical scene of aggressive encounters between young women and men. The

9. This case will have familiar overtones to anyone who followed the sensational 1979 murder trial in Kano involving the son of a prominent Kano businessman; however, this trial was presided over by the last British judge on the Nigerian bench—who retired to England immediately after the acquittal.

following case was sent to the emir by the *alKali* of Wudil: "Auta of Sakuya village insulted Garba's slave girl at the well. She said to him don't repeat that, and he repeated the abuse again. She was irritated. He walked about in front of her and struck her with both hands on her back. So she fell into the well and died." Three witnesses for Auta testified that the girl had abused him before he pushed her as she bent down to pull a bucket out of the well. Auta was made to compensate Garba for the value of the slave girl and was given the standard homicide punishment of one hundred lashes and a year in prison (115A).

Another case involved a girl named Khadija, whose father sent her to the well to carry water in a skin: "When she was carrying the water back, before her arrival, the skin broke. She came to her father crying, not saying anything. Afterward, rumormongers spread the lie that she had been hit by a man named Muhammad. He was called and denied this. The father forgave him" (93D). The tendency of a father to forgive sexual assaults on his daughter also emerged in another case, where two youths beat a girl, striking her on her private parts, and causing her death (97D).

One group of women who ran a particular risk of violence were itinerant traders (26D, 30D), for whom open assault (as opposed to surreptitious theft) seemed to be a greater problem than for their male counterparts. For instance, 'Aisha of Katsina emirate "came to Kano city with her trade goods. She arrived after nightfall. When she came to a place called Bulukiya, she was seized. A man told her to chose between her self and her goods, and she chose her self. So he took the goods. The emir asked if she had ever seen the man before. She said no. The emir told her to go and look for her goods" (33B).

The period 1913–14, with the arrival of the railway and the subsequent surge in trade caused by the groundnut boom, was one of considerable insecurity for all itinerant traders (Hogendorn 1978). No woman trader is mentioned in the records from March 1914 until the end of the records under study, in late November of that year. This may suggest that with the growing insecurity women became less involved in trade or that they were the first to withdraw from trade as the effects of the great drought hit. Of course, it may also mean that they had found a way to protect themselves, or that they had come to the conclusion that it was not worth the trouble going to the emir if they were only going to receive patronizing encouragement in the search for their stolen goods.

If violence was a common coin of the new commercial circuits, so was intimidation, albeit less visibly. A woman named 'Aisha, from Bakin Ruwa ward in Kano city, came to the council to claim 60,000 cowries and a horse from a prominent Kano merchant, Abdu Agogo. But once before the council she claimed that two men had pressured her into the complaint, claiming that if she did not make it "the *bature*" (the white man) would imprison her (187D). This case reminds one of the emir's ruling that widow-trustees could not pawn or loan their property and suggests that any thorough study of women and the economy in Kano needs to look at constraints, both legal and cultural, on women's involvement in transactions of lending and borrowing which are essential to one's entry into the modern commercial economy.

Other problems that occasionally arose were assault on a woman which caused the child to fall off her back, killing the child (151D, 185A), and cases in which women were run over and killed or injured by horses (69E, 78C). One Kano man, by the name of Yusuf, was gallant enough to stop his galloping horse, pick up the woman he had knocked over, and ride with her to the emir's judicial council—where he was exonerated (190C).

The most curious sort of case was that which involved the allegation of causing death through magical powers. One such case involved a girl named Fatima. She said to another girl, Dundu, "Let's go have fun. She [Dundu] refused. She said that there's no good in you. The result was that she [Fatima] did to her the thing called *kandunbaka* [casting the evil eye] and she died because of it." The Wambai of Kano, the official in whose district the incident had evidently taken place, reported this case to the emir, asking to be exonerated from "the ruses of the time and its nuisances," a request which was forthwith granted. The dead girl's guardian forgave Fatima, and "the *shari'a* [Islamic law] accepted his word" (9G).

Conclusion

The legal records from 1913–14 provide only a limited view of the life of women in Kano, but they do offer some critical insights and allow us to formulate some important questions. Several of the most important concern the effects of British antislavery measures. It is clear that a large number of slave women were redeemed for the purpose of marriage, concubinage, or a form of legally reinforced concubinage dressed up as marriage. The women involved, before the colonial era, would usually have been married to fellow slaves, but the emancipation of all children born after 1901 sharply reduced the attraction of this option for masters. At the same time, the banning of slave raiding and slave trading meant that the only feasible means of adding members to one's household was through marriage. Unmarried female heads of household, particularly widows, could not adapt easily to this change, for the availability of slaves had been important in maintaining their position.

The presence of independent widows as heads of household must also be seen as the result of deliberate choice on the part of the emir's judicial council, which consistently defended the property rights of widows with children, although it placed restrictions on a widow-trustee's ability to transform real estate into some other form of wealth by preventing her from alienating property. One way to interpret this is to see it as a reflection of the council's support for continuity within the household and its opposition to the expansion of landholdings either through wielding political power or by manipulating inheritance rights.

Perhaps the most serious problem faced by women as a group was the threat of violence. Some of this violence was related to changes which had come with colonial rule. Certainly this was the case for theft-related violence which was stimulated by the groundnut boom, and which may have involved a new class of rootless men, many of them male ex-slaves, whose rootlessness arose from their being denied access to land and to wives. It may also have been the case in some incidents of domestic violence, since new women were being recruited into the households of the well-to-do through redemption, either as wives or as concubines, and since traditional concubines now enjoyed a greater margin of power thanks to an uncertain British policy regarding their rights and status.

The case of Hafsa's death illustrates the tensions which could arise within an elite household. She protested against her husband's favorable treatment of his concubine and, in response, he beat her severely. She turned to her mother, but her mother evidently urged her to go back to her husband. When Hafsa died, her kin turned to the judicial council for redress, but they found the council unwilling to apply the *qasama* oath, so the husband was let off. It is not clear whether this decision reflected the council's tolerance of domestic violence or its fear that Hafsa's influential husband would complain to the British, who might have reversed the council's decision on the grounds that the *qasama* oath was an archaic, primitive legal device.[10] In any case, it is clear that women like Hafsa had no effective recourse against domestic violence.

Data from the emir of Kano's judicial council thus suggest an ironic conclusion. The British in northern Nigeria aligned themselves with the traditional ruling class, and because of this they took a gradualist approach to slave emancipation and overlooked disguised slave sales in the form of redemption by third parties. But if any group of women lost in power and status as a result of colonial legal policy, it was those of the wealthier classes:[11] for they now had much reduced access to slaves, who to them were especially crucial for running an independent household; and the concubines in their households gained new leverage as a result of British confusion over how to treat them.

---

10. Homicide law was to be a key issue in debates over the establishment of a Nigerian criminal code during the 1950s, and the *qasama* oath was a major focus for British jurists' criticisms of Islamic law. They saw this oath not only as archaic in principle but as unfair, since it could not be applied when the victim lacked male agnates to take the oath. The records of 1913–14 make clear that the British were already insisting on more thorough recording of homicide cases.

11. This conclusion is consistent with the findings presented in the introduction to Robertson and Klein 1983.

8 *Barbara J. Callaway*

The Role of Women in Kano City Politics

In Hausa society the social hierarchy, which is male-dominated, is defined in sacred rather than in secular terms. Kano City is 99 percent Muslim. Equality for women in an Islamic society is circumscribed by the teachings of the Qur'an, which defines women's role in both the family and society. The revelation of the Qur'an to the Prophet Mohammed and the articulation of the *shari'a* (Islamic law) through the ages by Islamic scholars have contributed to the formulation of certain assumptions concerning the rights and obligations of women. Muslim scholars maintain that the Qur'an explicitly demands the same standard for men and women, and thus the two are equal before God: "And whosoever does a righteous deed, be they male or female, and is a believer, we shall assuredly give them a goodly life to live; and we shall certainly reward them according to the best of what they did" (Qur'an 16:97).

In Islamic law, women are afforded explicit rights and protections, particularly in regard to inheritance, marriage, and support, but the general import of references to women in the Qur'an is that women are dependent on men and are fulfilled only through subordination to them. Although the roles of wives and husbands are viewed as complementary rather than "unequal," it is quite clear that relationships within the family are hierarchical and patriarchal in nature. Although "women have the same [rights in relation to their husbands] as is expected in all decency from them, men stand a step above them. God is mighty and wise" (Qur'an 2:228). The Qur'an dictates that women's inheritance rights are less than those of men, that the testimony of two women is equal to that of one man in *shari'a* courts, and that women should cover their bodies, live away from public view, and speak with no one but their husbands and designated male relatives.

In Kano today there is great pressure to conform to the prevailing interpretations of Islamic doctrine: women function in effect as minor wards of their husbands and fathers. Girls marry young, generally at the onset of puberty. Upon marriage, most women enter seclusion (*kulle*): they do not go out to shop, trade, or visit the market, and they confine many of their activities to the domestic side of human relationships. They observe postures of deference and service toward men. They do not question the patriarchal structure of the family. Public roles for Kano women are conceived of only in relation to Islamic concepts of "justice" and "equality."

Kano City Politics: An Overview

With an estimated 10 million inhabitants, Kano is the largest state in the Nigerian Federation and the only one with a homogeneous indigenous population (Hausa-Fulani). Kano is also the largest of the traditional Hausa states, and Kano City is increasingly recognized in the twentieth century as an important center of Islamic learning. Explicitly religious concepts of political authority and community have been important in Kano since the time of Mohammad Rumfa, who ruled from 1463 to 1500 and was acknowledged as the first Muslim emir.

From 1952 to 1983 two parties dominated political life in Kano (although during the periods of military rule parties were officially banned): the NPC/NPN (the Northern People's Congress, which metamorphosed into the National Party of Nigeria) and the NEPU/PRP (the Northern Elements Progressive Union, which metamorphosed into the People's Redemption Party). Both identified themselves with Islamic concepts of government, and Islamic themes have been strongly in evidence in their political rhetoric. The Northern People's Congress (NPC) was the dominant party in northern Nigeria during the period 1952–66; its successor, the National Party of Nigeria (NPN), won elections at the national level in 1979 and 1983. When addressing an exclusively northern audience, each claimed to represent the consensus of the society, the Islamic *Umma* (Ar.) and each asserted that not to accept this consensus was in fact heretical and un-Islamic. By the same token, the opposition Northern Elements Progressive Union (NEPU) and its successor, the People's Redemption Party (PRP), stressed the political implications of Islamic concepts of government and sought doctrinal support for their political ideology by emphasizing the Islamic content of their political program. The leaders interspersed Islamic themes in political speeches and poetry by using religious allusions and justifications. During periods of civilian rule in Nigeria (1960–66 and 1979–83), the primary source of identity for all politicians in Kano was as Muslims and northerners, in contradistinction to more ethnically conscious southerners: political leaders emphasized the universalistic teachings of Islam and saw themselves as members of the wider Islamic world.

However, there were significant differences between the two political parties. In a number of ways, NEPU/PRP challenged the "old order" supported by NPC/NPN. The themes of radical and opposition northern politics, as developed by the leader and spokesperson of NEPU/PRP, Aminu Kano, and others in the party, stressed the interrelationship between religion and the class-based nature of society. In their attack on the NPC and the significant roles played by the traditional leaders in that party and its government, NEPU leaders argued that Fulani rulers had betrayed the Islamic ideals set down by Shehu Usman dan Fodio at the time of the jihad. They then attempted to place the stamp of Islamic approval on NEPU's own political program.

A consistent theme of NEPU/PRP politics in Kano was an ideological attack on the entire traditional political structure, including the political position (or nonposition) of women. Reiterating and expanding upon the Islamic concepts of "freedom," "jihad," and "justice," Aminu Kano made the position of women a basic concern of his political party from the start. NEPU/PRP advocated the immediate adoption of a system of direct democracy with universal adult suffrage, including the enfranchisement of women, to replace the traditional class-based, hierarchical structures upon which the British had tried to build and which the NPC had protected, preserved, and elaborated. In the 1979 election, held after thirteen years of military rule, the NPN won the presidential election at the national level, but the PRP overwhelmingly won the elections in Kano State. The PRP, as NEPU had been two decades before, was essentially a Kano-based party, and Kano remained the locus of both its leadership and electoral strength. It was widely believed that women, voting for the first time in 1979, gave the PRP its large majority vote in Kano. After Aminu Kano passed away suddenly in the spring of 1983, his party lost the presidential election in Kano State, but his candidates again won the separate state elections in Kano.

In politics, as in other aspects of life, Muslims regard the Qur'an as the source of law defining personal responsibilities, values, interpretations, and community obligations. The teachings of the Qur'an may be made clear only through revelation and interpretation by Islamic scholars. Thus if a radical position in modern Kano politics was to emerge, it had to be formulated by learned Muslim scholars, who were recognized as the only legitimate interpreters of Islamic law and its moral and spiritual values. Three early leaders of NEPU— Aminu Kano, Sa'ad Zungar, and Isa Wali—were all trained and recognized as Islamic teachers. Aminu Kano was universally referred to throughout his adult lifetime by the Hausa term for teacher, *malam*. He gave Qur'anic read-

ings during Friday afternoon prayers in Kano and during the fasting period
of Ramadan, stressing the centrality of justice in Islam and its relevance to
the treatment of women. Amino Kano's advocacy of an expanding role for
women in the polity was deemed legitimate in part because he was regarded as
a religious as well as a political leader.

Of the political parties active in Kano over a thirty-year period, only NEPU
and its successor, PRP, expressed genuine concerns about the role and social
position of women and advocated public policies, especially education, for
them. In the 1950s and 1960s Aminu Kano and his colleague, Isa Wali, were
virtually alone in addressing this issue; by the late 1970s and 1980s the subject
had become part of the party platform of the PRP and was advocated by a wide
spectrum of its members. This advocacy was couched, however, in the language of Islamic justice, not feminist revolution. In 1959 NEPU supported the
right of women to vote, and in 1979 the PRP promised to promote women in
politics and to extend education to them. Aminu Kano himself had sponsored a
school for women, which convened in his home from 1952 to 1983. The school
offered courses in handicrafts, machine sewing, Hausa, and basic English literacy, but it offered nothing encouraging women to organize themselves for
political activism.

Aminu Kano was a modernist and progressive in his practice of Islam.
Throughout his lifetime, he was well known for his deep commitment to
Islamic teachings, his politically caustic poetry, and his writing and reading of
satirical plays which contained thinly veiled ridicule of the pompous ways of
traditional emirate rulers. His mother, most unusually, was herself educated:
she taught her son the Qur'an and started his study of Arabic (Feinstein 1973:
35). Aminu Kano felt strongly about his mother and the limitations placed
upon her life by Hausa society. To her memory he dedicated his lifelong efforts
to introduce change in the status of women, stressing education and their full
participation in the polity (interview #46, Kano, April 14, 1982).[1] While a
student in London (1946–48), he wrote all of his term papers on "The Problem of Girls' Education in Kano," and in 1956 he published articles on the
status of women in Nigeria in the *Nigerian Citizen*, where he was quoted as
saying, "It is impossible to promote the status of women and men (I now like
to say women and men) in this twentieth century while maintaining this medi-
eval form of government" (Paden 1973:288; Sklar 1983:101). When he died,
Aminu Kano's home became a place of prayer. Had he lived, his running mate
in the presidential elections of August of that year would have been the first

---

1. In 1981–83 structured interviews were conducted with eighty-eight women living in two
wards in Kano City. The women were assured anonymity and thus their interviews are cited only
by number, date, and place.

Nigerian woman nominated by any political party for high national office, Bola Ogunbo.

Aside from Mallam Aminu Kano, the public spokesperson most closely identified with concern for the status of women during the 1950s and 1960s was another student of Islamic law and an opposition political leader, Isa Wali. In the summer of 1956 Isa Wali wrote a series of articles in the *Nigerian Citizen* which provoked discussion and set the parameters of debate concerning the appropriate place of women in the polity (*Nigerian Citizen* July 18–August 4, 1956). Wali discussed the proper role of women in public authority, stating:

As for public life, there is nothing in Islam which prevents a woman from following any pursuit she desires. There is no distinct prohibition against her taking part in public leadership, as Aisha, the Prophet's widow, demonstrated (*Nigerian Citizen*, July 18, 1956, p. 6, quoted in Paden 1973:290).

When discussing the rights and scope given to women by Islam, I touched on some leading Moslem women, such as Aisha and "The Mothers of the Believers," the wives of the Companions of the Prophet, and their successors, who played a full and active part in public life, education and leadership in Moslem history. . . . Aisha . . . as a widow . . . turned her energies and talents more and more into political channels, until, for a time at least, she came to dominate the political situation with great spirit and energy (*New Nigerian*, August 4, 1956, p. 5).

In the same vein, a widely distributed article written by Alhaji Shehu Galadanci, a member of an important Fulani family in Kano and at one time vice chancellor of the University of Sokoto, advocated increased educational opportunities for women. Writing in 1971, during the period of military rule, Galadanci set out the framework for expanding the education system to include girls and women. Like Aminu Kano, he stressed that the search for knowledge was commendable and obligatory for all Muslims and that it should not be limited to men:

The Qur'an exalts those who have knowledge (not just men). Chapter 58, v. 11 states "God will exalt those who believe among you, and those who have knowledge, to high ranks."

Women have heavy responsibilities as wives and associates of men, and secondly as mothers and trainers of younger Muslim generations. (Galadanci 1971:6, 9)

Galadanci cited three examples which he maintained established Islamic sanction for the education of women: (1) that the Prophet himself had two educated wives, one of whom recorded 1,210 hadiths "direct from the mouth of the Prophet," and the other of whom was custodian of the authentic Qur'an manuscript; (2) in Nigeria, Shehu Usman ɗan Fodio allowed women to attend his lectures and preachings; and (3) the two daughters of Usman ɗan Fodio had acquired a high standard of Islamic education. As further evidence, he cited ɗan

Fodio's daughter, Khadijah, who wrote verse in Fulfulde concerning Maliki law, as well as an Arabic grammar. "Even in recent years a few learned women were known to be active in learning and teaching in their homes" (Galadanci 1971:10). According to Galadanci, it was Europeans who were responsible for the disappearance of learning for women in the North African Islamic world.

Galadanci further set forth the arguments which were to find their way into the PRP platform ten years later. He argued that in a good marriage a husband and wife should have "compatibility and harmony in a standard of general knowledge and intelligence," and thus the same educational opportunities should be afforded both sexes. Girls in the north should be educated, but a great deal of emphasis must be placed on teaching the "Islamic ways of life to girls so that they can provide a congenial Islamic environment at home and moral training for children" (Galadanci 1971:12). This leading educator did not advocate knowledge for women in order that they might discover their own intellectual interests and pursue them for their own sake; rather, he supported knowledge for women solely for the purpose of making them better Muslims, better wives, and better mothers in the "Islamic way."

Aminu Kano, Isa Wali, and Shehu Galadanci repeatedly criticized and challenged the exclusion of women from the public world. They asserted that the position of women had been misrepresented in Islam and that Nigerian women had suffered because of misinterpretations of the Qur'an. It was Mallam Aminu Kano who first made the point that taking four wives, for example, was sanctioned by the Prophet only if each could be treated equally; since this was, according to Aminu Kano, beyond human capability, the Qur'an never actually endorsed polygamy. He claimed also that education was advocated for both men and women, since the Prophet had said that the only way to understand Islam was through education. And since women were admonished to teach children, Aminu Kano believed that education for women was clearly called for (interview #46, Kano, April 14, 1982).

But exhortations for the education and public emancipation of women were being made at a time when a resurgence of Islamic fundamentalism limited women's public role. Girls continued to marry at puberty, if not earlier. Observers also noted an increase in female seclusion among urban Hausa families, in sharp contrast to developments in Islamic societies elsewhere in West Africa (M. G. Smith 1955, 1960; Abell 1962; Hill 1972, 1977). Aminu Kano argued that domestic seclusion of women did not necessarily mean that women should be excluded from the political process. Yet wife seclusion and a revival of Islamic fundamentalism clearly limit the public role of women while underscoring the static nature of domestic arrangements.

Women and Formal Politics: The First Republic (1960–1966)

The appeal to educate and give political emancipation to women was in conflict with what had become deeply ingrained patterns of male subordination of women. Challenges to such patterns engendered strong reactions, and therefore, in order to be regarded as legitimate, they were justified by appeal to Islamic religious injunctions. Largely in deference to strong Muslim lobbying, Nigeria's first constitution (1960) did not grant women the right to vote. The regional governments in the east and west enacted legislation extending the franchise to women, but the party in power during the First Republic, the NPC, strongly resisted such action in the north. Addressing the National Assembly on March 25, 1965, Waziri Ibrahim stated: "We in the North are perfectly happy: our women are happy about their condition and I appeal to other members of the Republic to please leave us in peace. There is not a single Northern woman who has told anybody that she is unhappy. We know what is right for women and our men know what is right for themselves" (quoted in the *Sunday Times*, May 27, 1979, in an article recapping the history of politics in northern Nigeria). Ahmadu Bello, premier of the north and president of the NPC, stated in his autobiography: "Female suffrage is inimical to the customs and feelings of the great part of the men of this region" (1962:223). NEPU did advocate female enfranchisement, but it was not elected to power, and similar legislation was strongly resisted in the regional legislature. Extending the franchise to women was seen as incompatible with the customs and feelings of the greater portion of the population. The low level of education for women in the north was also a serious problem—literacy in English, for example, was virtually nonexistent. Indeed, women's lack of education was cited by the regional government as a reason for not extending the vote to them: "The education of women must reach a far greater strength, and the number of properly educated women must be increased to many times the present number before the vote would be used to full advantage" (Bello 1962:233).

Despite the fact that the franchise was denied to women in the north during the First Republic, both major political parties in Kano had "women's wings" affiliated with them during this time, although the leadership and the central committee of the women's wings in both the NPC and NEPU were appointed by the party leaders and had little or no autonomy. The male leadership of the parties assumed a paternalistic relationship to the women's wings. In some parties women occasionally had a representative on the party's executive committee, but the women's wings of both parties relied upon the actual male party for membership recruitment and financial support.

Since women could not vote, the party was not concerned with involving women in politics per se. The NPC, in fact, expressly opposed women's suffrage and proposed no programs geared to women or their interests. Yet the women's wing was conspicuously in evidence at most political rallies. In the NPC in particular, it existed primarily to provide "entertainment" at political rallies. During the First Republic, participation in the women's wings understandably carried a derogatory implication, for it was popularly believed that only prostitutes were involved in politics.

Thus it has been suggested that most of the women who worked with political parties by providing entertainment (chanting, singing, and dancing at rallies) during the 1960–66 period were from the ranks of local prostitutes (*karuwai*). The publicly known active members of the women's wings of both parties were in fact *karuwai,* as were the presidents of both wings. In the absence of any substantive female role in the public sector, it was perhaps natural that political parties would turn for political support to the only women not in seclusion—the *karuwai.* This was so partly because most husbands, even if they were politicians themselves, would not allow their own wives to be involved in anything so public. Men came to the rallies to listen to politicians and to see and hear women perform the party songs and chants. The *karuwai* in turn received many benefits from their association with the parties. Most particularly, they were able to travel at party expense, and since their function was to mingle with the crowds and provide amusement, they presumably could conduct their own business as well.

The women's wings were staffed by female "officers" who were largely illiterate and acted on instructions from male sponsors. No issues of particular concern to women were raised, and the women's wings played no substantive role either in the generation of party platforms or in their presentation to the public. Because northern women could not vote prior to the 1979 elections, it is apparent that the women's wings of the party were not relevant to a women's vote but were an attraction to the male voting population.

Women and Politics: The Second Republic (1979–1983)

A military decree in 1976 finally extended the franchise to women in the north, and the ban on politics was lifted by the military government on September 23, 1978. The traditional leaders of the old north, particularly the Sultan of Sokoto, as well as all the political parties, then urged women to register and vote. Women did in fact register, and more women than men voted in the 1979 elections in the northern states. Thus in Kano, Aminu Kano's basic program for reform for women was subsequently adopted.

In spite of rhetorical emphases on issues largely removed from the immediate concerns of women, there is evidence that women voting for the first time did recognize a difference between the two parties in terms of the interests of women. This is illustrated by voting patterns in two wards, Kofar Mazugal and Kurawa, whose social characteristics have been studied in detail by Schildkrout

Table 8.1. Elections in Two Kano Wards, 1979

Party	Kofar Mazugal Vote by Party	Kurawa Vote by Party
National Party of Nigeria (NPN)	4,202	13,001
People's Redemption Party (PRP)	10,551	14,491
Greater Nigerian People's Party (GNPP)	136	451
Unity Party of Nigeria (UPN)	0	247
Nigerian People's Party (NPP)	0	47
Total	22,707	28,237
Voters registered		
Men	26,350	17,160
Women	23,650	17,840

Source: Federal Election Commission, Register of Voters, General Election 1979.

(1978a, 1978b, 1980, 1982) (see table 8.1). It was in the predominantly Hausa wards such as Kofar Mazugal that NEPU drew its votes during 1950–65 and that the PRP won overwhelmingly in 1979 and 1983. The NPN easily won the 1952–66 elections in the more middle-class, predominantly Fulani wards such as Kuwara and was expected to win easily in 1979 and 1983, with a small PRP factor evident. In fact, NPN barely won these latter two elections in Kuwara, lending credence to the PRP assertion that it was women voting for the first time that provided them with their overwhelming victory in Kano. A survey taken in Kuwara in 1982 indicates that women were very much aware that PRP was the party "supporting" women. It is reasonable to speculate that PRP votes there were largely women's votes, as they represented the new element in the political social structure of the ward (see tables 8.1 and 8.2).

In the 1979 elections Mallam Aminu Kano was defeated in his bid for the office of president of the country, although his party and its candidates for state offices won overwhelmingly in Kano State with 86 percent of the vote. Thus the governor of Kano State was a member of the PRP, even though Aminu Kano himself held no office as a result of the elections. In the Second Republic the rhetoric and continued efforts of Aminu Kano kept notions of Islamic justice and equality at the center of political debate. The dominant northern party, the NPN, he asserted, had corrupted Islam. As part of the Islamic reform that he proposed, Aminu Kano advocated greater involvement of women in public affairs. To demonstrate its commitment to this end, the PRP in Kano implemented large-scale education programs for women and appointed several women to public positions.

Shortly after the election, there was a subtle but noticeable change in radical PRP rhetoric, most notably in the speeches of the governor. He and other members of his cabinet, endorsed by newspaper columns written by young

Table 8.2. Does It Make Any Difference to Women Which Party Is in Power?

Respondents	Yes	No	No Opinion
Female university students (N = 114)	73	28	1
Girls secondary students (N = 144)	80	30	10
Urban women (N = 188)	90	62	15
Rural women (N = 138)	63	41	20
Male university students (N = 572)	241	315	12
Urban men (N = 97)	30	40	8
Rural men (N = 57)	15	25	5

Source: These data were collected as follows: female university students—Barbara Callaway in 1982–83; female secondary school students—Indo Aisha Yuyuda in 1982; urban women—Barbara Callaway and Bilkisu Mohammed in 1982–83; rural women—Bilkisu Ismail and Bilkisu Mohammed in 1982; male university students—Barbara Callaway in 1982–83; urban men—Mohammed Attihiru Jabo in 1982; rural men—Sani Mohammed Kura in 1981.

Notes: Indo Aisha Yuyuda, Bilkisu Mohammed, Bilkisu Ismail, Mohammed Jabo, and Sani Mohammed Kura were students of the author's at Bayero University in Kano during 1981 and 1982. They collected this data as part of their research for the B.S. degree. Missing cases are not accounted for.

intellectuals at Bayero University in Kano and Ahmadu Bello University in Zaria, renewed and elaborated upon the themes of the "antagonism of interests" and the "class struggle" between the ruling class and the common people (*talakawa*). In this discourse, there was much concern about the place and role of women. Education for women continued to be advocated, but increasingly concern was raised about "alien" notions of "women's liberation" and the superiority of the place of women in Islam in contrast to other religions. Radical intellectuals emphasized reform rather than revolution.[2] In later years Marxist themes emerged, but the Marxist analogy was taken only so far; until 1983 radicals sought to build upon the principles of the Islamic jihad, not the Marxist revolution. Equality was a notion extended to include women, but this extension was defensible on religious, not secular grounds. The PRP's advocacy of education for and political participation by women did not imply support for female independence and autonomy. Both men and women understood this.

In this context, the PRP demanded a restructuring of Nigerian society to allow more political and economic opportunity for the "oppressed" and the development of a socialist economy to benefit all the people. So that all would

2. During 1982–83 a group of radical women students at Ahmadu Bello University in Zaria founded a new organization, Women in Nigeria (WIN), dedicated to improving the status of women and changing the social conditions which frame their lives. National conferences were held in 1982 and 1983 where women's issues were addressed by academics, women in the professions, students, and political activists.

benefit, PRP leaders advocated education for both women and men. Fathers and husbands were urged to send girls to school in compliance with the 1976 decree establishing Universal Primary Education (UPE). The PRP began to suggest that, although education for girls was now voluntary, it would soon become compulsory, and fathers would be fined for not obeying the law. The PRP also proposed a gradual nationalization of state assets and freeing of the economy from domination by the forces of multinational capitalism in order to eliminate poverty in Nigeria. At this point, it was claimed, women as well as men would be emancipated, and all would live according to the principles of justice.

In its four years in power, the PRP did in large measure carry out its campaign promises to women. Girls' schools were built, women's centers were established which offered adult literacy classes to women at night, and women were appointed to public office. In all of this, there was no public outcry against government efforts, although there was enormous private pressure in individual cases. However, the practical difficulties in the way of the PRP's carrying through even its limited women's program were enormous. The effort to appoint women to public positions is illustrative. The PRP government appointed three women commissioners (Home Affairs, Trade and Industry, and Health), one woman permanent secretary (Education), and one woman to each of the ten parastatal boards, but the high visibility of the female commissioners and permanent secretaries was a double-edged sword. Their appointment set an example which was certainly noted and commented upon, and as a consequence, many girls for the first time began to contemplate a public life, as data from a survey of girls in secondary school illustrates (see table 8.3). At the same time, the appointees' lack of experience reduced their effectiveness, for the women had serious difficulties in performing their responsibilities: two of the commissioners were in their twenties and had no employment history, and the permanent secretary had no experience in the domain of her education ministry. Thus their appointments were destined to fail.

The government's difficulty in finding experienced, qualified women to appoint highlighted the serious lack of educational and professional opportunities for women. Although the party and the government wanted to make a dramatic statement concerning the new roles that women could be expected to play in a "radical" and "modernizing" regime, there were literally *no* qualified women available for appointment. With a literacy rate (in English) for women over twenty-one of less than 1 percent, the problems involved in finding women with any skills or experience at all to appoint were enormous. Clearly, it would take time before women of appropriate age and experience emerged who could play the roles to which "progressive" young men in the society were committed. In this specific instance, time was too short for the PRP government. The military coup of late 1983 preempted all efforts to sustain these developments.

Table 8.3. Career Aspiration: Dala Government Girls
Secondary School, Kano, 1982

Question: In the future, what do you want to be?
(mark only two choices)

Career	Number ($N = 144$)[a]	Percentage (rounded)
Teacher	41	28
Nurse	5	3
Doctor	10	7
Commissioner[b]	25	17
Politician	18	13
Engineer	3	2
Scientist	1	1
Astronaut	20	14
Lecturer[c]	2	1
Civil servant	5	3
Journalist (radio, TV, or newspaper)	7	5
Wife and mother	140	97

Note: Indo Aisha Yuyuda (who administered the ques-
tionnaire), Bilkisu Mohammed, Bilkisu Ismail, Mohammed Jabo, and Sani Mohammed Kura were students of
the author's at Bayero University in Kano during 1981 and
1982. They collected this data as part of their research for
the B.S. degree.

[a]Eleven of the 144 respondents marked only one choice.
Therefore column total does not equal 288.

[b]In this context, a commissioner is a political appointee
who heads a branch of the state government.

[c]A lecturer is a university professor.

Recent Developments

Coups in December 1983 and January 1987 brought two more military governments to power in Nigeria. Both continued to stress the importance of education, but Nigeria's declining oil-based economy has greatly reduced funding
for it. In Kano the military government continued to support the Mass Education Program for women and has managed to keep girls' secondary schools
open. Discussion of the proper place of women and their treatment according
to Islamic principles is continually stressed in the daily press. In particular, the
young age at which girls are married and give birth is being attacked, and educated Islamic women are speaking out to condemn abuses of women by men.
In 1985 an official government press issued a booklet entitled *A Degree Above
Them* elaborating on this theme:

This matter of women's rights, which affects all of the population and the whole of family life, is therefore of greatest concern for the future of Islam in Nigeria. And if we wish to uplift the Muslims in this country, this is surely an area of priority, where everyone needs to rethink his own attitudes. Does he recognize that a woman has rights over him similar to those he has over her? —and that he is only a degree above her, — one degree, not 100 degrees! Does he moreover appreciate that his degree above her is that of *responsibility* not *freedom from responsibility*? (Lemu 1985b:5)

The place of women as participants in the public realm seems assured, but their subordination in matters prescribed by the Qur'an remains underscored.

Conclusion

Even though women played only tangential roles in the PRP government between 1979 and 1983, this was the first time in the modern era when Hausa women were visible in any sort of legitimate and institutionalized public role. From these experiences a few women were exposed to organizational principles and learned how to operate in the public sphere. The PRP succeeded in politicizing women to some extent and brought them into the public domain: it offered educated women an outlet for their views, and by opening its patronage positions to women and bringing them into the government, it began to create a more socially heterogeneous environment for many isolated and class-bound Muslim Hausa women.

The circumscribed conception of the nature of women's political interests (from the male point of view), however, is illustrated by the fact that, even in a party headed by Aminu Kano, the women's wing was simply an adjunct to the men's party. Although NEPU/PRP advocated women's rights and the PRP appointed women to public positions, women were not politicized around their own issues. "Women's rights" were defined as the right to an education and the right to vote. Issues other than these of particular interest or concern to women, such as family planning or changes in the marriage laws and divorce rights, were not addressed. Women were not encouraged to confront any issues on their own, and when they did so, they were roundly condemned by all political factions. In terms of party organization, the "women's wings" were neither reformist nor revolutionary concerning women's issues, and no party made an attempt at appealing to the revolutionary potential of women as a suppressed group in changing society.

The male-female dichotomy in Kano is sharp, and nothing which directly challenges male authority is likely to be tolerated. Only those reforms that can be justified by an appeal to Islamic teachings can be absorbed and result in real change in the lives of women. Women seem to recognize this and seek reform under these conditions. The restrictions on women's roles in society required by Islamic teachings, however, must be understood and acknowledged in any attempt at discussing present or predicting future political participation by women beyond the act of voting.

Women's lives lived separate from those of men give them a potential psychological foundation for seizing separate opportunities (Callaway and Schildkrout 1985). But women still need the support of men if they are to function in the public arena. Most especially, they need religious sanction. Without this, they are not likely to produce change in the reality of most women's lives. By the same token, men who believe in more human equality and who are supportive of education and other opportunities for women can gain female support for their parties, programs, and policies, for there is female electoral support to be tapped.

Although a nascent ideology of sexual egalitarianism such as that begun by the PRP can integrate women into politics, their absorption does not necessarily challenge the male agenda or male control of the party and the government. Neither does it generate a specifically female agenda nor challenge domestic relationships. In the short run, co-optation of the women's issue sets constraints on the development of a female agenda decided by women. Although the co-optation of women's issues and concerns might provide entry into the political sphere and give legitimacy to questions concerning Islamic interpretations of the proper roles for women, it is not likely that the political "awakening" of women will be allowed to threaten mechanisms of male social control over them. The few women given leadership opportunities thus far have not specifically challenged sex-role norms and male authority, because they are seen as required by Islamic beliefs. Women are aware of men's hostile reactions to notions of "women's liberation" and avoid provoking them. In so doing, they reinforce such attitudes, resulting in little long-term change in the social relations between men and women.

The enfranchisement of women by the military government and the commitment to certain advances for women by the dominant political parties in Kano, the PRP and NEPU, have been very significant. Women, however, still face disadvantages because of the protections given, both in the Nigerian constitution and by the culture, to Islamic beliefs (Callaway and Schildkrout 1985). It will be a long time (if ever) before the society accepts the notion of sexual equality in such matters as inheritance, employment, divorce, free choice in marriage, and the right to keep children after divorce. For the moment, these matters are not defined as political issues but as religious prescriptions. For this reason, changes in matters which so affect women are not likely to come through political processes—either through the passing of laws or through the legal establishment of secular law above religious law at the national and state level. The reaction of Muslims to the provision of equal rights in the 1979 constitution is instructive. They launched an intense campaign to enhance the *shari'a* and "protect" it from the interference of the state. Hence any attempt at directly confronting the subordination of women as protected by the *shari'a* or the Qur'an will be vigorously attacked and is probably doomed to failure. Rather, it is legislation in areas that can actually be endorsed by Muslim leaders that will mark significant change for women. This is especially true in the area of education. Islamic leaders now agree that learning was advocated for women from the time of the Prophet through that of Usman dan Fodio. Hence education, offering women new knowledge and new horizons, is the real threat to continued female subordination.

Although a majority of the population and a majority of the voters, women are not in reality a political majority. All legislation directly applicable to women must respect Islamic teachings and fall within the teachings of the Qur'an. Liberation or emancipation for Muslim women in Kano will not be the same as for Western women. It does not begin with the struggle for voting rights but will emerge when scholars believe that within the Islamic tradition it is possible to give public recognition to women's existence separate from men and to women's position on issues affecting them.

PART 3. WOMEN IN THE CHANGING ECONOMY

9 *Catherine Coles*

Hausa Women's Work in a Declining Urban Economy: Kaduna, Nigeria, 1980–1985

This essay presents findings from research conducted in 1981 and 1985 on changes in Muslim Hausa women's income-earning activities in the northern Nigerian city of Kaduna. During July and August of 1985 while in Kaduna my attention was drawn to the substantial contributions women were making to basic subsistence and household maintenance for their families. These contributions appeared to have increased markedly from levels I had observed in 1980–81. Although Hausa women have long carried out income-earning occupations (M. G. Smith 1955; Hill 1969; Simmons 1975, 1976; Remy 1975; Jackson 1978; Pittin 1979a, 1984a; Schildkrout 1979, 1983; Mary Smith 1981), Muslim Hausa normative expectations associated with marriage continue to place the burden of providing food, clothing, and shelter for the family directly with the husband. In 1985, however, Kaduna Hausa women freely admitted providing cash regularly to their spouses, and their activities were a crucial source of income for the support of families.

Such changes in women's behavior were necessitated by severe economic dislocation which affected Nigeria in the aftermath of the 1970s oil boom. In 1980, 96 percent of Nigeria's export earnings were linked to oil production, as

Funding for fieldwork and subsequent data analysis and writing were provided by the University of Wisconsin; the Department of Anthropology Goodman Fund, Dartmouth College; and Dartmouth College faculty fellowship and research funds.

were 84 percent of federal revenues. Urban residents felt the effects of these increased revenues through government-sponsored development programs which
improved and expanded transportation, communications, and energy systems,
built new port facilities, stimulated and invested in new industries, and initiated universal primary education (Nigeria 1982; Bienen 1985:25–35; Watts
1987:9, 14–15). But this development and the distribution of revenues and incomes were highly uneven, and the boom had many negative consequences for
urban dwellers (ILO 1982; Watts and Lubeck 1983; Bienen 1985: ch. 3). As
Michael Watts notes:

The meteoric growth of cities such as Kano, Warri, Lagos, and Port Harcourt—over
10 percent per annum during the 1970s—is astonishing in relation to the conspicu-
ous neglect of basic urban services, low-income housing, spatial planning, and transportation. The gravitational pull of the construction boom drew thousands of migrants
into sprawling and underequipped cities, with the result that by 1980 two thirds of
all urban residents lived in single-room residences. The appalling condition of urban
waste disposal has created an epidemiological nightmare in some cities (such as Lagos),
which contain levels of general anarchy and crime almost unrivaled anywhere. (Watts
1987:61)

In 1982 the international oil crisis led to an immediate cut in Nigerian oil
production and a severe decline in oil revenues (from $27.4 billion in 1980
to $11 billion in 1983 [Watts 1987:59]). The civilian government of Shehu
Shagari, as well as subsequent military governments, found it necessary to
slash budgets, implement austerity plans, curtail imports, and drastically de-
value the naira (Olayiwola 1987:126–34). In Kaduna such changes were felt
by the Hausa community in increased levels of male unemployment, frozen
wages for those who remained employed, late or nonpayment of salaries for
teachers, rapid inflation in prices of basic foodstuffs and commodities, and frequent scarcity of many items. At various times in 1983–84 powdered laundry
soap was unavailable. In 1985, 50 pound bags of rice had risen from 30–35
naira to 200 naira so that many could afford only locally made noodles in place
of rice. Adult women, carrying infants and young children, went from house
to house begging for food, soap and clothing. For Hausa urban dwellers in
Kaduna, with limited access to land or agricultural produce that might have
been obtained from kin in rural areas, maintaining a cash income was essential
to basic subsistence. Hausa women's efforts to increase their income were not
unwelcome to their husbands under these circumstances.

Hausa women's occupational activities (indeed, their lives) in Kaduna are
not necessarily representative of those of Hausa women elsewhere. Kaduna
women are members of a community which originated when Hausa traders
left the old city of Kano and brought their families to settle in this new location in the mid-1920s. Unlike migrant communities throughout west and north

Africa that are part of the far flung Hausa trade diaspora (Cohen 1967, 1969; Schildkrout 1970b, 1974, 1978c; Works 1976; Benson and Duffield 1979; Pellow this volume), Kaduna lies outside of Hausaland proper, within an area of Islamic Hausa cultural hegemony. Hausa in Kaduna represent a point of moderate variation in the continuum of experiences making up Hausa culture as a whole. Such a milieu may be increasingly common within the overall range of Hausa social life, however, given contemporary changes in Nigeria. New opportunities for education and employment, participation in national political parties and a federal government, the growth of Hausa cities and towns to include substantial populations of non-Hausa residents, and movement of Hausa people to non-Hausa cities throughout Nigeria have all led to the development of a widespread pattern of existence similar to the Kaduna model of a heterogeneous local environment.

The lives of Hausa women in Kaduna and similar contexts are shaped by these surroundings: domestic arrangements, the degree and nature of seclusion practiced, their experience of both kin and extrafamilial social relationships, and the local economy in which they participate all reflect a milieu distinct from that of Hausa women in rural areas or in the old walled cities. Yet the success of these women in income-earning occupations and their increased share in providing for the subsistence needs of their families do not negate the patriarchal nature of Hausa society, even in the form it takes in this new urban center. Many changes in female work patterns identified here in their infancy do suggest the potential for significant future alteration in the division of labor by gender, in the relative control of wealth by men and women, and in equal access to education and the modernizing, formal sector of the economy.

The descriptive and analytical focus in this chapter is on Hausa women's income-earning occupations in Kaduna. Income-earning activities are initiated by women themselves, and represent individual interests, resources, skills, assessments of local market conditions, and strategies for gaining access to desired cash or services. Such activities frequently involve women in relationships with nonkin individuals and groups distinct from household and family, and result in income over which women have sole rights of disposal. Documenting these aspects of Hausa women's lives in various contexts is important for building an image of them as rational actors who participate in social processes beyond the realm of the household and family as well as for gaining a better understanding of their contributions to the local economy.

Many scholars have drawn attention to the linkages between productive and domestic labor (Edholm, Harris, and Young 1977; Beneria 1982). To distinguish between the two types of labor, I use the term income-earning occupations (productive labor) to include activities which, regardless of where they are performed, result in income either in the form of cash or some material good which may be consumed or exchanged for another desired item or in the form of a service performed for the women. Domestic labor refers here to unremunerated work performed by a woman, within or outside the residential compound: housework, marketing, food preparation and cooking for her children, husband, and others (kin and nonkin) who eat or reside with them, childcare, and all activities which contribute to the maintenance and well-being of such individuals. Beneria (1982) and others have used the terms *reproductive labor* and *production for use-value* to refer to many of the activities associated with domestic labor. Although not discussed at length here, they constitute a vital part of Kaduna Hausa women's total work. Domestic labor is intertwined with income-earning occupations in many situations: women who prepare food for sale often combine these activities with childcare; many also provide a portion of this food directly to their families for consumption without payment or else use their profits to help purchase food and other necessities for them.

In the discussion which follows I describe the context within which Hausa women live in Kaduna and consider the implications of this setting for their labor; I present data on female income-generating labor and changes in female work patterns between 1981 and 1985, and then use these data to illustrate strategies women have developed to achieve their goals; I conclude by assessing briefly the overall contributions Hausa women make to the local economy in Kaduna.

The Physical Setting and Cultural Context: Hausa Women in Kaduna

Kaduna originated as a British colonial administrative center early in the twentieth century, situated south of Hausaland in an area settled originally by the Gwari people. Today it is a commercial and industrial center and state capital, with more than 600,000 residents from every part of Nigeria. The Hausa community discussed here resides in two adjacent wards, one and a half kilometers from the central business district: Hausa arrived during the mid-1920s in response to a request from the British colonial administration of the Emir of Kano for a group of traders to settle there. Members of other ethnic groups entered the areas during subsequent years, obtaining land on which to live from the first ward head, the Hausa *Mai Unguwa* (ward head). In 1981 about 56 percent of the population identified themselves as Hausa, 11 percent as Ibo, 11 percent as Yoruba, and the remainder from various other ethnic backgrounds. Although many are recent migrants, in some families up to four generations have lived in the two wards. Over 60 percent of the population are Muslim; about 31 percent are Christian (Kaduna Polytechnic 1981). Although the areas are heterogeneous in terms of religion and ethnicity, they are clearly dominated by Hausa cultural forms.

In 1981 the wards had a combined population of nearly 30,000 in an area of 71.512 hectares, and had been designated by the Kaduna Capital Development Board (the major organization responsible for planning and implementing development in the metropolitan area) as "high-density, low-income" areas urgently in need of development efforts. They lacked adequate roads, water, and power supplies, and had virtually no drainage, sanitation, and refuse disposal systems. Such conditions remained essentially unchanged in 1985. A single primary school served the entire population of the two wards. Most residents live in mud-walled compounds with tin or thatched roofs: a single entryway leads into an interior courtyard open to the sky; bedrooms and parlors are entered from the courtyard; kitchen, latrine, and washing rooms are shared among residents. Few compounds have pipe-borne water: in 1981 most had wells inside the exterior wall or residents obtained drinking water from a public standpipe. About two-thirds of all compounds were wired for electricity, although the supply was sporadic (Kaduna Polytechnic 1981). These living conditions produce serious health hazards for local residents, and frequent illness is a significant impediment to greater productivity for both men and women. A single medical facility—a maternal and child welfare clinic—serves the entire area, although it is unequipped to provide medical care for the general population. Residents thus seek treatment at hospitals in the city center, and from herbalists, bone setters, midwives, and *bori* (spirit possession cult) practitioners.

Hausa residents of these wards include both the urban poor and what might be termed an urban middle class. Male Hausa earn income as traders, unskilled laborers (such as drivers or night watchmen), mechanics, or contractor-builders. A small number are clerks or low-level civil servants, and many former soldiers have retired here. Survey data (Kaduna Polytechnic 1981) suggest that about 42 percent of those recorded as employed (both male and female) earned 600 naira per year or less; another 34 percent earned between 600 and 1800 naira. Data were not recorded for the unemployed, nor for secluded women. Most Hausa women live in one or two rooms (bedroom and parlor) within a compound, along with children and other kin who are present. A woman usually owns a bed, one or more chairs, a table, clothing, and a cupboard filled with metal pots and glassware (which were part of her dowry at marriage). Wealthier individuals may have electric radios, fans, television sets, or even a small fridge.

Women in the study are members of the local Hausa-Fulani community, and are part of a kin, residential, and social network of which the descendants of the first *Mai Unguwa*, and those who came with him from Kano City to Kaduna, constitute the core. The oldest arrived as young married women in the mid-1920s; others were born in Kaduna or migrated there with husbands or other family members. Many of their children have remained in Kaduna, marrying and raising their own children. Research was conducted with an original sample of 125 women in 1980–81; 79 were still living in the areas in 1985. Data on 34 additional women not part of the original sample are also drawn upon because their income-earning occupations were not represented in the original sample or they were particularly important in the social and economic life of the local area.[1]

Two features of Hausa-Fulani society in Kaduna have particular significance in shaping women's income-generating activities: the nature of the residential group and female seclusion. Unlike large kin-based compounds in old walled Hausa cities such as Kano or Katsina, most Hausa compounds in the study areas include several unrelated family groups, usually sharing the same ethnic identity and language, and often the same location (village or region) of origin. Hausa families in these compounds usually consist of an adult male, his wife or wives, children, and perhaps a parent or younger sibling of the husband or wife, or young relatives being fostered. Some affines and consanguines of the husband or wife will be present in the local community, although close contact with kin in other towns and rural areas is maintained. In this context a network based upon both residence and kinship has emerged as the setting for significant social interaction in which ritual and religious events, marriages, naming ceremonies following births, funerals, and other important events take place.

Hausa females in Kaduna usually marry for the first time between the ages of eleven and fourteen. Many divorce and remarry three or four times. Married women of childbearing age are expected to observe seclusion: the normative expectation for this practice is so strong that few women admit that they are not secluded. Yet the degree of actual seclusion varies from nearly complete confinement to none at all, even among women who claim to be secluded (Coles 1983b). Women generally live in compounds owned by their husbands, or in which their husbands rent rooms for them, to which access is restricted for nonkin adult males so that only those accompanying residents may enter. These compounds are referred to as "secluded" even though nonkin adult males and females live side by side. Secluded wives may leave their compound to attend a *biki* (marriage or naming ceremony), to seek medical treatment for themselves or their children, to visit their families once or twice a year, in the evening to go to the homes of neighborhood women to chat, and increasingly since 1983, to attend segregated classes at the new Arabic schools on a daily basis. Where a wife is strictly secluded (more likely in a kin-based compound), her husband may hire a nonsecluded woman or find a younger relative to perform

1. Informants were studied through participant observation, a formal interview schedule, and collection of life histories in both 1979–81 and 1985. In 1985 some information was obtained from informants on a small number of other women from the original sample even though the latter were not present for formal reinterviewing. Thus the number of responses for women in data presented may be greater than 79. Data on the 34 women not in the original sample were obtained through observation and nonstandardized interviews and made it possible to include several generations of females in the same families in the study.

duties outside the compound such as shopping for food at the market, obtaining fuel for cooking, washing clothes, and carrying water inside for cooking and drinking. This secluded world of women is largely free of male intrusion, supervised by women in middle or old age (*dattijuwa* and *tsohuwa*, respectively) who take nearly complete responsibility for their own behavior and that of younger women.[2]

What are the consequences of this form of seclusion, and the mixture of nonkin compound residents, for Hausa women's income-generating activities in Kaduna? "Secluded" compounds provide the arena within which younger married Hausa women carry out productive activities, savings groups operate, childcare and domestic responsibilities are shared, experienced women teach others new income-earning activities, and information crucial to these activities is exchanged. The practice of seclusion constrains the choice of income-earning occupations of women of childbearing age by limiting their mobility and direct access to shops and local marketplaces. Certain income-generating activities are in effect "reserved" for older women (or those few younger who are not in seclusion) who are able to move about freely. Yet seclusion for Kaduna Hausa women is not absolute, and occasions for going out provide opportunities for trade, acquisition of goods for simple purchase or resale, and contact with others who might cooperate in or have news useful to the conduct of particular income-earning activities. Furthermore, "secluded" compounds are not cut off from public life or from the diversity which generally characterizes urban life. A degree of heterogeneity among compound residents not found in kin-based compounds (even those in Kaduna) is present, with nonkin women from a variety of backgrounds often bringing together a wider range of experience in income-generating activities. Compounds are open to all women and children and many men as well: Ibo women selling fish, Yoruba women peddling household wares, Christian friends of teenage schoolchildren, among others, are all frequent visitors. Thus the form of seclusion practiced in Kaduna, and the nature of compounds, place limitations upon women's mobility and activities, but do not prevent secluded Hausa women from being involved in and knowledgeable about the local economy, community life, and public issues.

Income-Generating Activities of Hausa Women
in Kaduna, 1981–1985

Recent changes in occupations, and opportunities for secular education, have led a small number of Hausa women in Kaduna into wage labor as primary

---

2. Men do attempt to exert control over the behavior of their wives, but are not present much of the time to observe female activities. If they attempt to enforce seclusion too strictly, the wife may leave and seek a divorce.

school teachers, others as herbalist-midwives working with orthodox medical hospitals, and one as a programmer for Kaduna Television. Yet most of the productive activities carried out by Hausa women here fall within the informal sector (see Trager 1985). Census data and labor statistics account for little of this productive work: classifying, identifying, documenting, and subsequently analyzing women's productive work activities all have inherent problems (Pittin 1984a). Productive activities are not carried out in a single location, but take place both inside and outside compounds within which women are secluded. Females as well as males have a vested interest in concealing the amount of their incomes, making accurate information on earnings elusive. And because income-generating labor overlaps with and is often an extension of domestic labor, distinguishing each clearly from the other and ascertaining the precise numbers of hours spent on either are problematic.

What are the implications for women's income-earning occupations of the close ties between productive activities and domestic labor (Beneria 1982)? In Kaduna, Hausa women's domestic labor is similar to that of Hausa women in other urban centers, involving tasks such as food preparation, cooking, childcare, socialization of children, housecleaning, washing and ironing clothes, and serving guests. It consumes many hours in each woman's day, especially with water and electricity not easily available and the use of wood or paraffin as cooking fuels. It falls more heavily upon the shoulders of childbearing and middle-aged women than upon females not yet married or in old age, even though the young and old play their part. Sometimes these unremunerated activities resemble work that in another context would result in income. For example, if a woman is the *uwar gida* (first and senior wife) of a male compound head she may take over the day-to-day running of the compound, since her husband is likely to be away at work, or in any case would not remain inside all day with the women. She is greeted by visitors to the compound, settles disputes among other wives and occasionally between a husband and wife, advises younger resident women about childcare, assists in childbirth if they ask her, often collects rent, and oversees the physical maintenance of the compound. These work activities are in some sense an extension of her domestic labor; at the same time certain of them might be considered unpaid labor in a "family firm." No remuneration is received for any such work.

The domestic labor of Hausa women arises out of their membership and participation in domestic groups, families, and households—which in the community described here are neither units of unified production nor consumption, and change frequently in the number and composition of residents.[3] This work

3. Precise definition of the terms household, family, and domestic group is crucial in assessing women's roles within these groups and in documenting the extent to which social obligations affect their work. Pittin describes a fluidity in Hausa domestic groupings in Katsina so that "recognition of a particular domestic unit depends on one's perspective and definition" (1984a:481). Similarly

is associated primarily with women's roles as wives and mothers (less so but also with their roles as female affines and consanguines), although it is likely to be carried out as service to males, children, and elderly kin in whatever compound women happen to live, even if they are single and childless. Obligations associated with women's roles in families, households, and domestic groups, such as seclusion, diminish their ability and limit freedom to carry out income-generating work (Longhurst 1982). For example, the physical burdens associated with bearing children (described for Kano women in Harrington 1983), are recognized by Kaduna Hausa women, who in 1985 were making increased use of family planning services to space children and prevent further pregnancies after their mid-thirties. Yet while women acknowledge significant expenditures of time and energy involved in childcare, most see no reason to choose *between* childbearing and income-earning occupations; rather the question becomes one of accommodating the demands and requisites of each with the other. Indeed, the needs of children and a husband may encourage or even make it necessary for women to engage in such work, particularly if the husband is poor or unemployed. Furthermore, many of the individuals who benefit from a woman's domestic labor have responsibilities and obligations to her that affect her material status, physical well-being, and the resources she has available to use in an income-earning occupation.[4] Women do not forfeit all rights to material and financial support in their own kin groups after they marry: many continue to own property—a house, land, or animals such as sheep or goats—which is kept at the home of their consanguines. Husbands are expected to contribute substantially to basic subsistence necessities of women and children; grown children frequently provide support for women in old age; and female consanguines and affines assist each other in income-earning ventures.

Jean Trevor's study of family change in Sokoto (1975b) indicates that problems still exist in defining the Hausa family as an operational concept. Adding to the problem of definition of concepts is the fact that such units are undergoing structural and morphological changes such as those described by Arnould for the Hausa *gida*, or household, in Niger (1984). I leave the definition and clarification of domestic and household forms to future efforts in the interest of focusing here upon the behavior and strategies of individual women (Guyer 1981; Hammel 1984). I do attempt to specify the precise relationships and individuals mentioned in relation to the Hausa women whose work is analyzed.

4. Jane Guyer (personal communication, May 1988) has drawn my attention to the implications of obligations toward a woman on the part of other individuals which her work may create. In the case of domestic labor, such obligations arise, I would argue, out of particular relationships as much as out of work performed by women—such as when individuals provide physical care for their aged kin. With regard to productive labor, obligations which will be activated in the future can be viewed as a form of delayed-return income. There are also other types of female labor not considered here since they are not undertaken specifically for the purpose of earning a living (Beneria 1982), such as work provided by one Hausa woman for her *kawa* (female friend) or for her partner in a patron-client relationship, in which the labor is expected as part of the relationship and a return of labor or gift is expected in the future.

Female Income-Generating Activities

In spite of both impediments and incentives present for women through their domestic labor and family obligations, a majority of Kaduna Hausa women carry out at least one income-generating activity (*sana'a*) on a regular basis. In 1981, 102 out of 114 women (80.9%) reported that they had at least one occupation; in 1985, 64 out of 80 women (80.0%) affirmed such participation. Nearly half of such women practice multiple income-earning activities: in 1985, out of 64 women engaged in income-generating occupations, 33 (53.2%) had a single occupation; 24 (38.7%) had two concurrent occupations; 4 (6.5%) had 3 occupations; and 1 woman (1.6%) maintained 4 occupations. Such women respond to opportunities which arise seasonally or otherwise periodically to purchase and resell food or other salable items, and to conditions of supply and demand in the local community itself, withdrawing from the sale of certain commodities if they become too expensive. Tables 9.1 and 9.2 illustrate the frequency of occurrence of specific occupations among women of different age groups.[5] In both 1981 and 1985, cooking and selling food was the most frequently practiced occupation: 45 out of 102 women with income-earning occupations in 1981 prepared or cooked food to sell; 42 out of 64 women reported this as an occupation in 1985.

Many occupations may be undertaken by women either in or out of seclusion, but secluded women require the assistance of older women, children, or adult male kin who sell goods and food which are prepared inside the compound and purchase food or required goods from markets for women's use at home. Secluded women prepare food for sale (such as bean cakes [*ƙosai*], fried groundnut cakes [*ƙuli ƙuli*], noodles [*taliya*], and tomatoes and spices for use in soup [*kayan miya*]); conduct petty trade (*sayasayarwa* or *ciniki*) in items such as kola nuts (*goro*), clothing, jewelry, soap, bread, cooking oil, and dried milk; sew men's caps (*hula*) or weave straw floormats (*tabarma*); pound grain brought in to them (*daka*); plait hair for other women (*kitso*); sew clothing with a machine; trade in larger items such as cloth; make small goods for sale such as leather jewelry or incense for fires (*turaren wuta*); and work for wages for other women. Young brides usually do not practice an income-earning occupation during their first year of marriage, when they are completely secluded, but begin soon after with the help of an older female relative or friend.

Particular trades, such as midwifery, require a woman to move around freely. Older women, or those few younger women who do go out, prepare and sell food both inside and outside their compounds, trade, grind grain or *kayan miya* (soup ingredients) by machine, purchase food items in bulk (traveling to markets outside of Kaduna by taxi each day, returning with foodstuffs then sold to

---

5. Several of the income-generating activities listed above are not reflected as occupations in these tables since they were carried out by women not formally interviewed.

Table 9.1. Primary Occupation at Time of Interview by Age and Seclusion Status of Hausa Women (*N* = 102)[a] (Kaduna, 1981)

Occupation/Seclusion Status (+/−)[b]	Age									
	9–15	16–20	21–30	31–40	41–50	51–60	61–70	71+	Totals	
Prepare/sell food	+1	+4	+9	+6	+1	+1	+0	+0	+22	45
	−7	−0	−2	−1	−6	−3	−0	−4	−23	
Weave/sew	+4	+10	+12	+3	+2	+0	+0	+0	+31	35
	−0	−3	−0	−1	−0	−0	−0	−0	−4	
Trader	+0	+0	+2	+1	+1	+0	+0	+0	+4	14
	−0	−0	−2	−1	−3	−3	−1	−0	−10	
Teacher	+0	+0	+0	+0	+0	+0	+0	+0	+0	2
	−0	−0	−2	−0	−0	−0	−0	−0	−2	
Plaiting hair	+0	+1	+1	+0	+0	+0	+0	+0	+2	2
	−0	−0	−0	−0	−0	−0	−0	−0	−0	
Prostitute	+0	+0	+0	+0	+0	+0	+0	+0	+0	1
	−0	−0	−1	−0	−0	−0	−0	−0	−1	
Midwife	+0	+0	+0	+0	+0	+0	+0	+0	+0	1
	−0	−0	−0	−0	−0	−0	−0	−1	−1	
Pounding/grinding	+0	+0	+0	+0	+1	+0	+0	+0	+1	1
	−0	−0	−0	−0	−0	−0	−0	−0	−0	
Wage job (NTV)	+0	+0	+0	+0	+0	+0	+0	+0	+0	1
	−0	−0	−1	−0	−0	−0	−0	−0	−1	
Totals	+5	+15	+24	+10	+5	+1	+0	+0	+60	102
	−7	−3	−8	−3	−9	−6	−1	−5	−42	

[a]Responses consisted of a single primary occupation carried out at the time of the interview by a single respondent.

[b]+ refers to seclusion being observed; − refers to lack of seclusion.

local women for preparation and sale), and become pawnbrokers (s. *dilaliya*). They also may sell items such as matches, candles, soap powder, tinned foods, toilet articles, and soda at small shops near or attached to their compounds but open to the street. One older woman cares for children in her home while their mothers are away working. Those few able to establish themselves as commission agents (in nonperishable goods—rice, sugar, semovita, salt, oil, dried milk) earn high incomes relative to other women in the area. Women in their seventies and eighties who are physically able continue to participate actively in such occupations, although they usually move out of the more labor intensive preparation and sale of food and instead trade, sell firewood, and prepare herbal medicines. Older women are more likely than younger women to own compounds, having inherited or bought them with their earnings, and may rent

Table 9.2. Occupations ($N = 100$)[a] at Time of Interview by Age and Seclusion Status of Hausa Women ($N = 64$)[b] (Kaduna, 1985)

Occupation/Seclusion Status $(+/-)$[b]	Age									
	9–15	16–20	21–30	31–40	41–50	51–60	61–70	71+	Totals	
Prepare/sell food	+2	+1	+15	+9	+3	+2	+0	+0	+32	51
	−1	−1	−1	−2	−4	−8	−1	−1	−19	
Trading	+0	+1	+7	+1	+4	+1	+0	+0	+14	18
	−0	−0	−1	−0	−1	−0	−0	−2	−4	
Weave/sew	+0	+0	+1	+1	+1	+0	+0	+0	+3	5
	−0	−1	−0	−0	−0	−0	−0	−1	−2	
Machine sewing	+0	+1	+3	+0	+0	+0	+0	+0	+4	4
	−0	−0	−0	−0	−0	−0	−0	−0	−0	
Uwar Adashi	+0	+0	+0	+3	+0	+0	+0	+0	+3	3
	−0	−0	−0	−0	−0	−0	−0	−0	−0	
Bulk buying at market	+0	+0	+0	+0	+0	+0	+0	+0	+0	3
	−0	−0	−0	−1	−2	−0	−0	−0	−3	
Plaiting hair	+0	+0	+2	+0	+0	+0	+0	+0	+2	2
	−0	−0	−0	−0	−0	−0	−0	−0	−0	
Selling firewood	+0	+0	+0	+0	+0	+0	+0	+0	+0	2
	−0	−0	−0	−0	−0	−0	−0	−2	−2	
Commission agt.	+0	+0	+0	+0	+0	+0	+0	+0	+0	2
	−0	−0	−2	−0	−0	−0	−0	−0	−2	
Midwife	+0	+0	+0	+0	+0	+0	+0	+0	+0	1
	−0	−0	−0	−0	−0	−0	−0	−1	−1	
Pounding/grinding	+0	+0	+0	+1	+0	+0	+0	+0	+1	1
	−0	−0	−0	−0	−0	−0	−0	−0	−0	
Food prep. wage labor	+0	+0	+1	+0	+0	+0	+0	+0	+1	1
	−0	−0	−0	−0	−0	−0	−0	−0	−0	
Leather jewelry	+0	+0	+0	+1	+0	+0	+0	+0	+1	1
	−0	−0	−0	−0	−0	−0	−0	−0	−0	
Turaren wuta	+0	+0	+0	+0	+1	+0	+0	+0	+1	1
	−0	−0	−0	−0	−0	−0	−0	−0	−0	
Teacher (prim.)	+0	+0	+0	+0	+0	+0	+0	+0	+0	1
	−0	−0	−1	−0	−0	−0	−0	−0	−1	
Child care in home	+0	+0	+0	+0	+0	+0	+0	+0	+0	1
	−0	−0	−0	−0	−0	−0	−1	−0	−1	
Prepare herbal medicine	+0	+0	+0	+0	+0	+0	+0	+0	+0	1
	−0	−0	−0	−0	−0	−0	−0	−1	−1	
Owns compound	+0	+0	+0	+0	+0	+0	+0	+0	+0	1
	−0	−0	−0	−0	−0	−0	−1	−0	−1	

Table 9.2. Occupations (N = 100)[a] at Time of Interview by Age and Seclusion Status of Hausa Women (N = 64)[b] (Kaduna, 1985)

Occupation/Seclusion Status (+/−)[b]	Age								
	9–15	16–20	21–30	31–40	41–50	51–60	61–70	71+	Totals
Ritual prep. of girls at	+0	+0	+0	+0	+0	+0	+0	+0	+0 1
marriage	−0	−0	−0	−0	−0	−0	−0	−1	−1
Responses[a]									
Subtotal	+2	+3	+29	+16	+9	+3	+0	+0	+62 10
	−1	−2	−5	−2	−6	−10	−3	−9	−38
Total	3	5	34	18	15	13	3	9	100
Respondents[b]	3	3	25	10	8	9	2	4	64
	4.7%	4.7%	39.1%	15.6%	12.5%	14.1%	3.1%	6.3%	100%

[a]Responses (N = 100) included the total number of reported income-earning activities carried out by the respondents.

[b]Respondents (N = 64) were women who reported currently carrying out at least one income-earning occupation.

[c]+ refers to seclusion being observed as reported by respondents; − refers to lack of seclusion.

rooms for income. And to older women is reserved the practice of particular occupations involving the exercise of ritual power and authority, such as midwifery (*ungozomanci*), the preparation of girls for marriage and of the bodies of women for burial, and the making of herbal medicines (*magani;* Coles 1990a).

Although *karuwanci* (prostitution) is practiced as an occupation by Muslim Hausa women in Kaduna, only one prostitute, a visitor, was part of the 1980–81 sample, and she was not present in 1985. Hausa prostitutes usually settle in a city or town some distance away from their consanguines, so it is likely that women from the 1981 sample who later entered prostitution subsequently left the area. However, it was quite common for newly divorced women to stay temporarily in the compounds of their female friends, moving later to locations where they engaged in prostitution. Hausa prostitutes are often involved in the practice of *bori* (a spirit possession cult), and although Kaduna Hausa women asserted that *bori* was antithetical to their roles as Muslim women, and no *bori* sessions were observed in their compounds, female adepts are active in the areas.

Although the occupations described here are virtually all individual endeavors, cooperation does occur among women as they work for income: vendors of the same cooked foods in a single location agree to sell on the street at different times of the day; childless women in seclusion have foods or other items they produce hawked by nonkin children whose mothers "donate" their labor; and nonsecluded women regularly purchase items at the market needed by secluded women to carry out their occupations. Some women hire others to work for them: in 1985 a divorced woman of twenty-eight who was living in the

Cooking and selling food is the most frequently practiced occupation. Photo by C. Coles.

compound of her maternal grandmother prepared noodles for sale to support herself. She hired two secluded women living in the same compound to assist her and paid each one naira for two hours work per day inside their compound. She was not secluded, and traveled weekly to the large city market to purchase needed supplies. Her profit was about ten naira every five or six days.

Women also assist other women in learning and starting an occupation. In 1981 women reported having learned their occupations in a number of ways: before marriage from their mothers (24.2 percent) or other female kin (22.1 percent); from female friends or other acquaintances (47.4 percent); through training in formal schools or classes such as in sewing (5.3 percent). The remainder did not recall how they had learned.

It is difficult to reach an accurate understanding of how much time women devote to income-earning activities (Dixon 1982). Occupations differ considerably in the time required to perform them and the regularity with which they are carried out (many are seasonal or otherwise periodic); and the intensity of activity for a single occupation may vary from one individual to another and from time to time for the same person. The least time-consuming among them, collecting rents or heading a rotating savings group, might involve only an hour or two once or twice a week. The preparation and sale of food varies as to daily and weekly duration depending upon the type of food produced: the range among women in the sample was from four hours weekly (cooking *cincin,* a sweet, twice a week for two hours each time, and giving it to a male

Secluded women require the assistance of children who sell in the street food prepared at home. Photo by C. Coles.

Some women purchase and resell food or other resalable items. Photo by C. Coles.

family acquaintance to sell) to six or seven days a week for about ten hours per day (preparing and selling *kosai* and *wainan rogo* [fried bean and cassava cakes]). Sewing or petty trading frequently continues off and on, interspersed with cooking and childcare activities.

To ascertain how much time women spent on income-generating activities, in 1985 they were asked to report their activities in standardized interviews conducted by the author, and subsequently many of the informants' actual activities were observed. Women were asked how often they carried out a particular activity (daily, off and on, or a specified number of times; number of times per week or month). Through detailed questioning they were then asked to estimate the numbers of minutes per day and hours per week which they spent on particular occupations both during periods of high intensity and low intensity activity. Most often these estimates were reached through discussion of specific activities carried out within a few days (or less frequently, weeks) of the interview itself. Observations were then carried out by spending entire days with particular women as they engaged in occupational (and domestic) labor, and by frequent, usually unannounced, visits to most others. Since several women live in each compound, a single visit usually provided time-use data on several informants. Analysis of data on various income-earning occupations provides a mean duration of work ranging from 12.7 hours per week (during periods characterized as less busy) to 17.4 hours per week (during periods of peak effort) for each occupation. Nearly half of all informants engaged

A secluded woman prepares food for sale. Photo by C. Coles.

A young Hausa bride with co-wives and friends. Photo by B. Mack.

in income-generating activities at this time were involved in multiple occupations concurrently. When total income-earning activities are examined for each woman, the mean number of hours per week during peak intensity periods is 24.4, and during less busy periods, 17.3. The range is from 2 (in each period) to 80 during high intensity and 70 during low intensity work, with medians of 20 and 12, respectively. Observational data confirm that Hausa women appeared not to be overreporting the time they spent on occupational activities, and in some cases their reports may have been low.

Spending Patterns and Income

A Hausa woman has the undisputed right to keep and dispose of earnings which accrue to her through her income-generating labor. It should be mentioned that in Kaduna, some occupations (such as midwifery, or preparation of herbs for use as medicine) bring payment in goods in addition to or instead of in cash. A midwife, for example, regularly receives the head of the ram slaughtered for the naming ceremony of a child she has washed following birth, along with a sum of money. At the time of the study, she was also likely to receive payment in food, toilet articles, other items, and cash each time she came to wash a baby.

In Kaduna women are much in need of such income. Apart from contributing to a woman's own maintenance and the subsistence of her children within a marriage, her occupation becomes even more crucial if she does not remarry after being widowed or divorced (thus losing support from a husband). Even if she lives with kin under these circumstances, receiving lodging and food from them, an occupation allows her to be more self-sufficient and comfortable, and to support any children who continue to stay with her.

Table 9.3 provides responses by Hausa women in Kaduna as to how they spent money earned in their occupational activities in 1981 and 1985. Because responses are *reports* rather than observations of spending (although numerous spending events and their outcomes were observed) they must be interpreted as general trends, and as including a potential bias toward spending patterns which women may have wished to project to others, not necessarily corresponding to actual spending. In 1981 spending on personal items for the woman herself (clothing, cosmetics, furniture for her rooms, television sets, radios, jewelry), reinvestment in business, sending money to consanguinal kin, and providing gifts, clothing, and snacks for her children appear to have been the most frequent uses for income. A number of women reported spending extensively on gifts for female friends as part of formal exchange networks. Money was rarely given by a woman to her husband. Although not usually mentioned in interviews, many women regularly gave alms in the form of coins or food to beggars who came by their compounds, and they also saved for their daughters' future first marriages. Like Muslim Hausa women elsewhere, those

Table 9.3. Spending of Earned Income by Women in the Sample
(Kaduna, 1981 and 1985)

Money Spent On	1981[a]	1985[b]
Clothing, snacks, personal items for self	85 87.6%	75 100.0%
Clothing, gifts, food for children	76 78.4%	59 92.2%
Education of children	16 16.6%	12 41.4%
Food, water, fuel for home	29 30.2%	18 69.2%
Reinvest for business	84 86.6%	63 92.6%
Give to husband	10 10.8%	3 16.7%
Send to own family members	83 85.6%	7 63.6%
Saving/paying for Hajj	4 16.0%	9 47.4%
Saving for unspecified needs	2 8.0%	20 80.0%
Female gift exchanges	13 52.0%	0[c]
Saving for daughters' marriages	0	22 61.1%
School fees for Arabic school	—[d]	7 35.0%

Note: The first 7 questions listed in the first column were asked in formal interviewing after they were identified in a pretest as significant spending areas. When formal interviewing was conducted, the next 4 responses were also volunteered by informants. These 4 were then included as questions in 1985.

[a]N varied for each response from 93–97 valid cases.

[b]N varied for each response from 11–75 valid cases; percentages calculated accordingly in both cases.

[c]Although women reported that they were not active in female gift exchanges in 1985, some small exchanges were observed.

[d]These schools did not open in the area until after 1981.

in Kaduna incur substantial expense when their daughters marry (Schildkrout 1988). Mothers are responsible for providing many of the items included in *kayan daki* (literally, "things of the hut," given as part of the dowry), primarily the *kwano* and *tasa* (enamel and glass bowls and dishes).

By 1985 women reported changes in many of these spending patterns, and their answers were confirmed through observation. Nearly 70 percent of women interviewed reported spending large amounts of their income on subsistence items—especially food and fuel—which previously their husbands had provided. The numbers paying for clothing and food for their children increased to over 90 percent, and over 40 percent claimed to be contributing to costs associated with their children's education. A substantial number of women admitted giving money to their frequently unemployed husbands, and fewer were sending money to their consanguinal kin than had done so in 1980–81. The exchange of gifts with female friends in *biki* networks had nearly ceased.

One further sign of changes in spending patterns was a decrease in participation by women in formal savings groups. Women have for many years joined rotating credit associations (*adashi*). The groups operate as each member contributes a fixed sum on a regular basis (such as fifty kobo per day, ten naira per week, or fifty naira per month); each in turn then receives the total pool. Those who join the same *adashi* group tend to have incomes within a common range. Some groups are based within a single compound, with the *uwar gida* acting as leader of the group (*uwar adashi,* mother of the pool), collecting and distributing the monies, even though she may be older and wealthier than other women in it. A second form of *adashi* operates with a single individual (not necessarily female or even Hausa) receiving and holding the savings of contributors until they wish to use them. In both types a payment is made by each member to the head of the group when she receives her savings. In 1985 observations and reports by women suggested a considerable decline in their participation in *adashi:* only 38 out of 78 women responding (48.7 percent) claimed to be participating, with the lack of money reported as the sole reason for other women's lack of participation. Several women also left occupations as leaders of *adashi* groups between 1981 and 1985.

These changes in spending patterns from 1981 to 1985 illustrate the predominant response of women to worsening economic conditions: to increase their own contributions toward the basic needs of their families. By 1985 Hausa women were allocating increasingly large portions of their earnings toward food, fuel, household expenses, and their children's subsistence needs and education. Yet just when demands upon them to contribute more to family subsistence needs were increasing, women's incomes were falling. Although no data on incomes were obtained in 1981, women in the study were asked in 1985 to report minimum and maximum profits per week for each occupation in which they engaged. Combining profits from all occupations, survey data show for each woman an estimated weekly mean profit of 10 naira minimum and 16 naira maximum. These figures may be somewhat lower than actual profits received because, as one informant said, "you and your children eat your profits before you finish working—you buy snacks, or kola nut, or give money to a visitor." She was pointing out that many subsistence items (such as food snacks) are paid for from earnings before a woman can "set aside" her profits.

Since women's responses on income could not be confirmed with observations as readily as were reports of work duration, the degree of data reliability with regard to actual income could not easily be assessed. To address this problem, a small number of informants especially well known to the author were approached to discuss their earnings in greater detail. Information from these conversations provides an indication not only of 1985 income levels but also of a decline in profits between 1981 and 1985. Overall, there were no large discrepancies between profit levels as reported in the survey and those examined in greater detail with particular informants. One of the latter, Hajiya Mero, a woman 40 years of age and the nonsecluded wife of a former soldier, explained changes in her income over the last few years in this way:

I used to trade many things—mostly cloth—in 1967, and I made a profit [*riɓa*] of 15 to 20 naira a week. From 1977 to 1980, I was making up to 30 or 40 naira a week. But now people have no money to buy, and I am lucky to make 5 or 7 naira in a week— many weeks, nothing. Alhaji [her husband] has not given me a wrapper for any *Salla* [Muslim holiday, when husbands usually give a suit of clothes to their wives] for three years now. Only the children have received them—there is no money.

The decline in Hajiya's personal income is typical of that experienced by many other women in the area during the period described. Yet Hajiya and her family were fortunate: her husband received a military pension of 225 naira per month, and they own two compounds from which rents amounted to 330 naira (15 naira per room) each month. This income is considerably more than the 60 to 100 naira per month that might have been earned by an unskilled male family head working as a night watchman and the 125 naira per month minimum wage, which other men in the area received in 1985. Hajiya spent much of her time in a shop attached to the front of their compound, where she and her husband sell soda, matches, candles, boxes of soap powder, and other small items. She also helped to maintain the compound in which her family and other tenants lived. She did not include any share of the rents from the compound or profits from the shop when reporting her earnings. With five children in school, most of the income from these sources was spent on school fees and maintenance of the compounds. In 1985 meat and fresh fruits, plentiful in 1981, were conspicuously absent from the family's diet, *salla* again brought no new clothing, and the purchase of a ram for the holiday caused hardship felt for some time.

Strategies for Survival: Changes in Work Patterns of
Kaduna Hausa Women

Work histories of individual Hausa women in Kaduna illustrate that over the course of their lives most undertake many different occupations. For each woman the selection and timing of particular occupations depend upon many factors: individual motivation and initiative; the degree of domestic labor required of a woman (in particular the numbers and ages of children she has borne and raised); her seclusion status and the availability of assistance to circumvent the limitations imposed by seclusion; her age (relevant to occupations involving the exercise of ritual powers); her physical capabilities (such as for strenuous activities—grinding or pounding); specific skills or educational qualifications; the availability of capital to begin an occupation; and a woman's assessment of current market conditions (Is there sufficient demand for the product or service she is considering? What level of profit can she expect given current prices?). Work patterns identified among Hausa women in Kaduna in 1981 and in 1985 are in effect "snapshots" of their choices and activities in two distinct socioeconomic contexts. When compared, they reflect aggregate changes in occupations as women aged, moved through the life cycle, acquired skills or educational qualifications, and responded both to needs which arose in their own lives for income and to local economic conditions.

Specific changes in women's work patterns from 1981 to 1985 are intertwined with several longer-range processes and trends in the society and economy. The most significant wider trends are the growing availability of secular education, a related increase in occupational opportunities for women, and the growth of Islamic consciousness and fundamentalism in northern Nigeria. The first of these, the growth of secular education, began during the colonial period and heightened in the 1970s (with initiation of universal primary education in the north in 1976) with both positive and negative consequences for women's occupations. Children are an important source of labor that can be enlisted both in women's domestic and income-generating work: from the age of six or seven they care for younger siblings, run errands such as marketing, and hawk prepared foods on the street. Thus increasing levels of attendance by children at secular schools present a very real threat to the continued viability of their secluded mothers' occupations by removing the child labor upon which much female work depends (Schildkrout 1983).

The availability of secular education and technical training for Hausa women themselves has produced many opportunities for them to engage in new occupations (C. Martin 1983). In Kaduna, Hausa women trained in secular schools are beginning, albeit in small numbers, to work as teachers and nurses, in state ministries and local government offices, and in other wage labor positions. Women who strive for education and work in these new occupations experience both benefits and disadvantages, as is evident in the cases of two young female primary school teachers. In 1981 one was married; the other was single and lived with her family. By 1985 the former had divorced and was completely supporting herself and her young son from her earnings. The latter had negotiated a marriage which permitted her further education and employment, and as a married woman was attending an advanced teacher training college in Kano. Yet by attending secondary school and not marrying until well into her twenties, this second woman relinquished the right to be considered a social adult, and many of her maternal kin would not admit her into their homes until she finally married. Had it not been for the moral support provided by her father, a former soldier, it is doubtful that she could have withstood the pressure from the rest of her family to marry and give up her career.

Changes in the economy and society in Kaduna during this century have made possible the transformation of some previously existing occupational roles for Hausa women, linking them with the formal sector, and have led to the demise of others. Several women reported abandoning occupational roles they had worked at before moving to Kaduna: for example, weavers from a village in Kano State known for its cloth ceased their activities when they left the village since they could not compete with machine-produced cloth from local factories in Kaduna. Women in other occupations have been more successful in adapting to change, and profiting from it. Two influential women in the areas, Hajiya Asabe, an elderly midwife and herbalist, and Hajiya Mai Magani, an herbalist and traditional healer, have both worked with orthodox medical hospitals for the testing of their medicines. Hajiya Asabe has also cooperated with these medical authorities in programs to improve health care for pregnant mothers and new babies. Hajiya Mai Magani's work has taken her throughout Africa and has involved her in a number of international studies, projects, and conferences sponsored by the World Health Organization of the United Nations. The following paraphrased excerpt from her life history describes some of her activities:

Hajiya Mai Magani (literally, "one who has medicine"), a well-known herbalist trained in traditional medicine, whose reputation extends throughout Nigeria and much of West Africa, lives in one of the wards studied. Here she holds a daily clinic for outpatients and maintains a small live-in unit for those requiring more intensive treatment for mental disorders. Hajiya originally learned to prepare and use *magani* (medicine) from her mother's father, and his father, in Gombe, where she was born and raised. She began as a woman in her twenties, and has continued to work with herbal treatment for both physical and mental illnesses for almost thirty years: she is now about fifty-five years of age. During this time, revelations in her sleep "from Allah" have provided her with knowledge about particular courses of treatment for illnesses she did not know. She employs both adult males and females to work with her in treating patients and preparing herbs as medicines in her compound. She has worked for several years with hospitals in Kaduna and Zaria, and with international organizations such as WHO, attempting to standardize the use of local herbs in orthodox medical treatment. She is a vice president of the National Association of Herbalists, which operates in Nigeria. Hajiya has never borne children, although she has fostered children of her brothers. She has become very wealthy through her work, and she owns several houses in the immediate areas and a house in Gombe, where her brothers remain with her family. Her present marriage is *auren silkiti*, in which her husband stays most of the time in a compound in another part of Kaduna with his other wives. Hajiya is highly respected in the local community and is recognized as a powerful and independent woman. She also organizes and supervises *bori* activities in the area.

Both Hajiya Asabe and Hajiya Mai Magani continue to participate in the informal sector of the economy, providing services as herbalists, healers, and in the case of Hajiya Asabe as the most respected midwife in the area, while carrying out activities in the formal sector as well. Their new relationships with orthodox medical authorities and with other herbalists have led to the development of new societal norms and expectations for the role of female herbalist (Coles 1990b).

The implications of secular education, new occupations, and changes in previously existing occupational roles for Muslim Hausa women are significant not only for the lives of individual women involved, but for the entire society. Both the process of secular education itself and the new occupations challenge the indigenous system of division of labor by gender as well as seclusion. Educational training may be acquired in coeducational institutions where young women not yet married, but of marriageable age in Hausa society, come in regular contact with males. Female teachers, nurses and other medical personnel, government workers, and other wage laborers work with male staff and clients as well as female. The fact that increasing numbers of Muslim Hausa women are moving into these settings, and that at least some Hausa males support women's efforts, suggest that current changes are neither temporary nor likely to be reversed.

A more recent impetus for change in Hausa women's work in Kaduna is associated with the call to closer identification of Nigerian Muslims with the international Islamic community. This phenomenon has been studied in Kano City: Callaway's account of a political party incorporating radical Islamic ideology makes a case for strong support by women (1987 and this volume); Lubeck (1986) illustrates the mutual effects of the development of (working-) class consciousness and an Islamic ethno-nationalist identity among male factory workers. In Kaduna it is striking that during a period of economic hardship and decline (1981–85) a large new mosque was built in one of the wards studied and that some Muslim women were able to save money for and make the hajj to Mecca. Out of 116 women responding in 1981, 17 had made the hajj; of these, 5 had gone more than once. By 1985 these numbers had increased: out of the remaining 82 women in the sample who responded, 23 reported having made the hajj. The cost of such a trip during the first period of the study was about 600 naira for plane fare and a similar amount for accommodation and travel during the stay in Saudi Arabia. Women invariably returned with gifts of stereo radios, casette players, and gold and coral jewelry for close relatives at home as well. It is not unlikely that the total spent by an individual for the entire trip could reach 2,000 naira, an amount representing years of saving for one hajj. Although wealthy kin sometimes pay for the journey of a close relative to Mecca, data collected in 1985 show that most frequently a woman pays for the hajj herself; for those sent by another individual, the husband most often provides the required amount.

For the majority of Hausa women in Kaduna, the most significant aspect of changes occurring in Islam has been the creation of Islamic schools, which they began attending in large numbers in 1982–83. In 1985, 47 out of 80 women reinterviewed (58.7%) were attending Islamic schools. Generally these were married women of childbearing age: those who did not attend were either old or younger divorcées living on their own; a few middle-aged women did not go. The cost was small (2.50 naira per month), and was paid by a woman's husband if he could afford it or by the woman herself. Those enrolled spent two hours a day, Sunday through Thursday, in graded classes; a few attended for longer periods. Aside from studying the Qur'an, *hadisi,* and Islamic history, women were instructed in reading, writing, and basic mathematics, and they frequently described class discussions relating to marriage, childbearing, and female health issues. A dramatic change appeared in these women between the conclusion of the 1981 study and 1985: virtually all had either become, or were well on the way to being, literate. Although the language of oral instruction in classes is Hausa, written materials are predominately in Arabic. Outside of school, most women spent at least an hour or two each day on homework, consulting the more advanced students among them for help. Furthermore, they had begun reading magazines and simple books available in Arabic.

Islam places a high value on education. With this justification few husbands have interfered with their wives' attendance at Islamic school. Three women living in the community teach classes in the local Islamic school; one is married to a *malam* (Qur'anic scholar). For most women who attend, Islamic school has not only opened the door to literacy and knowledge; it also legitimates mobility outside "secluded" compounds. Wearing identical long gowns (resembling the Middle Eastern chador), which cover them completely except for their faces (which are usually covered with a separate cloth), women move about en route to Islamic school, loiter while returning home, visit friends, or even conduct a bit of trade. Even young female children have begun wearing this type of dress to Qur'anic school. Whether its use will spread, allowing women to move out of their compounds for purposes other than attending Islamic school, and replacing seclusion with a form of veiling as occurs in other Muslim societies, is not clear at present. Income-earning activities of Hausa women appear to be affected most directly through these schools in the increased contact women are afforded with each other on a daily basis, the growing acknowledgment by both males and females in the community of women's rightful claim to education, the opportunities offered women for exchange of information, buying, and selling, and the potential use of literacy in women's personal and occupational development.

Against the backdrop of these large-scale trends occurring in the milieu that Muslim Hausa women inhabit in Kaduna, a number of specific changes in their work patterns are evident in the 1980–85 period. Although the same basic occupations were carried out by women studied at each time, by 1985 individual women had made changes in their occupations to maximize their earning power in light of current conditions in the local economy and the effects felt by their family. Many changes involved cooking and selling different foods or trading in different products: women moved out of trade in items such as palm oil, jewelry, and clothing (which they claimed many people could no longer afford to buy), and into petty trade in more basic foodstuffs. Some occupations were dropped entirely by large numbers of women: for example, weaving and sewing by hand declined significantly in frequency because there was no demand for the straw floor mats or men's caps which women had formerly produced and sold. Although fieldwork in 1985 was conducted during the month of Ramadan and over *salla,* women who earned income by machine sewing of clothing and who should have been very busy at that time had hardly any work. And with a lack of available cash, the purchase of prepared food from other women had dropped off: observation confirmed a lack of reciprocal activity among women who previously had bought and sold frequently from one another, particularly in small items necessary for daily cooking or food snacks.

When queried about prior occupations in 1985, 62 out of 80 women responded that they had previously but no longer carried out particular income-generating activities. Among occupations dropped by women within the last three years (1982–85), those most frequently reported were trading (15.6%), food preparation and sale (34.4%), weaving or sewing by hand (9.4%), and heading an *adashi* group (6.3%). Five young women (15.6%) had married for the first time, and so no longer engaged in hawking for adult women. Primary reasons given as to why women left these occupations were a lack of demand for the product or service (25.0%), no money to carry out the activity (15.6%), and the loss of a young person who could hawk food or other wares for them (28.1%). Many occupations of older women appeared in 1985 to have been hurt less by the decline in the economy than had those of younger women, possibly because the occupations (midwifery, trading in large items, buying in bulk) were less vulnerable and the women more secure and better established in them.

In summary, women's strategies during this period of decline in the economy were to continue to carry out, or else switch to, income-earning activities in which a good or service was produced for which there was still significant demand; and to reallocate their income, directing larger amounts into subsistence needs for their children and husbands, and smaller amounts into female exchange networks, luxury items for themselves, and money given to members of their natal kin group. At the same time they took advantage of increased freedom of mobility associated with attendance at Islamic school, and increasing access to both Islamic and secular education, to further their preparation for and conduct of income-earning activities.

Conclusions: Hausa Women's Work and the Local Economy

Through income-generating occupations, Hausa women in Kaduna contribute significantly to the local economy in two primary ways: first, in their monopoly of a small number of key activities through which existing demands for goods or services are met; and second, through their contributions to the subsistence of their families. Many of their occupational activities are linked to the preparation and sale of cooked food, which women (not only Hausa, but Yoruba as well) monopolize in the local economy. Schildkrout (1982) has suggested that Hausa men actually subsidize these activities through giving women money to purchase ingredients for domestic cooking, which the women then use to buy cooked food from each other. This practice is breaking down somewhat in Kaduna, where men have less money to give their wives for food generally. Yet a market for cooked food still exists: male laborers coming into the area, local men who do not regularly eat at home during the day, and some women and children continue to purchase food. This occupation and the related activities of those who supply and distribute the products meet a significant demand in the local economy that has persisted even in hard times. Other occupations monopolized by women include midwifery, hair plaiting, particular types of herbalism, and heading of one type of rotating credit association. Many of the remaining income-generating activities of women are not gender specific: men as well as women sew by machine and embroider men's caps, act as commission agents, and work as teachers and nurses.

The direct increase in contributions made by women to the subsistence needs of their families through spending from their own earnings between 1981 and 1985 has already been documented. Although data from the study do not make possible an estimation of the percentage of family-household income provided by Hausa women in Kaduna in 1985, in several families well known to the author an adult female provided 25 to 50 percent of the total.

Both the ability to provide cash or material goods to others and Hausa women's occupations themselves help to raise female status in the local community (among both women and men), for they provide women with prestige, material well-being, and the potential for increased power over other individuals. Financial success in her occupation(s) also brings a woman increased independence and control over her own life: if she can support herself she can negotiate conditions of a marriage with a prospective husband from a stronger position, perhaps contracting a marriage which does not require her seclusion or one in which she may remain in a home she owns, with her husband either joining her or living elsewhere. She has greater freedom of choice in deciding whether and when to begin living as *bazawara* (a single woman) and greater security if she is forced into this situation through widowhood or divorce.

A woman with sufficient wealth can make the hajj to Mecca, further increasing her prestige and social standing in the community. She can send other relatives to Mecca or pay school fees and expenses so that they can attend non-Qur'anic school. Wealthy Hausa women in Kaduna have donated money for community development projects of their own choosing; some act as patrons of younger neighborhood women. By giving gifts and sharing her earnings and resources with others, a woman increases her power and authority over the recipients, both male and female, and their responsibility to her in the future.

Many restrictions on the mobility, independence, and occupational opportunities of Muslim Hausa women throughout northern Nigeria persist, some associated with patriarchal cultural norms, others with the negative impact of colonial rule and related economic changes (see, e.g., Schildkrout 1986). Yet women pursue income-earning activities aggressively and have shown themselves determined and able to assume greater responsibility for subsistence within their families. Whether similar actions have been taken by Hausa women in other contexts (in which their behavior may be more circumscribed) is not clear from data currently available. Within Kaduna, women with wealth, occupational success, and prestige (relative to the overall sample) are more powerful than most other women, and than those men with less wealth, prestige, and lower status. But for the majority of women, struggling to feed their families, to facilitate their children's education and become educated themselves, issues of power may be negotiated increasingly as they perceive opportunity and need for them to move beyond behavior that conforms to cultural norms. Important questions remain: What effect will current strategies and activities have on the future development of women's occupational roles? Will their authority and power within the family, or community, increase as a result of their greater financial responsibility? Answers to such questions may provide insight not only into occupational roles but also into basic processes of social change.

10 *Alan Frishman*

Hausa Women in the Urban Economy of Kano

The role of women in urban economic activity in Third World nations has, until recently, been neglected or intentionally overlooked by planners and development economists. But women in every society play a crucial economic role both indirectly, by supporting other workers with household activities, and directly, by participating in the economic production of goods and services for sale. The first kind of activity has officially been omitted by the United Nations in its studies of Third World nations because, by definition, "women occupied solely in domestic duties are not considered as employed and therefore are not included in labor force data" (UN 1975:62). The intentional exclusion of household activity also omits those women who simultaneously carry on household duties and productive economic activity from within the house (Hill 1969). This production, which is "hidden" from view but which is quite common in Kano, will be examined in this essay. I will estimate the value of the hidden productive activity and the economic impact of women within the informal and formal sectors and thus attempt to show that women play a substantial role in the urban economy of Kano.

Women in Africa participate in the open economy to a small extent in industrial activity and to a great extent in the informal sector (Fapohunda 1983: 43). In many parts of the continent, women control retailing activity and are active small-scale entrepreneurs (Simms 1981). In other areas this activity is more restricted, because of custom (women are responsible for maintaining the household) or religion (the Islamic restriction of wife seclusion) or the power of men to restrict opportunities for women. Thus women are often constrained in their labor force participation and their choice of explicit economic activity.

The UN Economic Commission for Africa reported in 1975 that "the median participation rate of women considered economically active (in 24 countries with available data) is 28%; for men, it is 49%. In manufacturing, the median for women (for 19 countries with available data) is 8% of the manufacturing workers." The conclusion drawn by the commission was that women played "only a relatively small part in the modern wage employment sector" (UN 1975:62–66), which is the part of the economy most easily measured.

On the other hand, the UN report goes on to argue that "for many women—whether married or not and whether husbands are present or not—life in towns means a struggle to get income, and the only avenues often open to them are brewing, baking, hawking or prostitution, or the acceptance of unskilled employment at low wages and sometimes poor working conditions with little job security" (UN 1975:66). This informal sector activity in urban areas is often an extension of household activity. Women are strongly represented in the activities of trading; preparing food; laundering; cleaning; taking care of children, the old, and the sick; mending, sewing, and repairing clothes; hairdressing; sexual companionship; and the production of household handicrafts (Nelson 1979:299; Simms 1981:148; Sudarkasa 1981:54; Jelin 1982: 244, 253). There are a growing number of studies that focus directly on women's informal-sector activity, which led Jelin to conclude "It is likely that the pattern in Latin America of a predominance of women in informal sector jobs and in services and commerce is also widespread in non-Muslim Africa and Asia" (1982:252).

The existence of the explicit and "hidden" positions that women hold in an urban economy is highly dependent upon whether that sphere of the economy is expanding or contracting. Margaret Strobel, in her study of urban women in Kenya, argues:

In Mombasa, women's work became increasingly marginalized during the twentieth century. Unlike many men, most women were not drawn into the growing sector of the city's economy. . . . Women in traditional occupations faced government regulation or competition from those trained in European methods. Together with traditional skills, handicraft production that was not replaced by European imports represented a smaller and smaller portion of Mombasa's total output of goods and services. (Strobel 1979: 126)

She concludes that women have been forced into household work and marginal informal-sector activity.

Boserup has also argued that the evidence from Third World countries "strongly suggests that when larger industries gradually drive the home industries out of business, women lose their jobs, because the type of products they were making (home-spun cloth, hand-made cigars, hand-made matches, etc.) are replaced by products factory-made by a labour force composed of many more men than women" (Boserup 1970:111).

More recently, in a study of Ghana, Steele states that "industrialization policies favoring large-scale, capital-intensive production clearly worked to the disadvantage of small-scale female employment" (Steele 1981:165). However, he found that, while this is evident on the aggregate level, it is not as obvious on an industry-by-industry level. In summary, if women's occupations are transformed into formal sector jobs, then as countries develop, women will become even more marginalized in the labor force and in their economic activity than they have been already.

Hausa Women in Kano

Islam, which was introduced to Kano in the fourteenth century, had become the religion of all urban dwellers by the turn of the twentieth century. The major impact of Islam upon Hausa women has been to confine them to their husband's house from the time of puberty and marriage to menopause and old age. Although seclusion of women is a relatively new phenomenon in the rural countryside, it is a well-entrenched tradition in urban areas. Women do, however, pursue gainful occupations within the home (in both rural and urban areas) independently of their husbands (Hill 1977:85). Women rarely attend markets but are linked to the public sector via children, who buy and sell for them (Hill 1977; Schildkrout 1981). Some Hausa women work outside the home in small-scale industries and in large-scale industrial factories, but because their predominant activities are hidden, Hausa women have low participation rates in the work force (Pittin 1984a).

This result conforms to other studies of women's labor force participation. Guy Standing, in his study *Labour Force Participation and Development*, states that there are no general patterns of women's participation in low-income countries in general; however, he does find that female activity is low in urban areas in both Arab countries and in Africa (1981:14–15). In Islamic countries, several studies have found that low female participation rates can be traced to the cultural pattern of women's seclusion (see Boserup 1970 for Morocco and Iran; Youseff 1974 for the Middle East; Smock and Youseff 1977 for Egypt; Smock 1977b for Bangladesh; Papanek et al. 1982 for Pakistan).

Ester Boserup, in her book *Women's Role in Economic Development*, argues that women do not participate in formal industrial work both because employers are not willing to hire them at an extra cost (e.g., maternity leave or for night shifts) and because women prefer to work in home industries or service trades, which allow greater flexibility, ease of childcare, and the interspersing of household duties (see also Fapohunda 1983; DiDomenico 1983). In Arab countries, she argues, women who work in factories work in "harem conditions"—i.e., away from men (Boserup 1970:112–15). Renee Pittin has carefully studied the Nigerian census and found that "Hausa women's entrepreneurial activities . . . are often as invisible in censuses and surveys as the secluded women themselves. Indeed, statistically such women are doubly discriminated against: their domestic labour as wives and mothers is not treated as work, and their income-earning occupations, carried out in the home, are unseen and all too often unrecorded" (Pittin 1984a:477).

The conclusion that can be drawn from all of this evidence is that most women's work is systematically overlooked in Nigeria, just as it is in most less-developed nations.

Hausa Women's Household Economic Activity

Metropolitan Kano has two built-up areas which in the 1980s have blended together to form one city. The original walled Old City is 1000 years old; the adjacent "new town" was founded by the British in 1903. The newer part now contains well over half of the urban population, but most of the Kano studies of Hausa women's activities have either been based in the rural areas surrounding Kano (M. G. Smith 1952; Hill 1969, 1972, 1977) or in the Old City (Bashir 1972; Schildkrout 1981, 1982; Pokrant 1982). This study will rely upon that research to try to estimate the total effect of women's hidden productive activities upon the economy of the entire urban area of Kano.

Mohammed Bashir (1972) studied two wards in the Old City of Kano (Kurawa and Lallokin Lemu) in 1971–72 and found that women had many household (e.g., clothing for themselves and their children, luxury items) and social (e.g., gifts, daughters' dowries) obligations which they had to meet by means of their own earning power. They were autonomous in their economic activities and controlled the profits from those enterprises, although half of the women in his survey had obtained the original capital from their husbands. Other sources of start-up capital were the sale of personal property, a saving scheme, skimming money from the household food and miscellaneous budget, accumulating gifts of money given by suitors to daughters, and using their dowries or an inheritance (Bashir 1972; Schildkrout 1982:63) (see table 10.1).

Women invested in domestic animals (e.g., goats, sheep, cows), petty trading, menial services (e.g., pounding grain), and durable property such as jewelry and enamel bowls. They were heavily involved in food processing, knitting, embroidery, the sale of a wide variety of goods to meet neighborhood needs, the provision of services such as pounding and grinding grain, hair plaiting, and tailoring (see table 10.2). Trade was carried on by children, who could enter homes and interact with the secluded women, and it was competi-

Table 10.1. Source of Capital Funds (*Jari*) (%)

	Kurawa (N = 47)	Lallokin Lemu (N = 47)
Husband	53.19	42.55
Personal property and savings	10.64	6.38
Family	6.38	4.26
Noncapital occupations	4.26	23.41
Service occupation	23.41	17.02
Refused to comment	2.12	6.38
Total	100.00	100.00

Source: Bashir 1972:53.

Table 10.2. Occupations of Secluded Hausa Women in Kano

Type of Activity	Bashir's Study (1971) Kurawa (%)	Bashir's Study (1971) Lallokin Lemu (%)	Schildkrout's Study (1976/1978) Kurawa (%)	Schildkrout's Study (1976/1978) Kofar Mazugal (%)	Schildkrout's Study (1976/1978) Average Monthly Income	Average Across All Wards (%)
None	18.1	17.6	13	0	0	12.2
Selling food and processing food	13.2 ⎤	32.4 ⎤	⎤	⎤	⎤	⎤
Petty trading and retailing	10.9 ⎦ 24.1	2.8 ⎦ 35.2	41	63	₦15.93 (₦191.16/yr.)	40.8
Sewing caps, knitting, embroidery, and tailoring	42.2	18.5	37	28	₦6.72 (₦80.64/yr.)	31.4
Services (e.g., hair plaiting)	12.0	26.8	9	9	₦6.75 (₦81.00/yr.)	14.2
Other	3.6	1.9				1.4
	100.0	100.0	100	100		100.0

Source: Bashir 1972, Appendix; Schildkrout 1981, Tables 5 and 6, p. 92.
Note: Rate of Exchange ₦1 = $1.52 U.S.

tive, both between secluded sellers and with industrially produced substitutes (Bashir 1972).

Schildkrout studied women and children in two wards in the Old City of Kano (Kurawa and Kofar Mazugal) from 1976 to 1978, primarily with regard to the effects of parental economic status on children's activities. This led her to collect data on secluded women's household activities and the manner in which children helped to make those activities function smoothly. Some hidden market activities depend more heavily on the availability of children to hawk wares regularly (such as the sale of cooked food); others (such as sewing and embroidery) rely only on occasional help from children. The study indicated that women often changed occupations based upon the availability of children to help them (Schildkrout 1981:88).

Schildkrout found that most women had independent income-producing occupations and were heavily involved in the preparing and selling of cooked food. Women also traded in petty commodities and performed services such as embroidery, hair plaiting, and pounding grain for others (see table 10.2). The income from these occupations was used for household needs, gift exchange, security in case of divorce, and as capital to expand production. Husbands often extended credit to their wives, as Bashir found in other wards in Kano (Schildkrout 1981).

Finally, Pokrant studied tailors in three wards of the Old City of Kano (Soron Dinki, Yalwa, Hausawa) in 1975–76. He estimated that there were "many hundreds, perhaps thousands, of secluded Hausa women who engage in tailoring on a part-time basis from the privacy of their homes" (1982:205). Women made a substantial contribution to the production of specific lines of clothing— primarily hand-sewn items. Embroidered caps were the most common items and were produced for individuals as well as male cap dealers on a piece-goods basis. Women in the three wards specialized in different types of hand embroidery and usually worked on a "putting out" contract basis. The money obtained from sewing was used by women to fulfill domestic obligations. Finally, Pokrant argues that secluded women have a measure of economic independence from their husbands and make a substantial contribution to the tailoring trade in the city.

All three of these studies indicate that women are economically active, earn substantial incomes, and collectively make a significant contribution to the city's economy. The Old City tax data show that there were 83,163 adult women (virtually all of them Hausa-Fulani) living in the 133 wards in 1978– 79. If only 12.2 percent were not economically active at all (see table 10.2), then 73,017 women were not counted as part of the labor force! Head tax data are notoriously undercounted (since there is an incentive to exclude dependents and thus pay a smaller tax), so the true count is undoubtedly higher. Polly Hill has estimated a correction figure of 1.75 (Hill 1977), and my work indicates

that it may be as high as 2.5. If these figures are accurate, the number of economically active secluded women in the Old City might range from 127,779 to
182,542. It is probably safe to say that there are at least 100,000 Hausa women
who are economically active but hidden from view in the Old City alone.

According to Schildkrout's estimates, women were earning between ₦191
(naira) per year in the more lucrative food and petty trading areas (40.8 percent
of all women) and ₦80 per year in the sewing and service areas (44.6 percent
of all women). The average income, since the two groups are roughly the same
size, is ₦135 per year.

In 1973 a massive small-scale industry (SSI) study of Kano was carried out
by Ahmadu Bello University in Zaria. My analysis of that data indicates that the
average wage per SSI male employee was ₦161 (₦1 = $1.52 U.S.) per year
(Frishman 1979:21). Given the inflation rate from 1973 to 1977 of 61 percent
(Awosika 1980:3–4), and assuming that workers could keep up with inflation,
wages would have risen to ₦259 per year. Since poorer male workers cannot
afford more than one wife (although Islam allows up to four), the woman's
income of ₦135 in most families would be about a third of the total family
income and quite significant. In families with little or no regular male income
(because of part-time work or unemployment), the female contribution would
become even more important. Robert Sarly, in an unpublished World Bank Report on Kano, has estimated that in 1978 "at the relative poverty level (₦264
per capita per annum) about 48–62 percent of the population of Metropolitan
Kano falls into the poverty category; at the absolute poverty level (₦310 per
capita per annum) almost 52–67 percent are so classified" (1981:28). Given
this standard, a family unit of a father, mother, and one child would require
₦792 to be above relative poverty. The typical household that we have been
discussing would earn a total of ₦394 per year, which would put it well below
this poverty standard. It should be noted that the situation would be even worse
without the secluded wife's income. My estimates are that about 70 percent of
the male labor force in Kano is employed in the SSI sector or in low-paying
formal sector jobs, and therefore the majority of the urban population would
be represented by the "typical" family unit described above—earning a family
income in the poverty category.

Explicit Informal-Sector Activity

In the Ahmadu Bello University study of small-scale industries, students
combed the streets of Kano in 1973 and interviewed entrepreneurs. Although
they found 4,584 SSIs in the urban area and interviewed the manager-owners,
the procedure was haphazard in that only those firms visible from the street
were surveyed. Clearly all the hidden women's activity was excluded and much
explicit male and female activity as well. My estimates, based on the Ahmadu

Table 10.3. Survey of Small-Scale Industries, 1973 and 1980

Year	Total	Men	All Women	Hausa Women Muslim	Hausa Women Christian
1973	1,441	1,348	93	15	1
Found 1980	214 ⎱	198 ⎱	16 ⎱	0	1
	⎰ 772	⎰ 716	⎰ 56		
Missing 1980	558 ⎰	518 ⎰	40 ⎰		

Source: Frishman 1979, 1982.

Note: A random sample of 772 establishments were chosen in 1980 out of the original 1,441 from 1973, ensuring a distribution across all types of industries.

Bello survey and government registration of small-scale firms, are that the number of SSI businesses should have numbered at least 15,000 (Frishman 1979: 18). In spite of these drawbacks, a random sample of 1,457 was drawn from all interviews, and it provided a rich data base (which included the sex of the owner-manager).

Only 93 of the 1,457 owner-managers were female (6.4 percent), and only 16 were Hausa-Fulani (1.1 percent) (see table 10.3). This very small percentage results from the lack of direct economic activity available to Hausa women and the possible reluctance of male interviewers to approach female entrepreneurs. Most important, any generalizations made from such a small sample, although not useless, should be viewed with caution. Of the sixteen female Hausa entrepreneurs, only three were located inside the Old City, and only three were located in marketplaces which are dominated by men. Most were in neighborhoods in the newer part of the urban area established by the British under colonialism.

In other studies it has been argued that African women participate in small-scale activities because they involve little capital, compete minimally with childcare and other domestic duties (Strobel 1979:129), can be undertaken with women's traditional skills (Gilbert et al. 1982:71), and give women some independent income and a more open life-style. It is further stated that women are primarily self-employed, have few employees other than children to hawk goods, and are heavily engaged in retail trade (Hay and Stichter 1984:35). They work in highly competitive markets which are extensions of domestic activity and earn low incomes. Most of these women have little formal education, and "women between the ages of 30 years and 60 years are overrepresented in the entrepreneurial group, which suggests a high correlation between the high rate of illiteracy and the high average age of women traders" (Simms 1981: 148–49). It should be emphasized that these generalizations are made about women who are not in seclusion and who therefore have a great deal of freedom to begin with, regardless of whether they participate in economic activity.

However, many of the characteristics seem to apply to the secluded women as well.

It should be made clear that this essay is concerned with *legal* economic activity, and it therefore excludes many others—most notably prostitution. A significant number of Hausa women earn their livelihood from this activity, which has historically been one of the few ways for them to live independently. There have been no studies of prostitution in Kano, but a 1963 study of Sabo, a Hausa quarter in Ibadan, found that 250 of the 1,200 adult Hausa women (20.8 percent) were prostitutes. "In Sabo society, prostitution does not carry the same stigma which it does in Western or in some other societies. . . . Prostitutes frequently marry and slip into the anonymity of wifehood, and wives frequently divorce and emerge into the freedom and independence of prostitution" (Cohen 1969:55, 57). Although the number of women who have been active prostitutes may be inflated in this quarter, which houses many transient single men, the study does indicate that prostitution is quite common among Hausa women. Renee Pittin, in her dissertation and in "Houses of Women: A Focus on Alternative Life Styles in Katsina City," examines the significant number and role of prostitutes in an urban Hausa setting (Katsina). Unfortunately, there are no estimates of the earnings of these women, other than an indication that some women accumulate enough to invest in real estate (Pittin 1979a, 1983). In Kano it is impossible to estimate either the number of Hausa women who are active prostitutes or their earnings, so this aspect of women's activity will be ignored. It has been introduced here because it is a significant occupation and should be researched and included in a complete accounting of Hausa women's economic activity in the metropolitan area.

The occupations of the Hausa women interviewed in the ABU Small Scale Industry study of Kano were all extensions of domestic activity or traditional crafts (see table 10.4). Many women had adult employees working for them, and some used apprentices. The gross profit for these women was up to ₦190 per year, which, if increased by the inflation rate, would have been ₦306 in 1977. That is considerably more than the hidden female workers earned and exceeds the earnings of males in SSIs. Most of the businesses were founded between 1967 and 1972 (69 percent), although a couple had been in existence for a decade.

The range of ages for the female Hausa manager-owners was from twenty-eight to fifty-eight, with the average being thirty-six. Only 6.3 percent of the women had attended primary school; the rest had no formal education at all. A large proportion (84.6 percent) had received training in the occupation they were pursuing, probably from family members. Since the vast majority of Hausa women are married and in seclusion, it might be safe to assume that female owner-managers are "divorced or widowed older women who

Table 10.4. Occupations of Hausa Women in
the Informal Sector, 1973

Occupations	Frequency	Percentage
Food processing	7	43.75
Brewing	1	6.25
Grinding	1	6.25
Soap making	1	6.25
Snuff making	1	6.25
Bakery	1	6.25
Barber/hairdresser	1	6.25
Dyer	1	6.25
Mat making	1	6.25
Weaver	1	6.25
Total	16	100.00

Source: Frishman 1979.

have no expectation of remarrying" (Schildkrout 1981:91). In a more general statement, Gilbert argues, "Indeed, a disproportionate number of successful women entrepreneurs were barren. Other women began to expand and consolidate their business only in their late forties when most or all of their children had grown up and perhaps contributed to a joint household income" (1982:71).

Most studies of SSIs have indicated that the capital to start the business comes from personal savings. This is possible because of very low start-up costs. In this subset of nonsecluded Hausa women entrepreneurs, all those who answered the question claimed that their initial capital came from savings, but not one of the sixteen stated the amount of that initial capital. The overall study of male- and female-owned enterprises in 1973 found that two-thirds (66.7 percent) of the firms had start-up costs of ₦100 or less and that funds were obtained from savings (64.2 percent) (Frishman 1979:25–26). Bashir (1972), in his study of secluded women, found in contrast that the major source of capital funding was husbands (see table 10.3). However, if these SSI women are independent from men, which gives them the ability to function outside the home, then that source would not be available. Pittin found that many independent women in Katsina engaged in SSIs and generated their own funds independently of men (1983:295).

Half the Hausa women entrepreneurs claimed that they wanted to expand their business but were constrained by a lack of capital (70 percent) and good labor (20 percent). Some called for help from the government, others for government or bank loans, and still others for reduced rent. Although SSI entrepreneurs in general cry out for capital, there seems to be enough available from personal savings to meet their small needs. This may be more difficult for women in Hausa society, given their subordinate position, but considering independent women's demonstrated ability to accumulate savings, the lack of capital funds may not be a very significant constraint.

In 1980 an attempt was made at finding 772 of the 1,457 firms (53 percent) interviewed in 1973. Two hundred and fourteen were found (27.7 percent) after the seven-year lapse. Of the original group of 93 women-run firms, a search was made for 56, of which only eight were owned by Hausa women. A total of 16 were found, of which only one was Hausa-owned (see table 10.3). However, this one Hausa woman was Christian and originally had come from Ghana, and thus she is not representative of the typical Kano Hausa Muslim woman. This evidence implies that the occupations these women had in 1973 were generally precarious or unstable at that location (they could have moved elsewhere), although there was no way to determine why they were no longer in business.

Although this sample of nonsecluded Hausa women in SSIs is very small and generalizations are therefore difficult, it does seem to conform to generally held beliefs about women in the informal sector in Third World cities. Given the fact that most Hausa women are secluded, it is not surprising that the sample revealed so little explicit economic activity.

Hausa Women in the Formal Industrial Sector

Hausa women in the formal industrial sector in Kano have been studied by Lawan Abdu in his undergraduate thesis, "Female Labour in the Modern Economy of Kano." He examined the industrial sector of Kano and found that women were employed in standard semimanual labor and in the finishing stages in production. They were concentrated in the footwear, sweets and confectionary, and textile industries. Most women in his sample were young, between fifteen and twenty-nine, and they changed jobs frequently. Fifty-nine percent were married; the rest were single (30 percent), divorced (9 percent), or widowed (2 percent). Most had little or no education. Twenty-nine ethnic groups were represented, and only 11 percent of his sample were Hausa. The vast majority of these workers (79 percent) earned between ₦240 and ₦360 per year (Abdu 1973).

This sample indicates a low participation rate for Hausa women in industrial work, but the salaries are well above what they could earn via house trade (₦135) or from small-scale industry (₦190). Industrial occupations may be acceptable for short periods of time for a small number of young women who later marry and leave their jobs or accumulate funds to start their own businesses.

Conclusion

The overall impact of Hausa women upon the Kano economy is substantial. I have estimated elsewhere that the industrial factories in Kano in 1973 had a total wage bill (paid to male and female Nigerians) of ₦8.14 million; the small-scale industry sector added another ₦14.4 million in wages to the economy. Assuming a 25 percent growth rate in employment and a 61 percent inflation rate, the industrial and SSI sectors had wage bills of ₦16.38 million and ₦29.98 million respectively by 1977 (Frishman 1979:23). If the 100,000 Hausa women in the Old City engaged in hidden trade had each earned ₦135, their earnings would have been ₦13.5 million. It should also be noted that many Hausa women living in the urban area of Kano *outside* the Old City engage in house trade and that thousands more work in SSI, illegal activities, and nonindustrial formal-sector work. It would therefore not be unreasonable to estimate a total wage bill for Hausa women in 1977 of at least ₦16 million, which is comparable to the total industrial wage bill.

The economy in Nigeria and Kano expanded rapidly from 1977 to 1983, and the number and value of women's economic activities probably increased as well. However, since the economic downturn of 1983, women have not fared well. Since "manufacturing companies assume that women's salaries only serve to supplement the family income, . . . women tend to receive no training, are arbitrarily excluded from promotion and in many cases are employed on a strictly temporary basis" (WIN 1985c:51–52). The result of these attitudes is that women have been laid off from industrial jobs as those companies decreased operating capacity. In addition, with less consumer spending and high inflation, the sales from women's hidden activities most likely have declined. However, the extent of women's hidden economic activity will depend upon the importance of their goods and services to the subsistence urban economy and the prices that are charged. Given their preponderance in the production of necessities and their low operating costs, women's economic activity will continue to be significant and important to the well-being of the local urban economy.

The fact that Hausa women in Kano supply substantial income to their households enables many of their families to survive and function. This pattern undoubtedly holds for other urban areas as well. If some estimate of women's domestic activity could be made, it would show that their roles are crucial and indispensable to the economy and well-being of any city. This study shows that not considering women's roles in the economy leads to gross underestimates of urban economic output and to a policy of neglect in terms of women's needs and aspirations. The policy assumes that women will continue to shoulder household responsibilities and will continue to make implicit, hidden, crucial contributions to the economy, a dual role which has become known in development literature as the "double burden."

PART 4. WOMEN'S VOICES: FEMININE GENDER IN RITUAL, THE ARTS, AND MEDIA

11 *Nicole Echard*

Gender Relationships and Religion:
Women in the Hausa *Bori* of Ader, Niger

In the Ader region of Niger, the rules governing the functioning of the *bori* spirit possession cult, in which both sexes participate, assert the equality of the sexes. Participation for everyone is said to be subject to the same religious and cultural imperatives; women and men have equal access to the different roles that constitute the structure of *bori*. As such, there are in *bori* numerous symbolic and ritual expressions of the position and the role of both real female agents (adepts, referred to as mares of the gods), and imaginary and symbolic ones (female spirits). But the assumption of sexual equality in *bori* is in complete contradiction to gender relationships as they are defined in social practice in Ader. Hausa patrilineal society in this region provides a clear example of male domination legitimized by the reduction of women to their sexuality alone. The only social arena in which women are not forced into a class of inferior status and in which both sexes can enter into competitive relationships appears to be the institution of *bori*.

The aim of this study is to demonstrate that the actual practice of possession as observed in Ader between 1965 and 1981—without consideration of past situations or of those elsewhere in Hausa country—*contradicts* any affirmation of equality of the sexes. At the same time, however, *bori* does guarantee by particular means to women, as to men, opportunities for achievement not found elsewhere in the society.

The examination of *bori* has more general value with regard to understanding social relationships between the genders because it illustrates a common process, the reversal of discourse in practice. Such discourse, which expresses a recognition of women as social actors (a recognition that is contradicted in practice), thus appears as a sort of ideological "trap." Such processes of reversal, far from being fortuitous, contribute to the reproduction of unequal male-female relationships in the social realm and to the perpetuation of ideologies concerning them in certain societies.

The findings presented here are excerpted from an anthropological study begun in 1965 on non-Islamic religious expression in Ader, a region situated in the Republic of Niger at the northern confines of the Hausa-speaking area. The more specific study of *bori* itself focuses on the gap between theoretical norm and concrete social practice and is based on an analysis of a sample of 100 *bori* adepts (mares of the gods). This cult was the subject of the well-known research of A. J. N. Tremearne (1914), which was followed in 1948 by a brief study by Leroux and more recently by the work of Broustra, which focused particularly on women-mares of the gods (1972).

Before specifically discussing the situation of women in *bori*, it may be useful to review pertinent characteristics of male-female relationships in the Hausa society of Ader.

Women and Men in Hausa Society: A Clear Example of Inequality

With regard to male-female social relationships in Hausa Ader, two statements prevail: first, women and men have to be fundamentally different, and must never be or do the same things; and second, women, in order to live, have only their sexuality upon which to rely.

The assertion of this difference strictly delineates fields of competence and the division of male and female roles, excluding all possibility of competition between women and men, either in the sphere of productivity or in that of reproduction. The power of control and social decision making is masculine and determines the hierarchical organization of male-female class relationships. Furthermore, women can achieve status or relative autonomy only within their own sphere. This organization of social relationships between genders is particularly evident in the division of labor and in the organization of alliance systems and marriage.

In this way women in Ader are excluded from the greater part of grain production, whose principal products, millet and sorghum, constitute the base of their diet. In rare cases, they help out, but only if necessary. Since land is generally unavailable and the system of fallowing land is not practiced, private ownership of fields in Ader is rare; even the Hausa term designating it is barely known. This is not true in other regions. In Maradi, for example, the chief of the family distributes personal fields to younger brothers and to women to cultivate for personal profit (Levy-Luxereau 1983). Ader, moreover, is too far north to permit the cultivation of peanuts or the management of other small plantations which are often handled by women in other parts of West Africa. At most, women cultivate, where possible, only condiments and onions, which they sell fresh. Furthermore, the women of Ader own very little livestock, unlike the situation that obtains elsewhere—for example, in the Maradi Valley, where three-fourths of the goats are owned by women (Levy-Luxereau, n.d.). In southern Ader, where cotton cultivation has developed, women are beginning to acquire goats, which, according to Bonte (1969), signifies a more pronounced division of labor as well as men's increasing disinterest in small livestock.

Paid activities for women, outside of cultivation and the possible sale of fresh onions and condiments, consist primarily of the preparation and sale of cooked meals and the production and sale of pottery. Older women—widows and women past menopause—who are released from domestic and reproductive tasks, prepare and sell cooked meals at local markets or in the towns. Pottery is made and sold by young girls and women of certain patrilineages, the technique and production capacity being in fact linked to the patrilineage and not to the women themselves. For this reason, they engage in such activity only while they remain, by birth or by marriage, in a producing lineage.

These activities, associated exclusively with food preparation or with the production of utensils acquired, owned, and used only by women, do not extend beyond "the feminine sphere." None of them, no matter what the volume of production may be, permits a woman to attain economic autonomy, which is guaranteed to men in the peasant milieu by grain cultivation and remuneration for work during seasonal migrations. Moreover, comparative estimations calculated by the amount of time spent on comparable activities (production and sale by women of cooked meals and pottery and by men of objects made of animal skin or tools) show a lower rate of pay for feminine labor. Women and young girls obtain from their activities only a very small income, which they use to supplement the income of husbands or fathers for the purchase of food, trinkets for themselves or their daughters, or to meet gift obligations.

Given these limitations on their productive labor, women in fact survive only by exploiting their sexual capital. In Hausa Ader society only prostitution permits economic autonomy for women. In most cases it is resorted to only for a short period of time by women who find themselves temporarily unmarried or awaiting new nuptials, which generally come about quite soon.

It is marriage—the obligatory destiny of all—which constitutes the normal framework of life for women, as for men. Its organization is subject to a twofold requirement: maximization of fertility, because of the importance placed on the number of children, and masculine control over descendants, who, be-

cause of the patrilineal nature of the society, are considered the property of the
father and his patrilineage segment. This double requirement has many consequences. The banning of procreation outside of marriage is an element of male
control over descendants and is linked to the phenomenon of early marriage of
girls, who, as soon as they begin to menstruate (thus showing their fitness for
reproduction), are brought to their husbands and thereby "exposed to the risks
of pregnancy" (Tabet 1985). Although some scholars believe that first marriages formerly occurred at a later age, in Ader no information has been found
to confirm such a hypothesis. Similarly, the data do not indicate that matrimonial stability was stronger in Ader long ago. According to studies conducted
by Saunders (1978) in another Hausa region of Niger, 76 percent of marriages
end in divorce (which is institutionalized) and not by the death of husband or
wife. With the second marriage, bridewealth decreases, although possibilities
for a woman to influence the choice of her husband increase. Women who do
not change spouses in the course of their fertile life are rare; the average is
about three marriages per woman. Such marital instability is justified in Ader
by the belief that the movement of a woman from one man to another increases
chances of fertility. Thus the early marriage of girls (as compared with boys,
who do not usually marry before the age of twenty or twenty-five) and matrimonial instability appear to be the primary structural traits of marital organization
in Ader.

Accordingly, women first married between ten and twelve years of age—
and in any case, before the age of fifteen—subsequently change husbands,
and therefore houses and association with patrilineages, several times before
reaching menopause. They are transients who, deprived of all access to a status
based on a relationship to production and all rights to their descendants, are
clearly limited to tasks of biological and social reproduction. Recent changes
in Ader, whether of a cultural or economic nature (such as the spectacular
growth of Islam or the development of the market economy), have only accen-
tuated male domination through the suppression of certain practices and the
development of others which, until recently, remained marginal (most notably,
marriage with seclusion).

Women and Men in *Bori:* Egalitarian Volition

Contrary to what can be observed in the society as a whole, the spirit-possession
cult presents an image of an institutional area in which male-female social
relationships are egalitarian.

Far from being a religion in a strict sense—that is, an ensemble of representations and practices tending to interpret and control relationships with the
invisible—*bori* has numerous functions which are not religious in nature. Designated titles given to agents who have acquired status in it are the same as

those used in political chieftainships. This lexical equivalency reminds us that *bori*, like the former animist religion *asna* (pagans, heathens) and now Islam, is a component of social organization. Every spirit of the pantheon appears as a sociological, political, or historical significant, and the ensemble constitutes a code for interpreting various situations and events which confront all or part of the society. In this regard, *bori* currently provides the best forum in Ader for expressing contemporary social and political contradictions.

Numerous positive indicators confirm the role accorded to real or imaginary feminine agents in *bori*.

Participation of Both Sexes

The cult is accessible to all members of society with a few exceptions (witches, blacksmiths, butchers, and tanners, for example). Access to the cult is subject to the rule of heredity, according to which spirits are transmitted through matrilineal or patrilineal descent. New adepts, however, seem to be tolerated in small numbers and under certain conditions. The adepts, more female than male, form collectives under the authority of a chief and an assistant, either of whom may be male or female.

The *bori* pantheon is also composed of both sexes but with a double masculine dominance—on the one hand, because of the sex of spirits considered to be most important, and on the other, because of their number. Among 138 spirits inventoried in Ader, 90 "males" and 48 "females" were found, with 20 of the latter having appeared recently. In fact, the supply of spirits—that is, of available significants—is subject to: (1) the disappearance of spirits who lose their relevance as significants, (2) the transformation of other spirits so that the meaning they carry corresponds better to contemporary needs, and (3) the appearance of new spirits in response to particular changes or events.

Traditions of Origin

Diverse traditions, mythical or not, ascribe the origin of spirits and the organization of the cult to women. Thus a myth of origin which appears to be of recent invention, insofar as it borrows from Islamic tradition, names Adam and Eve as parents of the spirits. When their children had grown, the Master (God) asked them to come to him to present their children. Eve, thinking that he perhaps wanted to kill them, forced Adam to hide the fattest and the strongest children in the bush. The Master, who was of course ubiquitous, condemned those who had been hidden to remain so until the end of the world. Adam and Eve never found their children in the bush. From that time on, they were invisible; they proliferated and "attacked" men. It is this betrayal by Eve, with her lying, treacherous nature, that supposedly led to the emergence of the spirits which structure the Hausa realm of imagination.

Moreover, traditions of a historical nature (belonging to various population groups) attribute the development of the *bori* cult to one of two sources: hunters, who hold the position of "sons of women" with respect to the first occupants, or women, with the youngest sister of the leader having guided migration or movements of the group.

The Conjugal Metaphor

Male-female relationships, as they are constituted within the framework of marriage, serve as a model for the relationship between an adept and his or her spirits. Thus initiation rituals—that is, rituals of alliance between spirits and adepts—duplicate the marriage ceremony. This occurs first in their general organization (length, the unfolding of certain procedures, etc.) and afterward in their details, such as the lexical usage designating applicants by terms meaning "bride" or "groom" and the symbolic operation, divinatory in nature, which consists of sowing grain or bean seeds to see if they grow well in the place where ritual ablutions are held.

Control of the Emotional World

One of the characteristics which explains in part why women participate in relatively great numbers in such "cults" is the chance it provides for them to express and attempt certain emotional configurations not authorized elsewhere. Amorous passion, for example, is unwelcome within the framework of marriage, where it has the reputation of inhibiting procreation. It is, generally speaking, forbidden to women; men, however, may be subject to fits of passion, provided they are temporary. In *bori*, a spirit, seized by violent love-desire, "attacks" a person. The adept caught in this situation is socially unavailable until an "arrangement" takes place through *bori* ritual, which will organize and assuage the amorous passion. A sort of ongoing emotional reciprocity between adept and spirit seems to be necessary for the adept to play a particular role in the cult.

The characteristics described here show the extent to which *bori*, even though we are uncertain of its genesis, can appear to the observer as a unique arena for male-female social relationships: women and men are treated equally, which favors the emergence of feminine social personalities. Certain female spirits hold an important place in the hierarchy of the pantheon, and various possibilities for achievement—particularly in the sphere of emotions—are offered. Women are therefore assumed to participate directly in the construction and expression of different representations, especially those concerning them, and beyond that, in the ideological constructions in which they are at times integrated.

From Theory to Practice: The Duplication of Inequalities

How is the theory of the cult put into practice? In other words, how is it practiced at a given moment in a given place (for example, the actual presence of spirits manifesting themselves on the stage of possession and the division of functions between adepts)? Several excerpts from an investigation concerning 100 adepts belonging to a large collective in Ader (village of Funkwoi, February 1979) can perhaps help to answer this question. Such an evaluation can only be approximate because of the necessity for direct observation—that is, witnessing various manifestations—in order to collect most of the findings. Moreover, the information presented here concerns only adepts, who experience trance accompanied by possession, and not adherents, who do not become possessed (called "those who follow").

Average participation in *bori* in the 1970s varied, according to village, from 2 to 5 percent of the adult population (the nonadult population does not participate in the cult). The sample dealt with more than 100 adepts, of which 98 files were selected. Among the 98 adepts were 27 men, an optimal figure for male participation. The 98 participants were possessed by 82 spirits, of which 26 were female. These findings are summarized in table 11.1.

As represented in this collective, *bori* makes use of only a part (58 percent) of the supply of available spirits, female spirits being relatively less well represented than male.

The most important characteristics concerning the configuration formed by an adept and his or her spirits are the following: most adepts have three to five spirits, with the majority allied to spirits of both sexes; women have more female spirits than men; one spirit can often be allied to several adepts from the same collective (such as Arzanzana, who has 56 adepts, and Badaji, who has 48). These findings are summarized in table 11.2.

The data in table 11.2 show that the expression of matters of interest to women (conveyed by 167 spirits) has less chance of emerging on the stage of possession than do masculine concerns (conveyed by 296 spirits), the latter of which are produced nonetheless by the intervention of a majority of female adepts. Furthermore, there is a relative specialization of spirits according to the sex of the adepts—indeed, spirits possessing exclusively or primarily adepts of a given sex are more numerous than those allied equally with men and women, as table 11.3 illustrates.

Spirits primarily or exclusively allied with women can be divided in the following manner: (1) ancient spirits of both sexes, important in that they refer back to the old *asna* (pre-Islamic, pagan) society of Ader; (2) slave spirits of both sexes whose work it is to prepare the dance site, as well as to accomplish small tasks for the other spirits; (3) a singer spirit, comparable to a slave, whose chants call the spirits; and (4) female witch spirits, mostly of recent

Table 11.1. Mounts and *Bori* Spirits in Ader Sample

	Female	Male	Total
Mounts of the spirits	71	27	98
Spirits of the pantheon	48	90	138
Spirits in the sample	26	56	82

Table 11.2. Distribution of Spirits among Adepts in Ader *Bori* Sample

	Female Adepts	Male Adepts	Total
Total number of spirits or avatars	351	112	463
Average number per adept	4.94	4.14	4.70
Number of female spirits	133	34	167
Average number per adept	1.87	1.25	1.60
Number of male spirits	218	78	296
Average number per adept	3.06	2.88	3.02

Table 11.3. Alliance of *Bori* Spirits and Adepts in Ader Sample

	Female Spirits	Male Spirits	Total
Equal frequency	3	3	6
Spirits primarily allied with women	19	28	47
Spirits exclusively allied with women	11	13	24
Spirits primarily allied with men	4	25	29
Spirits exclusively allied with men	3	8	11

appearance, whose status varies and is often not yet defined. Spirits allied primarily or exclusively with men, however, are almost all male, important, and recent. Furthermore, five times more men than women inherited no spirit at all and were allied with the new spirits having contemporary sociopolitical significance. For example, there are the so-called spirits of the West, which originated with Zarma, a population that settled west of Hausaland in Niger and Mali. Appearing between 1970 and 1973, they proposed a sociopolitical interpretation of famine, thereby challenging the Nigerian government of the time. Alliance with these new spirits has become a prerequisite, in the last few years, for access to the role of chief of the *bori*. Since few women are possessed by the new spirits, few women have attained such status: the two women registered in Ader who have done so were both allied with recent female witch spirits. Thus the mode of access to the cult, as to various roles in it, contradicts in practice the assertion of egalitarianism on the basis of gender in Ader *bori*.

Table 11.4. Association of Female *Bori* Spirits in Ader with Different Concerns

	Signification							
	Deviant Feminine Figures		Association of Social History and Witchcraft		Servility Dependence		Control of Witchcraft	
	Number of Adepts		Number of Adepts		Number of Adepts		Number of Adepts	
Spirits (in order of frequency of appearance)	F	M	F	M	F	M	F	M
Arzanzana	47	9	—	—	—	—	—	—
Badosa (Dogwa Baka)	—	—	24	7	—	—	—	—
Ta'amu	16	2	—	—	—	—	—	—
Bagurma	—	—	—	—	11	2	—	—
Aljana (Dogwa Fara)	—	—	8	3	—	—	—	—
Magajiya	8	1	—	—	—	—	—	—
Zakuma	—	—	—	—	—	—	4	1
Halima	—	—	—	—	4	—	—	—
Wambey	—	—	—	—	—	—	2	2
Tsira Fako	—	—	—	—	—	—	2	1
Totals	71	12	32	10	15	2	8	4
	83		42		17		12	

On the stage of possession itself, where the male expression of various levels of social organization and history predominates, the "language" used by female spirits is of several types. If we set aside slave spirits and the singer spirit Halima, who signify above all servility and dependence, the female spirits represent concerns related to the history of society, illustrate deviant feminine figures, and express attempts by women at taking over the imaginary realm of witchcraft.

The best represented female spirits—that is, those having at least three adepts in the collective—can be divided as in table 11.4.

The *bori* view of history includes both sexes in that it is presented by spirits divided equally between the adepts of the two sexes. It recalls an alliance between indigenous cave-dwelling populations and hunters. This alliance is represented in oral histories as forming the base of sedentary peasant organization. Furthermore, witchcraft strength is also linked to the origins of society because of the adherence of.the two female spirits, Badosa, "the Fulani Bororo," and Aljana, "the spiritess," to the class of old, first-generation witch spirits (as distinct from contemporary ones). As a wandering Fulani, Badosa further expresses the ambiguity of relations maintained by the Hausa peasant society with the neighboring "Bororo" Fulani, known as the Woɗaaɓe.

A second representation of females in *bori* (and predominantly feminine with regard to its adepts) illustrates women figures other than the wife-mother —that is, individuals whose socially deviant behavior reveals an insufficiency, a lack, or a failure of the socialization of their sexuality, which bars their access to marriage and motherhood. Therefore, we find in decreasing order of frequency: a too-big young girl, Arzanzana; a woman expressing wild sexual desire, Ta'amu; and an aged "liberated woman" with habits that are unhealthy for the family, Magajiya.

Arzanzana is a *budurwa,* a term used to describe girls from the time their breasts begin to develop until they have given birth, even if the child is born dead. Generally girls are *budurwa* only for a short time, with marriage inter-vening as early as the beginning of menstruation. Age, and even a preg-nancy not brought to term, are sufficient to change a *budurwa* into a *mace,* a "woman." The name of Arzanzana, which means "smallpox woman," recalls the expression used in the work of Tremearne (1914:375) in the form of *'ya'yan zanzanna,* "children of *zanzanna*" (cutaneous eruption, smallpox). This ex-pression denotes a class of spirit children of both sexes which does not exist in Ader. In this region Arzanzana is a woman already adult—a too-big young girl—who, extremely seductive, is wooed and petted by the other spirits as their favorite, though she has already contracted several marriages. Her child-ish, capricious, and coquettish nature causes her marital instability; she has never given birth.

A woman of Tuareg origin, Ta'amu represents wild sexuality (aided by a blacksmith spirit), as if nonsocialized or badly socialized sexuality cannot be integrated into the social body itself. Instead, it is thrust into the margins of society: that which is outside but near, such as another ethnic group, or that which is distinctive, such as the metallurgists. In possession, Ta'amu evokes exhibitionism and sexual deviation (which prohibits giving birth)—the black-smith spirit, for example, is an eater of excrement.

Magajiya is a title used in Hausa political chieftainships to designate the mother or the sister of a political chief, but it is rarely used in this sense in Ader, where it denotes more commonly a woman who runs a house of pros-titution. Thus the spirit Magajiya has two principal avatars. In our sample, Magajiya is an agitated, shouting, turbulent woman, wandering endlessly, and also jealous—in particular, of one of her co-wives (Aljana, mentioned above). In short, she is a bad and fearsome woman.

The third theme associated with female spirits is that of the new witch spirits, who differ from the old ones (referred to above as "first-generation" spirits) in that they are not linked to the history of society. New witch spirits appear rarely in the table above, most of them having fewer than three adepts in the collective under consideration. Because of their excessive fertility, they prolif-erate, primarily attacking women deprived of *bori* heritage (usually those who

A *bori* spirit possession dance. Photo by N. Echard.

Woman possessed by new witch feminine spirit. Photo by N. Echard.

have not yet inherited spirits), even attacking girls as young as fifteen years
of age. Their appearance in *bori* occurs within the general context of the development of imaginary witchcraft to the detriment of human evil magic. This
class of witch spirits tends to monopolize mastery of fertility, thus bringing
about considerable transformation in the system. Previously, lack of fertility
was attributed to deviation from sexual propriety, implicating both partners.
Alternatively it was seen, to a lesser degree, as the action of various spirits,
with the two most important from this point of view not even represented in
the sample under consideration here. In any case, second-generation witches
tend to give weight to the idea that fertility is associated only with women, who
alone have control of it, and that biological reproduction of the society depends
upon the society of women, made up of real and imaginary individuals.

Conclusion

Contrary to the norms expressed about the *bori* cult with regard to equal participation by adepts of both sexes, there is in practice a veritable "sexual division
of religious work" (Balandier and Mercier 1952) in *bori* of the Ader region.
Male and female adepts constitute two distinct groups which have in common
a relatively small number of spirits. Specialization of spirits according to the
sex of adepts results in the masculinization of cult mastery: male adepts are
possessed more frequently by important, recent spirits and are more likely to
become chief of *bori*. Moreover, representations of women through possession by particular female spirits allied with adepts in the collective almost all
signify either dependence-servility or sexuality, thus recalling the imperatives
concerning the control of sexuality and its reproductive end.

This reduction of the potential for women's social presence, both real and
imaginary, is amplified by their infrequent participation in the construction of
new representations, which takes place by association with new spirits. As
we have seen, women's original production is limited to witch spirits (of the
second generation), which leads simultaneously to the development of a new
imaginary realm of witchcraft and the imprisonment of women in ideological
patterns of biological reproduction.

How can we interpret the gap between the prevailing discourse about the
bori cult and its observed practice? The principal hypotheses—far from exclusive—that can be formulated fall into two categories. The first are linked to
sociohistorical transformations from at least the beginning of the twentieth century that would have affected, negatively for women, the organization of social
relationships between genders. Other hypotheses concern the functioning of
the ideological system. Processes which serve to enhance women and reha-
bilitate them as social actors are present in numerous societies, marked, as in
Hausa society, by male domination. We have only to cite the importance placed

on maternity in our own society. As Leger-Hervieu (1983) puts it, this emphasis on the role of the genitrix-mother is accompanied by a negative perception of the body of women and, in the last analysis, serves to legitimize their imprisonment in the domestic sphere. Such processes are often analyzed either as furnishing proof of the power of women or in terms of internal contradiction. It seems more likely that they are part of the means by which a system creates, maintains, and reproduces inegalitarian male-female social relationships.

Marriage in the Hausa *Tatsuniya* Tradition: A Cultural and Cosmic Balance

Ga ta nan, ga ta nanku—"Here it is, here is a tale for you," the traditional storyteller begins. *Ta zo, mu ji ta*, the children reply—"Let it come, let's hear it." Storytelling is as old as humanity, and so it is among the Hausa, where folktale narrative (*tatsuniya*) is an important form of entertainment among children and adults alike.

Folktales are only one of many forms of Hausa oral literature. Other types include: the song poem (*waƙ'a*); the historical narrative (*labari*); the praise song (*kirari*); drama (*wasan kwaikwayo*); the proverb (*karin magana*); and fiction (*litafin hira*) (Skinner 1980). Many of these latter forms are contained in or overlap with the folktale narrative.

It is not surprising that women are the primary storytellers, entertaining the children they tend with didactic tales (M. G. Smith 1969; Skinner 1969; Stephens 1981). Yet it is a function of social circumstance that the earliest published Hausa oral narratives were told by Hausa men for inclusion in collections by European explorers like Frederick Schoen in the nineteenth century and British colonial officers at the turn of the twentieth century. Collecting Hausa tales and histories as language and cultural materials, British colonial officers made significant contributions to the preservation of early Hausa literature (M. G. Smith 1969). The most extensive such collection was made by Frank Edgar in the Sokoto region about 1911. The first of three volumes included materials given to him by Resident Officer, Major John Alder Burdon.

It was followed by two other volumes of material that Edgar collected later (Skinner 1969; M. G. Smith 1969). Translations of these materials to English came much later when H. A. S. Johnston published some of Edgar's collection in *A Selection of Hausa Stories* in 1966, and A. Neil Skinner translated the largest portion of Edgar's work for *Hausa Tales and Traditions*, published in several volumes in 1969 and 1977.

Although Hausa men still perform *tatsuniyoyi*, probably more so in Niger than in Nigeria, the tales are more often told by women. The steady growth of Islam, with its own narrative and poetic traditions, has encouraged the idea that men should concentrate on more overtly religious themes. Women, who generally spend less time in Qur'anic school and at the mosque, are more likely to perpetuate the pre-Islamic *tatsuniya* tradition. Contemporary folktales do incorporate many Islamic images, but they also reflect roles, rituals, and social relationships with a much longer history in Hausaland. They speak to the culture's dependence on nature—and on Hausa wives and mothers to nurture families in their agricultural milieu.

Both Hausa men and women are profoundly shaped by their agricultural subsistence economy. From early childhood girls anticipate a productive domestic role. Women contribute significantly to labor-intensive food preparation as mothers of numerous children and also as farmers on their husbands' or their own personal plots. Yet within this context, performers of the Hausa *tatsuniya*, a predominantly women's oral narrative tradition, argue in a feminist vein.[1] Their narratives suggest that women in traditional family roles are not dependent and inferior, but rather independent of and even superior to their male counterparts. Recognizing the self-esteem these narratives foster among women is especially significant in light of the recurrent accusation that Muslim societies accord women very low status.

Over 90 percent of some 40 million or more Hausa people in West Africa consider themselves to be Muslim; certainly many elements of Hausa Islam suggest a low status for women. Religious scholars teach that a virtuous woman always owes obedience to a man, either her father or her husband. Whereas men pray in public, women pray within the confines of their compounds because it is felt their presence might provoke lustful desires in men, for which women would be responsible. Under Islamic law a woman inherits less of the

---

1. Especially since the popular assimilation of Islam, men have elected to emphasize Qur'anic studies rather than the folktale tradition as an appropriate pursuit for serious Muslim men. However, especially in Niger, some men of all ages continue to perform *tatsuniyoyi*. In fact, in my own collection I found that these men count among the most outstanding performers. Two factors may contribute: (1) since they are at least somewhat nonconformist, only the most skilled male artists persist in performing the *tatsuniyoyi*, and (2) in general, Hausa men are much more accustomed than women to public speaking of any kind, and community roles may encourage their narrative abilities.

family property than her brother does; her husband can divorce her by pronouncement, but she must go through a complex legal process to divorce him. Economically, her options for generating income traditionally are far less remunerative than those open to men.

Narratives of the *tatsuniya* tradition repeatedly offer a counterpoint to this Islamic ideology. Although the *tatsuniyoyi* predate the mass adoption of Islam in Hausaland, contemporary narratives incorporate many Muslim images. Women are most often portrayed in traditional roles as cook and mother. But far from playing dependent wives, many of these heroines consistently challenge and best their husbands. Moreover, oppositions recur, aligning female antagonists with natural and supernatural powers against husbands who represent worldly, political authority. Conflicts occur between these counterforces and are mediated by women with supernatural abilities to nurture and produce life. If anyone must acknowledge dependency, it is a husband, whose political power is no match for his wife's supernatural power and whose cultural role is sustained by her culinary and reproductive abilities. In these tales women are separate and superior; they are highly esteemed in their traditional domain. Examining four narratives reveals how Hausa performers subtly build their argument. Their heroines are associated with other natural and supernatural figures, and they resolve conflicts through their womanly expertise in bearing and nurturing life.

The Narratives

One of the simplest Hausa narratives involves a marital competition (Stephens 1981:511–18). The daughter of a Muslim religious scholar (*malam*) desires to marry a prince. Initially her father objects because he prefers that she marry another Qur'anic scholar like himself. Although he capitulates, his hesitation reinforces the tension between the bride's association with her father's supernatural, religious authority and her groom's worldly, political power.

The marriage is made, and the *malam*'s daughter becomes a second wife. Immediately the prince launches a contest with his new bride. He offers rice to his first wife and stones to the new spouse, instructing each to make a meal. The *malam*'s daughter returns home, and her father miraculously turns the co-wife's rice to stones and his daughter's stones to rice.

This simple contest establishes important patterns. First, the bride, through ties to her supernatural father, is able to defeat her royal husband, despite his supreme political status. Second, the contest she wins is in the traditionally feminine domain of food preparation. She requires a miracle but fulfills her task to nourish her new family.

This pattern is varied but repeated in the second, more taxing challenge spelled out by the prince. As he mounts his stallion to ride to another country, he instructs his bride that before he returns, her mare must bear his stallion's colt and she must bear his son. Once again her *malam* father works a miracle, this time by disguising her as a prostitute and transporting her to her husband's lodgings. Her man is smitten, and she bargains for their horses to mate before she accepts him as a lover. Thus when the prince returns, his new bride has had his child and her mare the required colt. The senior wife is cast out and the marriage is at last stabilized.

A female contest affiliated with supernatural power has bested her male, political rival a second time. Moreover, her triumph concerns another traditionally female province, the bearing of children. Even the prince is dependent on his wife to produce his heir, and he is incapable of preventing that miracle. Symbolically, their stabilized marriage portrays a viable balance between supernatural, female authority and worldly, male authority, a balance that assures new life. As established in the tale of the *malam*'s daughter, a woman and her supernatural affiliation play an equal, if not a superior, part in that equilibrium.

The first two major conflicts in another popular Hausa tale specifically pose the question of whether sons or daughters are more valuable (Stephens 1981:531–43). The King of the East, father of several sons, is indebted to the King of the West, whose children are all daughters. The debtor refuses to make good his loan until his friend has a son come collect the debt. Sons, as opposed to daughters, thus represent superior wealth; without them the debt cannot be claimed.

However, the King of the West has a daughter, 'Yal Baturiya, a bold girl who declares that she is just as suited as a brother would be to collect her father's due. So she disguises herself as a boy and queries her father's stallion, "Kili, horse of my father, if you take me, will you bring me back?" Receiving an affirmative reply, 'Yal Baturiya mounts her steed and sets off.

Along the way she politely greets an ant who joins her quest. Once at her destination she announces her mission, and the men at court give her a series of tasks to prove that she is indeed a son, not a daughter. Each trial involves a choice, and each time alternatives are presented, the stallion Kili reveals the appropriate response for a boy. First she chooses correctly between two staple foods. Next, she sorts, rather than mixes, a collection of grain; her new friend, the ant, gives invaluable help. Finally, she must go swimming to expose her private parts. Kili distracts her audience by charging after the king's horse. In an alternate version of the narrative, the horse's supernatural powers enable him to exchange sexual organs with his mistress (Stephens 1981:551). This final test passed, the debtor's nobles conclude they must pay off the disguised princess. As she departs, she taunts them with her proven equality, "I'm 'Yal Baturiya and I came to fetch my father's money. I'm a girl, not a boy"

(Stephens 1981:537). They mount a chase, but the heroine, master of nature and magic, throws thickets, water, and fire in their path.

The bested King of the East is furious at the deception and seeks revenge by marrying 'Yal Baturiya. Once again he disadvantages her and sends her off to poverty as an outcast leper's wife. She resolutely accepts this fate until a messenger appears from the palace in search of cooking fire. Along with the fire, the messenger takes home tales of 'Yal Baturiya's dazzling gold draftsmen. When the same messenger returns to borrow the draftsmen, their mistress insists first on having a night with the king while the king's wife sleeps with 'Yal Baturiya's leper husband. Disguised, each wife conceives a son who looks like his actual father.

Later 'Yal Baturiya takes her son to the palace, where the courtiers immediately recognize him as a prince. They set a trial to identify the king's and the leper's respective offspring; her son reveals his royal origins. 'Yal Baturiya and her prince are promptly installed at the palace, establishing a final equilibrium within both her marriage and the kingdom.

This tale argues forthrightly that girls are equal to and as independent as boys. By disguising herself as a son, the heroine effectively portrays both genders simultaneously; her challengers are unable to tell the difference. She matches any brother she might have had in defending her family's fortune, and her deception makes her superior to a large group of male adversaries. Moreover, she is strongly associated with supernatural powers which are, in turn, related to the life-sustaining female roles identified in the previous tale of the *malam*'s daughter.

Through her religious father, the earlier heroine gained supernatural powers to defeat her royal husband. 'Yal Baturiya also performs supernatural feats to defy her male political adversaries, but the sources of her magic are the animals and plants of nature. Her father's stallion becomes her collaborator at the beginning of her quest, and his supernatural powers increase as the tale continues. He magically discerns the responses his mistress must give to preserve her disguise as a son. In the version in which he exchanges sexual organs with her, he can also manipulate the physical world at will. The heroine acquires another ally in the ant, who also displays supernatural abilities when it helps sort her grain. Additionally, when she escapes with her father's money, she fends off her pursuers with her command of nature by hurling thickets, fire, and water to block their path.

Like the *malam*'s daughter, 'Yal Baturiya displays supernatural powers in cooking and childbearing, two ways Hausa women traditionally nurture life. With help, she is able to preserve her disguise by choosing the correct staple food and sorting grain for food. Once married, she attracts the attention of her husband's household because she controls the fire they need for cooking. As in the previous *tatsuniya,* her final triumph occurs because, disguised, she can bear her rightful husband's child despite his efforts to the contrary. Motherhood assures harmony in her domestic life and in the cosmic balance between her natural and supernatural affinities and her husband's political world. By dominating traditionally female roles, the heroine resists oppression.

'Yal Baturiya's story also juxtaposes sexual oppression with other forms of cosmic disequilibrium and social oppression. As she sets off to prove her sexual equality, she draws a parallel with the equality between man and nature necessary to their mutual harmony. When the ant asks to accompany her, she answers, "A person is going to refuse another person?" (Stephens 1981:533). By granting equal status to even the smallest of nature's creatures, she gains the ant's help to preserve her disguise as a boy. Then following her marriage, the narrative criticizes another social equality. When her husband orders her banished to a life of poverty as a leper's wife, she responds, "So be it. A leper is human" (Stephens 1981:539).[2]

Tyranny, she suggests, has no rightful place in Hausa culture. To be humane is to acknowledge the equality and interdependence of diverse elements of the Hausa milieu: nature and humanity, rich and poor, powerful and weak, male and female. Man and woman may be as distinct as man and animal, king and subject, but each plays an independent role vital to the other.

'Yal Baturiya's affiliation with nature and its supernatural potential was strongly suggested through her collaboration with Kili. In other Hausa tales a young bride bridges the human and natural realm even more explicitly. She is a creature of two identities, the first expressing her origin in nature, and the second reflecting the royal human identity she gains by marrying a prince. Moreover, her links to nature permit her to lead her husband to a stable cultural and political identity and full adulthood. The heroes of these *tatsuniyoyi* portray Hausaland's highest authority, the *sarki,* or emir. But in these narratives the *sarki*'s authority depends on his wife's natural and supernatural ties, which are once again associated with women's traditional role of sustaining human life.

La6o is the heroine of one such narrative (Stephens 1981: 731–58). Her mother is a python impregnated by "a great stud of a man." The daughter they produce is born an exquisite human child. However, her snake mother promptly swallows and regurgitates her as a pitiful urchin with festering sores whom she calls "God's poor slave" (Stephens 1981:731). Then she sends the girl away from the wilderness to beg for a home in God's name, as if she were a Muslim Qur'anic student. La6o is thus an ambiguous heroine, simultaneously

2. In the Hausa practice of Islam, leprosy is viewed as the punishment of those who have committed the heinous sin of swearing falsely on the Qur'an. This belief and the increasingly repulsive appearance of lepers as the disease progresses combine to give them a supremely low social status.

a child of the human, natural, and supernatural realms. Combined with her natural origins, her supernatural characteristics reflect the beliefs of Islam.[3]

An old woman from the royal palace takes the sorry Laɓo home, where Maman, the spoiled prince, threatens to kill her. However, the girl joins the household as a servant and maintains a relationship to her animal mother by visiting her when she fetches wood for the cooking fires.

When the prince gives a grand party, Laɓo reveals that she is something special, worthy to be his royal mate. Like the other maidens vying for his attention, she cooks him a tempting sweet. Before she attends the festivities, her mother swallows and regurgitates her in her original stunning human form. Maman is enchanted, and as she leaves he offers her his ring and promises to pursue her.

Before her suitor comes to visit, Laɓo's mother retransforms her to an urchin. This time, when she prepares his favorite sweet, she hides his ring inside. Discovering the ring, he realizes that the urchin and her dazzling alter-ego are the same Laɓo. His earlier threat to murder her changes to a marriage proposal. Laɓo's role as nature's bride is reinforced when her python mother attends the wedding accompanied by many other wild beasts. Just before the ceremony the snake swallows and spits forth her daughter in a form befitting royal splendor. The marriage of man and woman, culture and nature, and political and supernatural power seems to have been made.

Yet the narrative further elaborates the relationship of these spheres. Laɓo must help her prince establish his own relation with nature before their marriage is fully cemented. This process is initiated when Maman's father, the king, plots to usurp Laɓo for himself by sending his son away to be killed in the bush. As Maman leaves, his bride gives him dates and her ring. Far into the wilderness the king orders that his son be buried alive at the bottom of a well.

The dates, Laɓo's gift from nature, permit Maman's resurrection. They nourish him, and their seeds produce the tree that he climbs to the top of the well. Maman's rebirth thus symbolizes his passage through nature. He emerges as nature's wild man, unshaven and barely clothed. By dropping Laɓo's ring into her servant's calabash of milk, he signals her that he has returned to life. She rides out to meet him with barbers and royal clothing to transform him permanently into a ruler. When his father appears, Maman deposes him and assumes the royal throne.

The repeated images symbolizing the heroine's identification with the natural and the supernatural have been noted in the narrative summary and need be only briefly listed here: Laɓo's mother is a snake whom she visits regularly

---

3. As a part of their religious training, Qur'anic students are literally expected to beg for their food. Thus La'ɓo at least partially assumes this religious role when she sets off with instructions to beg for both food and shelter.

when she collects firewood in the wilderness; a variety of wild beasts attends her wedding; her animal mother is also magically able to transform her into God's poor beggar, the Muslim guise in which she joins the royal household; the dates that she offers her husband represent the food man reaps from nature; supernaturally, they save his life by sprouting a tree he climbs to new life.

Laɓo's portrayal fuses both the religious elements of the *malam*'s daughter and the aspects of nature manifested in 'Yal Baturiya. And like her narrative counterparts, Laɓo relates these affiliations to women's culinary skills. However, she varies their pattern of producing new offspring. Instead, she orchestrates another life-giving miracle, the rebirth of her prince and husband.

She repeatedly helps nourish her household. Initially she is responsible for fetching the wood to feed the cooking fires. When Maman is still threatening to murder her, she twice signals her exquisite second self by preparing his favorite sweet, first when she attends his party and then when he returns to visit her. The second time he discovers his ring inside the cake, and their marriage is sealed. Later she sends him off to certain death with dates to nourish him and bring about his rebirth. Moreover, the servant who discovers the resurrected prince and returns with his ring has been sent to fetch a foodstuff, milk, from the palace herds.

Laɓo's image as a female nurturer is closely tied to her mediating role between nature and culture. She ventures into the bush of her birth to find firewood and brings it back to fuel the palace kitchen. The *nakiya* sweet she prepares for the prince functions to link her dual natural and human identities in his mind. The dates are nature's food. They are eaten raw but contain the seed which, grown into a tree, brings the hero back to his human realm. And milk too is a natural product which the Hausa normally ferment and add to other foods. Figuratively, Laɓo's nurturing and life-giving roles merge.

Laɓo's function as the source of life is somewhat altered from the image of the *malam*'s daughter or 'Yal Baturiya. Each of these earlier heroines equilibriated an imbalanced marriage by giving birth to her husband's child, despite the obstacles he established. Each son so perfectly resembled his father that he was forced to acknowledge the child's mother as his wife—a wife whose life-giving power outweighed his efforts to deny her marital and (for 'Yal Baturiya) royal status. In narrative terms, the sons express a man's dependency on his wife to reproduce his family line and sustain Hausa culture. The birth of the children also mediates the narrative conflicts, transforming marital conflict into domestic harmony.

The Laɓo tale portrays her prince's dependency in terms of his own person, although her life-giving power is still the source of her ability to achieve a balanced marriage. Rather than producing a new life, Laɓo resurrects the prince himself. His dependency and transformation mirror her own. Earlier he was the cultural figure who enticed her away from nature's space toward marriage and a permanent cultural identity. She in turn performs the same function for him. He is incompletely acculturated until he too merges with nature and the supernatural and returns a composite character. He is resurrected as nature's creature, and only through Laɓo's actions does he become a properly acculturated human ruler. They are balanced and interdependent, not only as woman and man but also as nature's and culture's respective offspring. Expressed in other stereotypes, this is not a tale of "civilized" man taming an "earth mother" or of "civilized" woman socializing a "man of the wilderness." It is both these dramas at once, and woman's source of power to assure this domestic and cosmic balance is her life-giving potential.

A final *tatsuniya* portrays a royal wife of natural and supernatural origins who explicitly challenges her royal mate's political power. This is the tale of the Squash Girl, who publicly kills her king when he claims that he is greater than she. In a graphic demonstration of her own life-giving power, she then resurrects him.

The version discussed here, performed by Baba Ladi in Mirria Niger, is a veritable political satire (Stephens 1981:447–76). Like storytellers everywhere, Hausa *tatsuniya* performers weave their narratives from familiar plot sequences. But Baba Ladi, an emir's daughter and wife, performed beneath the shadows of the palace for women and children of multiple royal connections and added a daring and delightful touch to her rendition of the tale. She named her characters after Mirria's own rulers sitting inside the royal quarters just yards away. Her villainesses were played by the royal wives. Satirizing these privileged women, she fictitiously beheaded them in retribution for their pompous attitudes. In doing so, she added a unique dimension of humor and immediacy to her narrative, a critique not only of men who underestimate the resources of their female counterparts but of all oppressive rulers.

Baba Ladi's story of the Squash Girl illustrates now familiar patterns: the heroine is associated in multiple ways with nature and the supernatural; she demonstrates her superior culinary abilities; she acts out her physiological and cultural ability to perpetuate life.

The Squash Girl, like Laɓo, is affiliated with nature and the supernatural when she is born. Her old and barren mother pleads to Allah to bless her with a child, even "if it's no more than a squash" (Stephens 1981:447). And so it is. Following this immaculate conception, she bears a squash.

The tie between nature and culture is further developed when the Squash Girl reveals her existence to her mother. The older woman goes out one day, leaving behind the cotton she had teased to make into thread. While she is away, her disguised daughter pops out of her squash and spins the thread. In this way the daughter signals her dual, natural and human identities by transforming a natural product into a cultural article. And she also suggests her supernatural powers by performing this minor miracle.

The heroine's link to the supernatural is reinforced when she is alone spinning one day and a Qur'anic student comes by to beg. He is the first human being to see her. Immediately he rushes to the emir to tell his ruler that he alone must marry this exquisite young woman. Off go the king's courtiers to claim her. Despite the old woman's protesting sobs, they cart her squash off to the royal compound.

The Squash Girl expresses her nurturing role as a cook at the same time she reveals her stunning human identity. While she is still a squash, the king demands that she and her future co-wives prepare food for a wedding feast. Her old woman attendant despairs, because a squash obviously cannot cook. Cooking food, however, like spinning thread, is work that women do transforming natural products into cultural forms; the girl inside the squash emerges a second time. She sends her attendant off for pots and condiments. All the raw ingredients are placed in the pans, and by morning there has been another miracle. Fragrant pots of porridge (*tuwo*), the Hausa staple dish, are ready for the ruler. Moreover, the other wives, who have mocked the squash bride, are unable to cook their food. This supernatural event, permitting an exemplary wife to cook while preventing her antagonistic co-wives from doing the same, recalls the tale of the *malam*'s daughter.

Once she has fulfilled her traditional nurturing role, the Squash Girl demonstrates the emir's dependence on her life-giving powers. Dazzling everyone in her human form, she promptly challenges her mate,

"Emir, am I greater than you are, or are you greater than I am?"
"No question, I'm greater than you are, Squash Girl."
"Tell all the drummers to stop" (Stephens 1981:469).

The emir does so, to no avail. But when his bride looks their way, they disappear. The couple repeats a similar challenge to dispose of the crowd, with the same result. The spectators ignore the husband's command to die, but the Squash Girl obliterates them all. Finally, she destroys the emir too, leaving him headless on the ground.

This hybrid heroine is explicitly more powerful than her royal spouse. The root of his dependency is ultimately not so much her power to destroy, but to create. She resurrects first the crowd and then her husband and ruler. He confesses, "You're greater than I am" (Stephens 1981:471). The crowd picks up the chant, her malicious co-wives are beheaded, and a new, stable royal household is established.

The Squash Girl plays an even stronger role in her marriage than Laɓo did. The former bestows and nurtures life, and she also destroys it. Metaphorically the dying crowd and emir interpret the implication of a woman's absence from the marriage bond; the implication is no less than the inability of Hausa culture to perpetuate itself.

Conclusion

Collectively, the four heroines act out the miracles of reproduction and resurrection in a specific context in these *tatsuniyoyi*. Their physical identities, the spatial movements they make, the actions they perform, and the resolution of their conflicts combine to depict Hausa wives as separate and often superior partners in their marriages. Their royal husbands may be more worldly and active in the community life outside the family compound, but their political power is limited to human dimensions and unable to extend itself beyond a single generation. In contrast, the heroines have close natural and supernatural affiliations by birth, originate from natural spaces, and even have alternative physical identities as natural products or creatures. They often nurture and create life itself as a result of these extracultural qualities. When their politically powerful mates attempt to obstruct their life-giving efforts, the women triumph.

These Hausa narratives present marriage as a microcosm of the wider universe. Wives and husbands represent distinct but interdependent domains. Women are natural and supernatural; men are political and cultural. Although the need to socialize natural and supernatural forces is portrayed in terms of maidens marrying princes, there is a clear argument that men are not therefore free to dominate completely. To the contrary, 'Yal Baturiya and the Squash Girl explicitly humiliate the men who advance such notions.

The narrative spouses are mutually dependent. Each helps to fully socialize the other—whether to change from a squash to a wife or to return from death in the bush to life in the palace. Each is vital to the partnership, just as natural and supernatural forces interact with cultural activities to produce the Hausa world. However, if one side of these forces sometimes needs to dominate, or at least to direct the other, it is more often the supernatural-natural domain that shapes the human culture rather than the reverse. Man transforms natural products, but without them he would quickly perish. Nature's need for man is not so clearly evident. Similarly, men shape women in important ways, but without women the culture they often seem to dominate would die. *Tatsuniya* performers have long communicated this message in image form.

13 *Janet Beik*

Women's Roles in the Contemporary Hausa Theater of Niger

Women are assuming an increasingly important place in Niger's Hausa theater, demonstrating their changing roles in contemporary society. In the past, Orthodox Islam discouraged public theatrical manifestations, although it has never entirely eliminated spirit possession cult (*bori*) ceremonies, the market comedies of the '*yan kama* (storyteller), or other dramatic and poetic performances. The Nigerien theater as it appears today—in planned, staged productions— was introduced by the French colonial administrators in the past half-century through Western schools and cultural associations. Since independence, Nigerien actors have created their own national theater, expanding the colonial models to incorporate local languages and a variety of cultural traditions in a unique form of improvised drama.[1] Whereas the colonial theater was largely the province of educated men, both in the schools and in the cultural centers for

My research in Niger (1980–81) was funded by a Fulbright-Hays Doctoral Dissertation Research Abroad Fellowship and facilitated by equipment from the Laboratories for Recorded Instruction, University of Wisconsin–Madison, and tapes from the Archives for Traditional Music, Indiana University. I am grateful to the Government of Niger, the Institut de Recherches en Sciences Humaines (IRSH) of the Université de Niamey, the Office de Radio-diffusion Télévision du Niger (ORTN), and the Centre d'Etudes Linguistique et Historique par Tradition Orale (CELHTO), Niamey, for their generous assistance.

1. For a fuller history of the Nigerien theater, see Beik 1987: ch. 1; Chaibou 1978–79; and Salifou 1973.

the elite, the current plays enjoy a wider popular base of village participation. As more women have entered public life and have become active in national development programs, the theater has begun to incorporate their presence and their concerns as well. A dynamic tool for national development, the Nigerien theater now both reflects and promotes the changing status of women in a society in transition.

The Hausa plays are nearly all comic, but they combine humor with an educational function. Troupes improvise the plays from a scenic outline which they arrange from a chosen theme. Although the dialogue is never written out, scenes may be intensively rehearsed to ensure that the intended message will be clear to the audience. The theme contains the essence of a play—a problem within the community, a moral dilemma, or an illustration of a new national program, such as the government's recent campaign for the Development Society.[2] Themes are topical, usually political in nature, and carefully selected to convey the troupe's views of current issues. The actors work through the sequence of scenes together, elaborating the theme, adding and refining the actions and characters that best portray their story. Most of the characters are stereotypes, quickly sketched, whose function is to further the action of the scene. Their titles, names, or costumes are often enough to identify them as a familiar comic or serious type whose actions the audience anticipates. Plays use multiple characters, and actors frequently take two or more roles in the same play. Rehearsals incorporate the improvised segments of actions, always with the troupe's members as a group discussing the play's development. It is a communal process, and although the director or a small group of actors may dominate the discussions, the troupe as a whole comes to a consensus before the play is set for performance. Each performance varies in detail, in the interaction with the audience, but the basis of the play is forged within the earlier rehearsals.[3] In this sort of process, women must become participants in order to be heard.

The plays are performed in Nigerien schools, at the village cultural centers (*Maisons des Jeunes*), and on national radio and television. As the most widely understood language in Niger, Hausa remains the primary language of this theater, though village performances may occur in the dominant local language or in a mixture of several languages. Students stage productions as entertainment for visiting dignitaries or sports teams and for national holidays. Village troupes under the aegis of the *samariyas* (from *samari*, "youths"), local self-help associations, perform for similar occasions and for the competition to attend the national festival.[4] Each of the nation's seven *départements*

2. For a more detailed treatment of the plays' themes, see Beik 1987.
3. For the troupes' rehearsal process, see Beik 1987: ch. 2, 1986.
4. The festival's official title is Le Festival National de la Jeunesse. It was held annually the week

chooses one troupe to perform its play at the national event. These plays have been televised since 1979, and they are frequently rebroadcast throughout the year. Other well-received plays have been added to the videotaped repertoire, a popular component of the evening programs. In addition to all of this theatrical activity, there are two radio troupes who perform weekly dramatic serials in Hausa; they too have attracted mass audiences. Strengthened by government support—its sponsorship of the *samariya* troupes, the national festival, and the media—this theater is nonetheless rooted in popular culture. It attracts performers and audiences from all social classes and ethnic groups. It has become a truly popular theater.

Despite this tremendous growth of the Nigerien theater in the past two decades, few women attend its live performances. Most married Muslim women are not seen at any public events. However, seclusion does not prevent them from being avid listeners of the radio serials and, for those whose families or friends can afford a television set, avid viewers of the broadcast plays. In recent years, the national festival competition has attained such prestige that many government officials now bring their wives and children to performances. If this trend continues, more women and their daughters will probably appear in the audiences for other theatrical performances as well.

Women also remain a minority within the troupes, but their numbers are growing. Most of the troupes I observed and interviewed had between thirty and forty active members, of whom five to ten were women. There are no professional troupes yet in Niger; all actors have other occupations within their communities. Yet the primary occupation for most Hausa women—that of wife and mother—usually precludes acting, because of prevailing Muslim sanctions. Therefore, most of the women involved in the theater are either unmarried girls or women "who live alone" (*masu zaman kansu,* referring to divorcées or prostitutes). These women generally leave the theater when they marry, and the troupes now must actively recruit new actresses on a regular basis.

Opinions among the troupes' directors, all men, differ over choosing their actresses. Abdoullahi Bagoudou, the theater director of Gaya, prefers to work only with young girls, who are not as strong-willed as independent women and who adapt better to the group's rehearsals.[5] The Matameye troupe's leaders, on the contrary, stated that there were too many problems working with unmarried girls, especially chaperoning them when the troupe traveled; their troupe prefers women who are independent of families.[6] Two of the leaders of Zinder's Troupe Amadou ꞌDan Bassa explained that women were only beginning to

of April 15 from 1976 until 1982, when it became a biennial event. The festival includes sports competitions, art exhibits, and the like, in addition to theatrical, dance, and musical performances by the best troupes from each region.

5. Interview with Abdoullahi Bagoudou, Gaya, Niger, December 10, 1980.

6. Interview with members of the Samariya of Matameye, Niger, January 17, 1981.

understand the work of the theater; they had difficulty separating their daily lives from rehearsals, and they often quarrelled with the men.[7] These comments suggest the degree to which the theater presents an unusual social context for Hausa communities. In bringing men and women together to work on a project for an extended period of time, rehearsals break the traditional pattern separating men's and women's spheres of activity. Moreover, as a public event, the theater is much closer to the men's customary world—the marketplace, political meetings, public debate. The women who choose to act are venturing farther from their traditional roles in the home. One of the results of this leap is the instability of women remaining with the troupes. Another is *kunya*.

In Hausa, *kunya* carries the meaning of shame as well as propriety, modesty, and appropriate conduct. Feelings of shame, fear, and inhibitions in acting before an audience affect men as well as women, but less frequently. In many of the rehearsals I observed, significant attention and time were directed toward training actresses to speak up, to hold their heads up without hiding their faces in their headscarves, a modest gesture common to Hausa women outside their homes.[8] In the Maïné Soroa Troupe's 1981 production of *Alhaji Shagali* (Alhaji Pleasure-Seeking), a key scene portrayed Shagali visiting a prostitute, Gimbiya. The role of Gimbiya was played by a teen-aged actress, Ladi Garba. In an interview after the troupe's performance at the national festival, Mahamadou Lido, a leader of the troupe, said that they had tried eleven young girls (*budurwa*) in the role, but none of the others could play it to the group's satisfaction. He attributed this to fear (*ɗaurin kai*) and shame. Even with only the members of the troupe present, the girls were ashamed to play the scene.[9] Ladi Garba said that she too had been afraid of acting the role at first, but that she cast her fear aside (*na hidda shi*): "If one feels *kunya*, one cannot work in the theater."[10] She felt *kunya* to be the greatest problem for a new actor, man or woman, playing a role in front of people, but that one becomes accustomed to it. She said that she would rather play a respectable wife than a role like Gimbiya but denied that she felt any shame in her festival performance.[11] Nor was any apparent to me; her lack of inhibition on the stage kept the audience in fits of boisterous laughter throughout the scene.[12]

The number and variety of roles women play has been increasing as more women join the troupes. Zinder's Troupe Amadou 'Dan Bassa, the leading

7. Interview with Abdou Louché and Yazi Dogo, Zinder, Niger, April 22, 1981.

8. Rehearsal notes, Zinder, Niger, March, April, August, September 1981.

9. Interview with Mahamadou Lido, Maïné Soroa, Niger, April 18, 1981.

10. Interview with Ladi Garba, Maïné Soroa, Niger, April 18, 1981. Her comment is expressed in the local Hausa dialect; standard (i.e., Kano) Hausa would render it as *na fidda shi*.

11. Ladi Garba, April 18, 1981.

12. *Alhaji Shagali*, by the Troupe Théâtrale de Maïné Soroa, performed at the national festival in Diffa, Niger, April 12, 1981.

Hausa troupe in the country, had only three women acting with them in the late 1970s. By 1981 there were seven.[13] Their most famous play, *Gado Karhin Alla* (Inheritance, Strength from God), was created in the early 1970s, and its published version, a transcription of a 1973 performance, is still the only Nigerien Hausa play to see print.[14] No women appear in that version. In 1979, when the troupe performed the play for television, women appeared in three minor roles.

The play concerns the election of a new village chief (*sarki*) from among a series of candidates, two of whom try to rig the election by bribery and magic. The most honest of the heirs is chosen; he then demonstrates true wisdom by reconciling his jealous brothers to his rule. In the 1979 filmed performance, Jekahwadiya (an attendant) ministers to the dying *sarki* in the first scene, and she begins to wail as he breathes his last. In the third scene, a crippled woman appears among the beggars who are rudely sent away by Mushe (*Monsieur*), the Western-educated prince, as he schemes to sell the grain provided by the government for famine relief. Later in the same scene, Alhajiya, Mushe's wealthy, well-dressed mistress, comes to visit him and he arranges to send her several sacks of grain as a gift.[15] These three women's roles were included in the re-creation of the play that I saw performed in Zinder in 1981.[16] They had become integral parts of the play, but they remained peripheral to the central story.

In 1980 the Troupe Amadou 'Dan Bassa won first place in the national competition with *Ba Ga Irinta Ba* (There's Nothing Like It).[17] In this play, the three women's roles are more significant than those of *Gado Karhin Alla*, but still minor compared to the roles played by men. *Ba Ga Irinta Ba* focuses on problems within the school system—the delinquency of students, drunken and negligent teachers, inefficient administrators, public prejudices about education, and the like. The play begins in the home of Mamman Arrivé (Mamman Who Has Arrived), a rich but ignorant and boastful merchant, whose son Sanussi runs home crying that his teacher has beaten him. Mamman immediately sets out to berate Madame, Sanussi's teacher, and creates a scene at the primary school as he fights with all the teachers and refuses to believe that his son, a spoiled brat, has not come to class for over a week (scene 2). Both Madame and Gimbiya, Mamman's wife, are central to this plot, but neither character dominates her scene. In the first, Mamman and his male friend discuss their business affairs and then move to his son's crisis, calling on Gimbiya to bring

13. Abdou Louché, April 22, 1981.

14. *Gaadoo Karhin Allaa (Waasan Kwaykoyoo na Zinder a 1973)*, transcribed by Abuubakar Mahamman (Niamey: CELHTO, 1977).

15. *Gado Karhin Alla*, by the Troupe Amadou 'Dan Bassa of Zinder, videotaped by ORTN (Niamey, 1979).

16. *Gado Karhin Alla*, performance by the Troupe Amadou 'Dan Bassa, Zinder, Niger, September 13, 1981.

17. *Ba Ga Irinta Ba*, by the Troupe Amadou 'Dan Bassa of Zinder, performed at the national festival in Niamey, Niger, April 1980.

them food early in the scene and sending her off when she becomes angry over her son's humiliation. Gimbiya taunts Mamman into action, but she must remain at home. In the second scene, at the primary school, a group of teachers and the principal, all men, are correcting exams when Mamman storms in. They send for Madame to tell her version of the beating, but it is the men who defend her against Mamman's verbal threats and plan what further action they should take.

The next few scenes carry the crisis through the governmental hierarchy, as the principal complains to the school inspector, who telephones the mayor (scene 3). The mayor calls for a town meeting to discuss the issues that have gathered in the wake of Mamman's outburst; he is not the first parent who has publicly condemned the teachers, and some have more justifiable complaints. The formal town discussion (scene 4) includes Madame, but she says very little. The representative parents and officials are all men, as they typically would be in a village assembly in real life. In the following scene, a gathering of Mamman's neighbors and colleagues, the only woman to appear is a young vendor who sells some meat to the men. Again, as in daily Hausa life, the women remain at home while such public affairs are discussed in the marketplace. Both groups of men—the official and the unofficial—find Mamman at fault, and his friends warn him that he must apologize to Madame and the school administrators (scene 5).

In the final scene of the play, Mamman's sister Jatu and Gimbiya briefly talk about the family's reaction to the scandal (scene 8). This interchange shows the women's parallel to the meeting of the men in the market; it takes place in the home, within the circle of women relatives and friends who regularly visit one another. On his return home, Mamman greets his sister, but he discusses the family's reaction not with her but with his elder brother, who arrives after Jatu leaves. In this series of actions, the play achieves verisimilitude to the patterns of Hausa social life. Mamman reconciles his family crisis in the public sphere, among men, and in the domestic sphere with his brother, rather than with his wife or sister. The women's equivalent debate takes place among themselves, and in this theatrical portrayal, it is secondary. Yet plays like *Ba Ga Irinta Ba* have begun to explore the domestic side of public issues, and others have brought these themes into greater prominence.

A year after *Ba Ga Irinta Ba*, with its two household scenes and token female teacher, the same troupe created a play with four of seven scenes occurring inside people's homes and with eight women's roles. The troupe's confidence in the strength of its actresses is evident in the key roles they were given in *Talala Mai Kaman Sake* (A Long Tethering Rope Is Like Freedom).[18] This play did not fare as well in the national competition as its predecessor, receiving only third

---

18. *Talala Mai Kaman Sake*, by the Troupe Amadou 'Dan Bassa of Zinder, performed at the national festival in Diffa, Niger, April 8, 1981.

place. Its themes are not as forthrightly nationalistic as either *Ba Ga Irinta Ba* or the plays given first and second honors in 1981, both of which portrayed corrupt entrepreneurs taking on government construction projects. Nevertheless, I found *Talala Mai Kaman Sake* to be a richer work, having deeper social themes in the conflict between the Islamic Hausa values of family responsibility and a Western-derived model of materialistic individualism.

Talala Mai Kaman Sake depicts the personal corruption of Talala after his brother's death. The community entrusts the inheritance to Talala to administer in caring for his brother's family, two widows and their children. This story is framed by formal scenes of public ceremonies; it opens with the funeral prayers and the decision of the elders to have Talala take charge of the estate, and it closes with a courtroom scene in which a judge condemns Talala to repay everything he has usurped from the widows and children. In the four scenes between these official decrees, the action unfolds in people's homes, with strong roles for the female characters. Talala has two wives, two girlfriends, a niece, and two sisters-in-law, all of whom raise their voices against his betrayal. The younger wife leaves him to return to her parents because, she asserts, he is rarely at home and he continually fights with her (scene 3). Talala's first wife more stoically watches the progression of his self-aggrandizement, as he sells off his brother's herds of cattle to build himself a new house and to make the pilgrimage to Mecca. But she too protests when he refuses to help his married niece after she has been robbed (scene 5).

Talala builds his new house in Western style—with electric lights, elegant fixtures, even a bathtub (scene 3). When he returns from Mecca and the house is completed, he and his friend plan to use it as a retreat in which to entertain young women (scene 4). Their talk is interrupted by El Giya, Talala's former mistress, who rails against his neglect of her ever since his newfound wealth has given him airs. The voluptuous young woman Talala sends for through a pimp also refuses to cooperate with his plans; she insists that he come and court her properly at her father's house. Finally, curtailing these amorous adventures, news arrives that Talala must return to his old house to see his niece Tsaibatu (scene 4).

Tsaibatu asks Talala for a loan from her share of the inheritance because her husband's house has been robbed. He adamantly refuses to give it to her (scene 5). The following scene portrays the despair of the widows, who feel they must sell their dowry items to pay for food, a last resort after months of Talala's neglect. A friend of their late husband, who lives in another town and has not visited since the funeral, hears of their plight and Tsaibatu's story of the loan. He advises them to take the case to the judge (scene 6). In the final scene, Tsaibatu and her mothers present their complaint in court and Talala receives his punishment (scene 7).

It is the women, upholding the values of the family and mutual responsibility, who condemn Talala. The court's formal sentence merely concludes the judgment that the action of the play has already borne out. Instead of emphasizing the public aspect of Talala's actions, as did *Ba Ga Irinta Ba* for Mamman Arrivé's arrogance, *Talala Mai Kaman Sake* focuses on the domestic side of Talala's wayward course: the neglect, abuse, and injustice suffered by the women of the extended family. In this play, the Troupe Amadou 'Dan Bassa has expanded its range of themes and perspectives by giving critical roles to its talented actresses.

A similar theme of traditional values in opposition to Westernization was developed by the Radio Club Troupe of Zinder in its 1981 production of *Darajar Kasa Al'adarta* (The Value of a Country Is in Its Customs).[19] The conflict of this play takes place within one family, and the troupe continually juxtaposes the different worlds of the women and the men, the young and the old, the modern and the traditional, the public and the private, as the story evolves. In the rehearsals I observed while the troupe was developing the play, the women played a very active role, strongly voicing their opinions in discussions and providing ideas for changes in the action.[20] The play reflects their contributions in its array of realistic female characters.

The structural basis for *Darajar Kasa Al'adarta* is the well-known tale of the good sister and the bad sister, each of whom embarks on the same series of adventures but reacts in different ways: the good sister is kind, helps the characters and creatures that she meets, and receives a reward (a husband, riches, etc.); her greedy sister hurries along, ignoring or scorning those she meets, and receives her due reward (a beating, disease, etc.).[21] The Radio Club Troupe adapted this familiar story to its current theme of the attraction of Nigerien youth to Western disco music, drugs, and alcohol, and the resulting corrosion of values.

The play follows the paths of the two daughters of a pious man, Alhaji Na Alla (Alhaji of God). In the opening scene, Na Alla calls his wives, Hajiya Pantaika and Hajiya Karama, and announces that they are not to permit their daughters to go about in the town any longer; he intends to find suitable husbands for them now that they are of age, and they must stay at home. He tells his wives to call their daughters, Taxi and Cha-cha-cha, and then repeats his edict to them. The women are all sent inside as Na Alla entertains two male friends, pondering the problem of controlling children in today's world. However, after the men leave, the women reemerge to discuss their views of the new order.

19. *Darajar Kasa Al'adarta*, performance by the Radio Club Troupe of Zinder, Niger, June 21, 1981.

20. Rehearsal notes, Zinder, Niger, June 1981.

21. For Nigerien Hausa examples of the good sister–bad sister narrative, see Stephens 1981, performances 605 and 606, pp. 1043–1107.

Pantaika disagrees with her husband, but Karama believes they must obey him. A young *fonctionnaire* visits to invite the girls to his house for a disco party that evening. When Pantaika learns that he works at the bank and has a lot of money, she urges her daughter Taxi to go to the party, while Karama forbids Cha-cha-cha to attend (scene 1). Unlike *Ba Ga Irinta Ba*, where Mamman Arrivé's wife and sister briefly comment on the scandal he has created, *Darajar Kasa Al'adarta* gives predominance to the women's views. Their reactions, rather than Na Alla's pronouncement, are the focus of the dialogue and provide impetus to the plot.

The second scene repeats and expands the arguments of the first, but in the home of a neighbor. Gagarau, one of Na Alla's friends, rebukes his wife for sending their daughter Rariya on an errand in town, claiming that she always returns with a pack of men, like dogs, following her. A young suitor does indeed appear to see Rariya, and Gagarau chases him out of his house. Later in the scene, when Taxi arrives to fetch Rariya for the party, her mother forbids her to go, but Rariya defies both her parents and leaves with Taxi (scene 2). This repetition of the conflict between the fathers and their daughters underscores the theme of the play. The ensuing scene is a comic portrayal of the parents' worst fears—an orgy with loud music, alcohol, drugs, and surreptitious sexual encounters in the back room. The police come to investigate the noise and arrest all the young people present (scene 3).

Meanwhile, Na Alla is arranging marriages for both his daughters with the sons of prominent men in the community. The police interrupt these negotiations to inform him that his daughter is in jail (scene 4). Na Alla and the other fathers go to the police station and are shocked to see their daughters wearing trousers and their sons sporting long-haired wigs (scene 5). An even greater shock than her attire is the news that Taxi is pregnant. After this public humiliation, Na Alla returns home and calls Pantaika and Taxi. He repudiates both of them: Taxi is no longer his daughter, Pantaika no longer his wife because he holds her responsible for Taxi's behavior. He then announces the divorce to Karama and tells her to prepare Cha-cha-cha for her wedding (scene 6). Not only does the good daughter receive the traditional reward, a husband, but Na Alla also remarries in the festive wedding scene (scene 7). In direct contrast, Pantaika takes Taxi to visit a religious scholar (*malam*) to see if he can provide her with "medicine" for an abortion. Instead, the *malam* arranges for the two women to be arrested by the police, a final repetition of the fate of the errant sister (scene 8).

Unlike many of the plays, *Darajar Kasa Al'adarta* has no single central character, and the women share the comic roles. Where Mamman Arrivé and Talala dominate the plots of their respective plays and become the central comic figures, Alhaji Na Alla remains a flat portrait of conventional morality. It is Pantaika, as played by Maryama (she uses no surname), who develops a comic rapport with the audience. An experienced actress, Maryama engages audiences with her sly wit and quick, uninhibited reactions to new twists of the plot. Karama may be cowed by her husband's commands, but Pantaika argues back. When she is cast out of her husband's house, Pantaika tries to find a solution to her daughter's dilemma. Pantaika and Taxi find defeat in the end; their immorality will be punished. Nonetheless, their outrageous actions provide the comic tension that sustains the plot and the audience's interest throughout the play.

The variety of portrayals within this play—the other wives, the other daughters, the young men, the neighbors, the *malam*—assures that Pantaika and Taxi do not become falsely stereotyped as women representing the trend toward loose, foreign morality, in contrast to the men who uphold Islamic values. Nor does Taxi become isolated as youth gone astray, since her mother supports her actions. The intricacy of the plot's parallel scenes suggests the complexity of the real social issues that the play explores. Through the dedicated participation of the troupe's actresses in rehearsal, the female characters present equal, active, and diverse roles in that exploration.

Of the plays I observed, very few portrayed women with formal education or occupations outside the home. Like the teacher in *Ba Ga Irinta Ba*, the few female characters in nontraditional roles had minor parts to play. Yet their presence signals a changing awareness of women's occupations within society. The play that won the national competition in 1981, *'Dan Kwangila* (The Entrepreneur), included female secretaries in two scenes, one at the bank and the other at the office of city planning (scenes 4 and 5). A third educated woman in this play is the wife of the corrupt commissioner who grants the government contract to 'Dan Kwangila. She speaks French and has a job, but she listens to her husband chastize her for being more interested in her coiffure than in joining the local organization which is working to better women's status (scene 2). In this brief dialogue, the troupe suggests a consciousness of women in the workplace through ironically reversing the couple's views of the working women's association.[22]

The only Nigerien play I found that focused on women's positions outside of the home was developed by the secondary students of Tchin ,Tabaraden. These students performed *Madame Sidikou* on the eve of Niger's Republic Day, December 17, 1980.[23] They dedicated the play to the holiday for Nigerien independence as a demonstration of the role that women are to play in the new society. The central character, Madame Sidikou, is the first woman to head a

22. *'Dan Kwangila*, by the Troupe Théâtrale de Maradi, performed for the national festival in Diffa, Niger, April 9, 1981.
23. *Madame Sidikou*, by the CEG Troupe, Tchin Tabaraden, performed for Niger Republic Day, December 17, 1980.

customs post in Niger (*chef de douanes*). To my knowledge, no woman had yet taken such a position at that time; Madame Sidikou was entirely a fictional creation.

The play opens at Madame's office on her first day at work. She immediately establishes a reform of the typically corrupt practices of the customs officials: there is to be no drinking on the job, and no one will accept bribes. Two traders, who are accustomed to paying bribes rather than duty, commiserate with Madame's subordinates, who may no longer consume the liquor they confiscate. In the second scene, Madame returns home at noon, changes her uniform for a housedress, fixes lunch for her two children, helps them with their schoolwork, and then attends to her husband when he arrives. Not until the third scene does any trace of conflict stir this idyllic balance between home and career, and then it is caused not by Madame but by Monsieur Sidikou.

Monsieur, a doctor, receives a series of patients at his clinic. When one of the spurned traders tries to discuss his wife's incorruptibility with him, Monsieur abruptly dismisses him. But he is much more cordial to a young woman and asks for her address in order to meet her after work for a personal house call (scene 3). Learning of her husband's affairs, Madame Sidikou fights with him and leaves for her parents' home (scene 4), a significant step for a Hausa woman to take toward ending her marriage. This rift is reversed, however, in the following scenes as the young woman jilts Monsieur for the corrupt trader, and Madame's mother persuades her to go home and give her husband a second chance (scenes 5 and 6). Madame returns to the house just as Monsieur is leaving to apologize to her (scene 7). The play concludes with a meeting of the rich men of the community discussing the changes wrought by a woman official (scene 8) and then a press conference in which Madame Sidikou answers reporters' questions on the dual role of women in the new society as worker and wife (scene 9). *Madame Sidikou* represents a youthful, optimistic vision of women as equal, productive participants in the modern sector of Nigerien life.

Madame Sidikou is not as polished a piece as the entries for the national festival or the productions of more experienced troupes. The students, under the guidance of a zealous director (the principal of the school), overemphasized their didactic theme. Yet the play demonstrates the range of material such improvised drama can accommodate. Any current topic of interest to a group of people can become the theme of a play. As more women become involved in the educational system, in national affairs, and in the theater itself, the plays will create new and richer characters for them. The appearance of *Madame Sidikou* portends exciting roles and themes to come.

In discussing the purpose of the theater for women, the young actress in Maïné Soroa, Ladi Garba, declared that it is to raise their consciousness (*jawon hankali*) "If a role does not touch women's affairs, they will not learn anything from it." [24] If the theater is to speak to women of the nation, it must reflect their world, what they know and do. The theater is seen by Nigeriens in all walks of life—government officials, actors, teachers, students, farmers, fathers, mothers, children—to have an educational function within the society as well as to entertain. With talented actresses joining and participating in the troupes and their creative process, women's affairs and their multiple roles in society will find full expression in the Hausa plays.

24. Ladi Garba, April 18, 1981.

14 *Ayesha M. Imam*

Ideology, the Mass Media, and Women: A Study from Radio Kaduna, Nigeria

Ideology has been defined as "a 'representation' of the imaginary relationship of individuals to their real conditions of existence" (Althusser 1977:152). In other words, ideologies are the ideas and beliefs through which people make sense of and relate to the world. Ideologies are not simply imaginary, however; they do not exist only in people's heads. They are material in at least two senses: first, ideologies arise from material conditions of existence (Marx 1977), and second, they are actualized in practices and have definite effects (Althusser 1977). It should be noted, however, that although ideology is conditioned by the material base it cannot simply be read off from an examination of the economic base in a mechanical way. The relationship is complex, and there is a point at which ideologies are relatively autonomous and work according to their own rules (Althusser 1977; Hall 1977b).

Although other (oppositional) ideologies may exist, the dominant ideology in any social formation is that of the dominant group—that group which not only has the means (for example, education and leisure) to formulate ideas, but also the means to ensure dissemination of those ideas (e.g., through patronage of suitable artists or mass media ownership and control; Marx 1965). Such ideologies work to maintain existing relations of domination and subordination by persuading subordinate groups to believe in and accept the status quo (Gramsci 1978). That is to say, dominant ideologies do not merely reflect existing conditions, but represent the interests of the dominant group and work to secure its continued existence. Hausa society, for example, is a male-dominated society, but the ideology that women are dependent wives and mothers can be contrasted with empirical analyses which show that women work extremely hard for a measure of economic independence and may contribute substantially, if not totally, to their own and their children's maintenance (Simmons 1976; Matlon 1979; Watts 1983). But the dominance of this ideology means that both women and men see women chiefly in terms of their domestic roles (Imam and Pittin 1984; Imam 1988). As a consequence, women's roles are neglected in development planning and policies (Knowles 1985; WIN 1985c; Jackson 1985), which militates against the possibility that women can develop as active and autonomous agents in social production instead of remaining socially and economically subordinate to men.

In contemporary Nigeria the communications media act as the major vehicle for dissemination of ideology (Ibrahim 1983). They are certainly more important than formal Western education for Hausa women, most of whom do not finish primary school, if they start at all (WIN 1985c; Imam 1988). It might also be argued that religious ideologies reach more people via the mass media (not only through coverage of actual prayers, services, and sermons but also through numerous articles in the print media and question-and-answer programs on radio and television) than through physical attendance at mosque or church. This is particularly true for women who are in total or partial seclusion (Imam 1985).

There has been considerable debate as to whether the media only reflect existing norms in society or whether they represent preponderantly dominant interests and play a conservative role. Numerous studies have demonstrated, however, that the mass media are owned and controlled by ruling classes (Murdock and Golding 1977; Ibrahim 1983) and that they represent the ideological interests of these classes (Hall 1977b; Mattelart and Siegelaub 1979; Ibrahim 1983). Thus it can be concluded that the mass media contribute to the acceptance of the status quo. They do so by providing a framework bounded by the dominant ideology with which to make sense of the world, and through which other ways of understanding are ignored, trivialized, or condemned (Hall 1977a; Imam 1980, 1985). It has frequently been pointed out that the mass media worldwide underrepresent, trivialize, and condemn women and issues important to women's interests (Cielemans and Fauconnier 1979; Gallagher 1979). Such a situation has been noted in Nigeria (WIN 1985c: ch. 6). Akpan's (1979) case study of the *Daily Times* and *New Nigerian* newspapers notes that women are grossly underrepresented in news stories, and Iwerierbor's (1981) analysis of the image of women in Nigerian films shows that only when women portray villains are they given active roles. Even then they are subordinate to male villains. Similarly, Ogundipe-Leslie's (1984) consideration of Nigerian literature shows that male writers marginalize women in their work.

The vast majority of the studies of women and the Nigerian mass media relate to newspapers, books, magazines, and television. Yet most Nigerian (including Hausa) women live in rural areas and are both illiterate and poor: they cannot read print media, nor could they afford television sets even if electricity were supplied to their villages. Radio, as a relatively cheap medium requiring neither literacy nor electricity, is thus very important. Another factor to be noted, given the average working day of ten to sixteen hours for rural women in Africa (UNECA 1972), is that listening to the radio, unlike reading or even watching television, allows women to engage in other activities at the same time. Finally, many radio stations broadcast predominantly in indigenous languages so that it is not necessary to understand English. This is not the case with most print media and the majority of television programs. Radio is therefore the most widespread and important medium of mass communication for the majority of Nigerian women.

This essay analyzes the content of three programs broadcast in Hausa by the Federal Radio Corporation of Nigeria's substation in Kaduna. Each episode of each program is broadcast twice a week. The programs analyzed were taped over a period of seven weeks from January 19 to March 9, 1985. (It might also be noted here that since what is now Radio Kaduna was set up in 1962 as Radio-Television Kaduna to cover the whole of northern Nigeria, its audience is far wider than Kaduna State alone—listeners live not only in adjacent Kano State but as far away as Gongola State.) The programs are *Uwargida Barka da Warhaka* (Good Day to the Wife [literally, "mother of the house"], aimed at women), *Maigidanta Barka da Rana* (Good Day to Her Husband, aimed at men), and *Don Matasa* (About Youth), which deals with youth. All three programs follow the same format: a topic is raised by a listener's letter and commented on by a studio panel, the members of which are placed in the position of authorities and experts. This "expert" position is further reinforced by the Hausa term of respectful address, *malam,* which also connotes teacher, although the panelists were not teachers or sociologists or other "accredited experts." The weight of the panelists' advice is strengthened by the rarity of disagreement on an issue. Thus, in effect, each piece of advice is repeated in four or five different ways—a very effective teaching method.

Twenty-nine topics were raised in all, some in two different programs and some several times in different episodes of the same program. (Topics raised in each program are listed in the appendix.) Of these, some 22 topics dealt with women or male-female relations. They are broken down in table 14.1 by theme and program (some topics dealt with more than one theme).

It is clear from Table 14.1 that the vast majority of themes dealt with con-

Table 14.1. Themes in the Topics Relating to Women and Male/Female Relations by Program

Themes	Program			
	Uwargida	Don Matasa	Maigidanta	Total
Control of wives				
Economic dependence	2	—	4	6
Restriction of movement	1	—	3	4
Injunctions to submissiveness				
and patience	2	—	3	5
Husband is judge in home	—	—	4	4
Total	5	0	14	19
Control of daughters				
Choice of husband by girls	1	1	3	5
Relationship of father and suitor	—	—	3	3
Early marriage	—	—	2	2
Total	1	1	8	10
Maltreatment of women				
Beating and harsh treatment	2	—	—	2
Withholding of maintenance	1	—	2	3
Male extramarital relationships	—	—	3	3
Total	3	0	5	8
Negative characteristics of women				
Greed	1	1	2	4
Fickleness	1	1	—	2
Sulkiness	—	—	3	3
Idle strolling (*yawo*)	1	2	3	6
Total	3	4	8	15
Learning for women				
Pro	1	—	—	1
Con	—	2	2	4
Total	1	2	2	5

trolling females as wives (19) or daughters (10), and condemning the negative characteristics of women (15). These ideological themes appeared far more often (44 times) than those deploring the maltreatment of women and calling for improvement (8). Even granted that all the programs focus on problems the predominantly negative treatment of women can be contrasted unfavorably (see table 14.2) with the generally positive images of men (29) and the infrequency of negative male images (14).

The discussions about negative characteristics in men were confined to those men who exhibited them (e.g., the irresponsibility of men who do not provide

Table 14.2. Themes Relating to the Characteristics of Men by Program

Themes	Uwargida	Don Matasa	Maigidanta	Total
		Program		
Positive roles/characteristics				
Family provider	2	—	6	8
Authority figure	1	3	9	13
Fairness	—	—	8	8
Total	3	3	23	29
Negative roles/characteristics				
Harshness and injustice	2	—	—	2
Promiscuity	—	—	3	3
Irresponsibility	1	—	2	3
Partiality/favoritism	1	—	2	3
Greed	—	—	3	3
Total	4	0	10	14

for their families or the harshness of men who beat their wives too much [sic]). They were not generalized into tendencies of all men, as was the case of the discussions on women's negative characteristics, which included statements, for example, on the general tendency in women to sulk or to be greedy. In addition, in none of the programs analyzed was there any praise for women or their qualities. Even the discussions about women's submissiveness were cast solely in terms of injunctions and one episode of *Maigidanta* likened women to lizards who will escape if the wall of male authority is breached ("*in bango ya saka ƙadangare zai samu wurin fita*").

Themes dealing with male control of females were by far the most preponderant. Women were seen as under male control by definition ("*mace tana karkashinka,*" in *Maigidanta*). Women were not to be allowed to leave the compound, even to collect firewood or locust bean pods or to trade in the market. Men are seen as the judge and arbiter in all family matters. For instance, fathers (but not mothers) were frequently called upon to exercise maturity and discretion in deciding upon the choice of a husband for their daughter. Even where the rectification of bad situations was discussed, the issue of where control lay was clear. Men were pleaded with, in terms of their own self-interest, to correct their behavior. For example, men who do not provide maintenance should not expect to go home and get a meal. Women, however, were to be stopped from behavior about which men complained, such as moving about in public outside the compound.

The importance of men as authorities was also implicitly ratified in the structure of program presentation. Although *Uwargida* is aimed at women there were always one or more men among the panelists; *Maigidanta*, which is aimed at men, never had a single female panelist; *Don Matasa*, aimed at both parents and youth, never had more than one woman out of four or five panelists. Thus men advise women but women do not advise men, and male advice on youth is given three or four times as much weight as women's.

In only two cases was the issue of women's decision making raised, but even then only in the context of ultimate male authority. In the first case, mothers were blamed for not allowing their daughters to go to school, even though fathers were willing (*Uwargida*). (The reverse situation was not raised in any of the programs in the sample.) In the second case, girls were to have some freedom in the choice of their husbands, but the father (not the mother), because of his greater wisdom, was to approve (or disallow) the daughter's choice. This topic, incidentally, was also the only area in which there was disagreement among panelists. In discussing girls who change their minds about suitors, the single woman panelist in *Don Matasa* argued that this might be justified when the suitor's behavior changed for the worse after acceptance (i.e., once he was sure of her). The other panelists (all male) simply condemned such behavior, and one of them disagreed strongly with the woman panelist, saying that if a girl has been given an element of choice she has no right to change her mind.

That women might be able to make decisions on issues affecting their lives was thus hedged with restrictions, as in the cases above, but more frequently it was trivialized or ignored altogether. The possibility that women could decide for themselves to pursue learning and develop their minds was also trivialized, being seen merely as an excuse to leave the compound. The possibility that women might have the right to decide not to live within polygynous marriages, even within Islamic law (Kabir 1985; Imam 1986), was not raised at all; rather, women were urged to behave with patience and forbearance toward co-wives. In fact, in *Maigidanta* the issue was presented as if men's sole aim in taking another wife was to benefit the existing wife or wives with companionship—why then should she/they be upset? Finally, the right of women to pursue independent trades for income was ignored, although numerous studies testify that it is an accepted feature of Hausa life (Bashir 1972; Simmons 1976; Pittin 1979a).

The issue of females' pursuit of learning was dealt with several times. Only in the case from *Uwargida* described above was it given definite encouragement. Girls' schooling was linked unfavorably with indecent dressing in *Don Matasa* and with immoral male-female relationships in *Maigidanta*: in the latter, intergender platonic and innocent friendships, even among school children, were considered unacceptable and impossible. The desire of married women to be educated was specifically treated as an excuse for *yawo* (idle strolling). Since most Hausa women are married by the time they reach fourteen years of age, the possibility of education is severely limited. Listening to the programs in this sample, a man who has refused to allow his wife or daughter access to education might well congratulate himself on his wisdom.

Conclusion

In general, all three programs treated women's roles and contributions negatively. The work women do was seen as being of little value: for instance, it was suggested that mothers should allow daughters to go to school because the work the daughters would otherwise do in helping their mothers, work such as growing peppers or grinding beans, was not very important. Women's attempts at gaining a measure of economic autonomy through such means as petty trading was castigated, in *Maigidanta* particularly, as greedy attempts to gain "pin-money" (H. *kudin-kashewa*) or as selfish, because hawking by young girls, whom secluded women must employ, exposes the girls to sexual advances from men while they sell their wares. (The recently passed Kano State Petty Trading Control (Amendment) Edict of 1988 to "protect young female children . . . from moral danger and exploitation" "protects" them by having the police arrest the girls, while ignoring the men who make sexual advances to or otherwise harrass them.) At the same time, however, women's expectations of anything more than basic maintenance from their husbands (e.g., soap, jewelry, or clothes) was treated rather ambivalently. A male panelist on *Uwargida* stated, for instance, that some husbands did provide these items but that wives did not use them. It was agreed in one episode of *Maigidanta* that it is helpful for a wife to be able to aid her husband with a loan of maintenance money. Nonetheless, the discussions overall suggest that independent cash generation for women is not viewed favorably.

So far this analysis has considered all three programs together. There are, however, differences in emphasis among them. In *Uwargida* the negative and positive themes on men are equally balanced (three each), but in the other two programs positive themes on men are mentioned more often (no negative themes in *Don Matasa* at all and a rough ratio of 5:2 in *Maigidanta*). In *Uwargida* the negative characteristics and bad treatment of women are mentioned the same number of times; in the other programs the themes of women's bad character are presented more often than maltreatment of women—4:0 in *Don Matasa* and 8:5 in *Maigidanta*. As has already been mentioned, none of the programs put forward any positive images or roles for women.

Overall then, all three programs put forward predominantly negative images of women and themes sanctioning the control and subordination of women. The programs aimed at women did so less often than those aimed at men or at both women and men. (It should be remembered that in the latter programs a woman panelist was either not present at all or greatly outnumbered by men.) Since all three programs explicitly advise people on how to behave, the

conclusion must be drawn that these radio programs play a significant and conservative role in persuading women to acquiesce to men, and men to continue
strengthening their control over and subordination of women. This study therefore confirms other, similar analyses, both worldwide and in Nigeria, which
demonstrate that the mass media present ideological themes that are narrow,
unrealistic, and demeaning to women. It must be remembered, however, that
the media do not do this in a vacuum. They represent the ideologies of dominant groups. Thus any attempt at changing this pattern of media treatment can
be fully effective only in the context of fundamental changes in the economic,
political, and cultural relations that operate to subordinate and marginalize
women. Nonetheless, recognizing that there is an interplay between structural
change and consciousness and that these changes are only likely to occur in
conditions of conscious direction, there is a place for efforts to change media
treatment of women and women's issues. Such efforts include:

1. The development of mass media materials that portray women in a positive
   manner and in a wide variety of roles.
2. The redefinition of "news" and "newsworthiness" to include women as
   active participants in societal processes.
3. The creation of positive attitudes toward the integration of women in
   the mainstream of social life among mass communication controllers and
   workers.
4. The expansion of education, training, and employment opportunities for
   women in all fields of media work from camera operator to manager.
5. Spontaneous and organized action from media consumers to protest against
   bias and sex stereotyping via letter-writing campaigns, articles, protests,
   and so on.
6. The need for organizations such as the Nigerian Association of Media
   Women and Women in Nigeria to work together to support and supplement each other's efforts to improve women's conditions, combined with
   the support of trade unions and other such organizations.
7. The creation (and patronage, by women particularly) of independent feminist media organizations and products.

Appendix

1. *Topics Raised in Uwargida*
   Patience with daughters-in-law
   Patience with co-wives
   Thrift
   Daughter's education
   Beating of women

Harsh-unjust treatment of women
Girls' short marriages
Women strolling (*yawo*)
Provision of soap or jewelry by husband

2. *Topics Raised in Don Matisa*
Indecent dress by school children, particularly girls
Disrespect for elders
Girls' fickleness
Pride
In-family fighting
Refusal to follow Islamic norms
Maliciousness

3. *Topics Raised in Maigidanta*
Control of wives
Girls' hawking
Showing off in front of women
Husband-wife disputes
Women going out of the compound (3 times)
Married men and "outside" women (3 times)
Daughters' marriages (5 times)
Interaction between male and female youth
Treatment of half-siblings
Co-wives
Preharvest crop selling
Control of children's movements
Wealth and charity

Glossary of Hausa and Other Foreign Terms

'Aar (Ar.)	Loan.
'Abaya (Ar.)	Cloaklike wrap, originally woolen.
Adashi	Money pooled in a collective.
Ajami	Written matter in any script when language is not Arabic—specifically, Hausa or Fulfulde in Arabic script.
Al'ada, Al'adu (pl.)	Local customs.
Alƙali	Islamic court judge.
Amarya	Bride.
Amma (Ar.)	Slave girl.
Arne	Pagan.
Armen kulle	See *auren kulle*.
Asali	Origins, pedigree.
Asna	See *arne*.
Auren ɗauki sandanka	Marriage in which a husband and wife each own their own home; marriage in which the husband periodically leaves the wife at home, returning to his parents' home.
Auren kulle	Marriage in which the wife is secluded.
Auren silkiti, auren sulkuci	Marriage in which the wife has her own home, separate from her husband's.
Auren tsare	Arranged marriage with partial seclusion.
Auta	Youngest of several brothers and sisters.
Azumi	The fast of Ramadan.
Bature	European.
Bazawara	Woman no longer married.
Bid'a (Ar.)	Blameworthy practice.
Biki	Celebration, especially for wedding and naming ceremonies.
Bikin suna	Naming ceremony.
Birni	Walled town, city.
Boko (from the English, "book")	Secular education.
Bori	Spiritual possession cult.
Budurwa	Unmarried girl of marriageable age, virgin.
Cikin gida	Private women's quarters of the home.
Cucunawa	Slaves born in slavery of slave parents.

255

Ɗan kama, 'yan kama (pl.)	Minstrel, player.
Ɗariƙa	Mystical organization.
Dattijawa	Woman of middle age.
Ɗaurin kai	Silly shyness, fear.
Dilaliya	Woman broker.
Diyya	Compensation payable for accidental homicide or wounding.
Fiƙihu	Islamic law.
Gara	Presents given by the parents of the bride to the parents of the groom.
Gida	Compound, home, house.
Goggo	Term of address for the wife of one's father (except one's own mother), father's sister, and mother's brother's wife.
Gwaggo	See *goggo*.
Haɓe (pl.)	Indigenous peoples in Hausaland.
Hadisi, hadisai (pl.), (*hadith*, Ar.)	Muslim oral tradition transmitted by the Prophet.
Haji (Hajj, Ar.)	Pilgrimage to Mecca.
Harim (Ar.)	Community of wives and concubines to one man. (Anglicized form is "harem."
Hawi (Zarma)	See *kunya*.
Hiba (Ar.)	Donation.
Hubbare (Fulfulde)	Tomb of a religious leader.
Idda	Period during which a divorced or widowed woman may not remarry.
Ijma' (Ar.)	Consensus of community of Muslim scholars.
Ijtihad (Ar.)	Independent judgment.
Ikhwan (Ar.)	Brotherhood.
Imam (Ar.)	Officiating Muslim prayer leader.
Iya	Mother, maternal aunt, man's or woman's title.
Jari	Capital, assets.
Jihadi	Campaign of religious reform.
Jinn (Ar.)	Spirits.
Kambunbaka, kandumbaka	Cast the evil eye.
Karin magana	Proverb.
Karuwa, karuwai (pl.)	Prostitute, courtesan.
Karuwanci	Prostitution.
Kasar Kano	Kano region.
Kasida	Ode.
Kawa, ƙawaye (pl.)	Girl or woman's female friend.
Kasuwa	Market.
Kaya	Load.
Kayan ɗaki	Dowry, trousseau (lit. "things for the room").
Kayan miya	Ingredients for stew.

Khul' (Ar.)	Divorce requested by the wife.
Kilishi	Title for the official charged with spreading the emir's rug and entrusted to communicate with women in the harem.
Kirari	Praise song.
Kishi	Jealousy.
Kishiya	Co-wife.
Kudin kashewa	Pin money.
Kulle (*kubble,* Nigerien Hausa)	Locked, wife seclusion.
Kunya	Modesty, shame.
Kwaraƙwara	Concubine.
Labari	Historical narrative.
Lawth (Ar.)	Grounds for presumption of guilt in homicide cases.
Liman	See *imam.*
Littafin hira	Fiction.
Ma'aji	Native Administration treasurer.
Mace, mata (pl.)	Woman.
Mace tana ƙarƙashinka	"The woman is under your control."
Madahu	Eulogizing the Prophet.
Magajiya, magada (pl.)	Heiress (also used as an official title).
Magani	Medicine.
Mahaifiya	Birth mother.
Mai Babban Daki	Kano title for the female relative of the emir who presides over the Babban Daki (grand residence) near the palace.
Mai gida	Head of the household.
Mai unguwa	Ward head.
Makaranta	School.
Makarantan allo	Qur'anic school.
Makulliya	Concubine, slave girl.
Malam, malami (m.), *malama* (f.), *malamai* (pl.)	Literate person, teacher, term of respect (Mr., Mrs., Miss).
Marikiya	Foster mother (lit. "one [f.] who supports").
Mass al-jinn (Ar.)	Attack of spirits.
Masu sarauta	Rulers, officials.
Masu zaman kansu	Divorcées or prostitutes (lit. "those who live alone").
Mata	See *mace.*
Mayafi	Large cloth covering a woman's head or a man's shoulders.
Mauludi	Date of the Prophet's birth.
Mma	See *umma.*
Mu'azzin (Ar.)	One who calls Muslims to prayer.
Muƙaddam (m.), *muƙaddama* (f.), *muƙaddasai* (pl.)	Deputy, representative, and (m.) one who initiates others into Islamic mystical organizations.

Muqaddam (Ar.)	Islamic mystic official.
Nahawu	Arabic grammar.
Nakiya	Confection of flour, honey, and peppers.
Qasama (Ar.)	See *yamin al-qasama*.
Qiyas (Ar.)	Islamic analogy.
Rahn (Ar.)	Pawning.
Ramadan	Annual Muslim month of fasting.
Riba	Monetary profit.
Sadaka	Alms, charity.
Sadaka	Concubine.
Sadaki (*sadaq*, Ar.)	Bridewealth given to the bride by the groom through her guardian; marriage payment.
Saki	Dialectical pronunciation of *sarki*.
Salla	(1) Post-Ramadan celebrations (*babbar/babban salla* [*Id-el-fitr*, Ar.] and *ƙaramar/ƙaramin salla* [*Id-el-kabir*, Ar.]); (2) each of five daily Muslim prayers.
Samari	See *sauraya*.
Samariya	Local youth groups (from *samari*, "youths").
Sana'a	Occupation, trade, profession.
Sarauniya	Queen.
Sarauta	Kingship.
Sarki	Emir.
Sauraya, samari (pl.)	Young man.
Shari'a	Muslim law.
Sira (Ar.)	Biography of the Prophet Mohammed.
Sosai	Well, correctly.
Suna	Name, naming ceremony.
Tafsiri	Scholarly analysis of the Qur'an.
Talaq (Ar.)	Phrase used in declaring divorce initiated by husband.
Talaka, talakawa (pl.)	Subordinate, peasant.
Tarbiyya	Training, education.
Tariqa, tarika (Ar.)	See *ɗariƙa*.
Tatsuniya, tatsuniyoyi (pl.)	Fable, story, oral narrative.
Tauhidi	Proclaiming belief in the oneness of Allah.
Thayyib (Ar.)	Widow.
Tsariƙa	See *ɗariƙa*.
Tsohuwa	Old woman.
Tuwo	Porridge.
Umma	Mother.
Umma (Ar.)	Community.
Umm walad (Ar.)	Concubine who has borne her master a child.
Ungozoma	Midwife.
Ungozomanci	Midwifery.
Ushiri	Tenth part paid as a commission to the court in cases involving action for debt.

Uwar adashi	Woman in charge of holding pooled money.
Uwar gida	Mistress of the home, head wife.
Wahayiya	Slave who has been freed after bearing a child for her master.
Waƙa, waƙoƙi (pl.)	Song, poem.
Wala (Ar.)	Patron-client relationship between master and freed slave.
Wali (m),	Guardian, saint, holy man; Executor of a blood feud.
Waliyya (f.), *waliyyai* (pl.)	Saint, saints.
Wali-al-dam (Ar.)	
Wasan kwaikwayo	Drama, play.
Wasiyya	Plea.
Waziri	Vizier.
Yamin al-qasama (Ar.)	Oath of compurgation.
Yatim (Ar.)	Orphan.
Yawm al-qiyama (Ar.)	Day of resurrection, reckoning and final judgement.
Yawo	Stroll, wander about.
'Yan kama	See *ɗan kama*.
'Ya'yan zanzanna	Smallpox.
Zaman turawa	Colonial period.
Zango, zongo	Camping place of caravan, strangers' quarters.
Zumunci	Blood or marital relationship, clan feeling.

Bibliography

'Abd al'Ati, Hammudah
1982   *The Family Structure in Islam*. Lagos: Islamic Publications Bureau.

Abdoulaye, Diallo Hassane
1978   "Islam in Niger." *Sahel Hebdo*, August 3, pp. 50–51.

Abdu, Lawan
1973   "Female Labour in the Modern Economy of Kano." B.Sc. thesis, Ahmadu Bello University, Zaria, Nigeria.

Abdulwaheed, Hafsatu M. A.
1983   *'So Aljannar Duniya'—Love, the World's Delight*. Zaria, Nigeria: Gaskiya Press.

Abdurrahman, Alhaji M., and Peter Canham
1978   *The Ink of the Scholar: The Islamic Tradition of Education in Nigeria*. Lagos: Macmillan.

Abell, H. C.
1962   "Report to the Government of Nigeria (Northern Region) on the Home Economics Aspects of the FAO Socio-Economic Survey of Peasant Agriculture in Northern Nigeria: The Role of Rural Women in Farm and Home Life." Rome: FAO. Mimeograph.

Abraham, R. C.
1962   *Dictionary of the Hausa Language*. London: University of London Press.

Adamu, Mahdi
1978   *The Hausa Factor in West African History*. Zaria: Ahmadu Bello Press; London: Oxford University Press.

1976   "The Spread of the Hausa Culture in West Africa, 1700–1900." *Savanna* 5 (June): 3–12.

Akpan, S. D.
1979   "News Photos and Stories: Men's and Women's Roles in Two Nigerian Newspapers." Ph.D. diss., Ohio State University.

Al-Attas, S. N.
1979   *Aims and Objectives of Islamic Education*. London: Hodder and Stoughton.

Al-Hajj, M. A.
1973   "The Mahdist Tradition in Northern Nigeria." Ph.D. diss., Ahmadu Bello University, Zaria, Nigeria.

Ali, Abdullah Yusuf
1975   *The Holy Qur'an*. London: Islamic Foundation.
Alkali, Mohammed Nur
1978   "Kanem-Bornu Under the Sayfawa." Ph.D. diss., Ahmadu Bello Uni-
               versity, Zaria, Nigeria.
Allott, Anthony
1960   *Essays in African Law, with Special Reference to the Law of Ghana*.
               London: Butterworth.
Althusser, L.
1977   "Ideology and Ideological State Apparatuses (Notes Towards an In-
               vestigation)." In *Lenin and Philosophy*, ed. L. Althusser, pp. 121–76.
               London: New Left Books.
Ames, David W.
1970   "A Sociocultural View of Hausa Musical Activity." In *The Traditional
               Artist in African Society*, ed. Warren d'Azevedo. Bloomington: Indiana
               University Press.
Amiruddin, B. E.
1939   "Woman's Status in Islam." *Muslim World* 32, no. 2.
Anderson, J. N. D.
1970   *Islamic Law in Africa*. London: Frank Cass. Orig. pub. London: Her
               Majesty's Stationery Office, 1954.
Archives National du Niger
1936   "Coutumier Haoussa." Vol. 4 of *Coutumiers juridiques de l'Afrique
               Occidentale française*. Publications du Comité d'Etudes Historiques et
               Scientifiques de l'A. O. f., ser. A, nos. 8, 9, 10. Paris: Larose, 1939.
Arnould, Eric J.
1984   "Marketing and Social Reproduction in Zinder, Niger Republic." In
               Households, ed. Robert M. Netting, Richard R. Wilk, Eric J. Arnould,
               pp. 130–62. Berkeley: University of California Press.
Arnould, E. J., and H. K. Henderson
1982   *Women in the Niger Republic*. University of Arizona, Tucson: Consor-
               tium for International Development. Office of International Agriculture
               Programs, Women in Development Program, Working Paper no. 1.
Awosika, Keziah
1981   "Women's Education and Participation in the Labour Force: The Case
               of Nigeria." In *Women, Power, and Political Systems*, ed. Margherita
               Rendel, pp. 81–93. New York: St. Martin's Press.
1980   "Nigeria's Anti-Inflationary Policies in the 1970s." Paper presented to
               the Nigerian Economics Society, Kano, Nigeria.
Baier, Stephen
1980   *An Economic History of Central Niger*. Oxford: Clarendon Press.
Balandier, Georges, and Paul Mercier
1952   *Particularisme et évolution: Les pêcheurs Lebou*. Dakar, Senegal: In-
               stitut Français d'Afrique Noire.
Bargery, G. P.
1934   *A Hausa-English Dictionary and English-Hausa Vocabulary*. London:
               Oxford University Press.

Barkow, Jerome
1973   "Muslims and Maguzawa in North-Central State, Nigeria: An Ethno-
              graphic Comparison." *Canadian Journal of African Studies* 7, no. 1:
              59–76.
1972   "Hausa Women and Islam." *Canadian Journal of African Studies* 6,
              no. 2:317–28.
1971   "The Institution of Courtesanship in the Northern States of Nigeria."
              Geneve-Afrique 10, no. 1:1–16.
1970   "Hausa and Maguzawa: Processes of Group Differentiation in a Rural
              Area of North Central State of Nigeria." Ph.D. diss., University of
              Chicago.
Barth, Heinrich
1857   *Travels and Discoveries in North and Central Africa: Being A Journal of
              An Expedition Undertaken Under the Auspices of H.B.M.'s Government
              in the Years 1849–1855*. New York: Harper and Brothers.
Bashir, M. K.
1972   "The Economic Activities of Secluded Married Women in Kurawa and
              Lallokin Lemu, Kano City." B.Sc. thesis, Ahmadu Bello University,
              Zaria, Nigeria.
Baveja, Malik Ram
1979   *Women in Islam*. Trans. Abdul M. Ali. Delhi: Academic Literature.
Beattie, John, and John Middleton, eds.
1969   *Spirit, Mediumship and Society in Africa*. New York: Africana.
Beik, Janet
1987   *Hausa Theatre in Niger: A Contemporary Oral Art*. New York: Garland
              Publishing.
1986   "Plays Without Playwrights: The Community Creation of Contempo-
              rary Hausa Theatre in Niger." In *African Literature in Its Social and
              Political Dimensions*, ed. Ellen Julien, Mildred Mortimer, and Curtis
              Schade, pp. 23–32. Washington, D.C.: Three Continents Press.
1984a   "Hausa Theatre in Niger: A Contemporary Oral Art." Ph.D. diss.,
              University of Wisconsin–Madison.
1984b   "National Development as Theme in Current Hausa Drama in Niger."
              Research in African Literatures 15, no. 1:1–24.
Bello, Sir Ahmadu
1962   *My Life*. Cambridge: Cambridge University Press.
Beneria, Lourdes
1982   "Accounting for Women's Work." In *Women and Development: The
              Sexual Division of Labor in Rural Societies*, ed. Lourdes Beneria, pp.
              119–47. New York: Praeger.
1981   "Conceptualizing the Labour Force: The Underestimation of Women's
              Economic Activities." In *African Women in the Development Process*,
              ed. Nici Nelson, pp. 10–28. London: Frank Cass.
Benson, Susan, and Mark Duffield
1979   "Women's Work and Economic Change: The Hausa in Sudan and in
              Nigeria." *IDS Bulletin* 10, no. 9:13–19.

Berger, Iris
1976   "Rebels or Status-Seekers? Women as Spirit Mediums in East Africa."
                    In *Women in Africa*, ed. N. J. Hafkin and E. G. Bay, pp. 157–81.
                    Stanford, Calif.: Stanford University Press.
Besmer, Fremont E.
1983   *Horses, Musicians, and Gods: The Hausa Cult of Possession-Trance.*
                    South Hadley, Mass.: Bergin and Garvey.
1975   " 'Boori': Structure and Process in Performance." *Folia Orientalia* 16:
                    101–30.
1973a   "Avoidance and Joking Relationships Between Hausa Supernatural
                    Spirits." *Studies in Nigerian Culture*. Occasional Papers of the Centre
                    for Nigerian Cultural Studies 1, no. 1:26–52. Zaria, Nigeria: Ahmadu
                    Bello University.
1973b   "Praise Epithets for Some Important *Bori* Spirits in Kano." *Harsunan
                    Nijeriya (Languages of Nigeria)* 3:15–38.
Bienen, Henry
1985   *Political Conflict and Economic Change in Nigeria*. London: Frank
                    Cass.
Bonte, Pierre
1978   "Aînés et prophètes: Religion et classes sociales chez les éleveurs
                    d'Afrique de l'Est." Mimeograph.
1967   *L'élevage et le commerce du bétail dans l'Ader Doutchi-Majya*. Etudes
                    nigeriennes 23. Niamey and Paris: IFAN-CNRS.
Boserup, Esther
1970   *Women's Role in Economic Development*. London: George Allen and
                    Unwin.
Bourguignon, Erika, ed.
1973   *Religion, Altered States of Consciousness, and Social Change*. Colum-
                    bus: Ohio State University Press.
Bovill, E. W.
1968   *The Golden Trade of the Moors*. 2d ed. London: Oxford Univer-
                    sity Press.
Boyd, Jean
1989   *The Caliph's Sister. Nana Asma'u, 1793–1865: Teacher, Poet and
                    Islamic Leader*. London: Frank Cass.
1984   "The Role of Women Scholars in the Sokoto Caliphate." Manuscript.
Boyd, Jean, and Murray Last
1985   "The Role of Women as 'Agents Religieux' in Sokoto." *Canadian
                    Journal of African Studies* 19, no. 2:283–300.
Bray, Mark
1981   *Universal Primary Education in Nigeria: A Study of Kano State*. Lon-
                    don: Routledge and Kegan Paul.
Broustra, Jacqueline Monfouga-Nicolas
1978   "La 'femme libre' de Birnin Koni (Niger) ou la parole des lieux inter-
                    médiaires." *Ethnopsychiatrica* 2, no. 1:7–36.
1974   "Signification de la possession en pays hausa." *Bulletin du Centre
                    Thomas More* 7:3–8.

1972   *Ambivalence et culte de possession: Contribution a l'étude du bori hausa.* Paris: Editions Anthropos. (Published under Jacqueline Monfouga-Nicolas.)

1967   *Les juments des dieux: Rites de possession et condition féminine en pays hausa: Vallée de Maradi Niger.* Etudes nigeriennes 21. Niamey: IFAN-CNRS. (Published under Jacqueline Nicolas.)

Bujra, Janet

1986   "Urging Women to Redouble Their Efforts . . . : Class, Gender, and Capitalist Transformation in Africa." In *Women and Class in Africa*, ed. Claire Robertson and Iris Berger, pp. 117–40. New York: Holmes & Meier, Africana Publishing.

Burdon, J. A.

1909   *Historical Notes on Certain Emirates and Tribes in Northern Nigeria.* London.

Callaway, Barbara J.

1987   *Muslim Hausa Women in Nigeria.* Syracuse, N.Y.: Syracuse University Press.

1984   "Ambiguous Consequences of the Socialization and Seclusion of Hausa Muslim Women in Nigeria." *Journal of Modern African Studies* 22, no. 3:429–50.

Callaway, Barbara, and Enid Schildkrout

1985   "Law, Education, and Social Change: Implications for Hausa Muslim Women in Nigeria." In *The Women's Decade, 1975–1985*, ed. Lynn Iglitzen and Ruth Ross, pp. 181–205. Santa Barbara: ABC Clio Press.

Chaibou, Dan-Inna

1978–79   "La théâtralité en pays Hawsa." Master's thesis, Université Nationale de Côte d'Ivoire.

Christelow, Allan

Forth-coming   "Theft, Homicide, and Oath in Early Twentieth Century Kano, Nigeria." In *Law in Colonial Africa*, ed. Kristin Mann and Richard Roberts. London: Heinemann/Currey.

1986   "Slavery in Kano, 1913–14: Evidence from the Judicial Records." *African Economic History*, pp. 57–74.

1985a   "Property and Theft in Kano on the Eve of the Groundnut Boom." Paper presented at the African and Middle East Studies Associations Conference, New Orleans.

1985b   "Records of the Emir's and Alḳali's Courts in Kano, Nigeria." *Fontes Historiae Africanae* 9–10:35–40.

Cielemans, M., and G. Fauconnier

1979   *Mass Media: The Image, Role and Social Conditions of Women.* UNESCO Reports and Papers in Mass Communications no. 84, Paris.

Clapperton, Commander Hugh

1966   *Journal of A Second Expedition into the Interior of Africa from the Bight of Benin*, 2d ed. London: Frank Cass. Orig. pub. London, 1829.

Cohen, Abner

1969   *Custom and Politics in Urban Africa: A Study of Hausa Migrants in Yoruba Towns.* Berkeley: University of California Press.

1967   "Stranger Communities: The Hausa." In *The City of Ibadan*, ed. P. C.
                      Lloyd, A. L. Mabogunje, and B. Awe, pp. 117–27. London: Cam-
                      bridge University Press.

Coles, Catherine M.

1990a   "The Older Woman in Hausa Society: Power and Authority in Urban
                      Nigeria." In *The Cultural Context of Aging: World-Wide Perspectives*,
                      ed. Jay Sokolovsky, pp. 57–81. New York: Bergin and Garvey.

1990b   "Social Change in Urban Africa: Three Generations of Hausa Women
                      in Kaduna, Nigeria, 1925–1985." New Hampshire International Semi-
                      nar Series Working Paper. Durham, N.H.: Center for International
                      Perspectives, University of New Hampshire.

1983a   "Urban Muslim Women and Social Change in Northern Nigeria."
                      Working Papers on Women in International Development 19. East
                      Lansing: Michigan State University.

1983b   "Muslim Women in Town: Social Change Among the Hausa of North-
                      ern Nigeria." Ph.D. diss., University of Wisconsin–Madison.

Collier, Jane Fishburne

1974   "Women in Politics." In *Woman, Culture, and Society*, ed. Michelle
                      Zimbalist Rosaldo and Louise Lamphere, pp. 89–96. Stanford, Calif.:
                      Stanford University Press.

Comaroff, John L.

1987   "*Sui generis*: Feminism, Kinship Theory, and Structural 'Domains.' "
                      In *Gender and Kinship: Essays Toward a Unified Analysis*, ed. Jane
                      Fishburne Collier and Sylvia Junko Yanagisako, pp. 53–85. Stanford,
                      Calif.: Stanford University Press.

Coulon, Christian

1989   "Women, Islam and *Baraka*." In *Charisma and Brotherhood in Afri-
                      can Islam*, ed. Donald B. Cruise O'Brien and Christian Coulon, pp.
                      113–33. Oxford: Oxford University Press.

Crooks, John J.

1923   *Records Relating to the Gold Coast Settlements from 1750 to 1874*.
                      Dublin: Browne and Nolan.

Cys, Monique

1975   "Vers la Fin." *Sahel Hebdo*, December 12, 1975, p. 37.

'Dan Fodio, Sheikh Usman

1981   *Nurul Albabi*. Kaduna, Nigeria: Jama'atu Nasiril Islam.

Decalo, Samuel

1979   *Historical Dictionary of Niger*. Metuchen, N.J., and London: Scare-
                      crow Press.

Denham, D., et al.

1826   *Narrative of Travels and Discoveries in Northern and Central Africa in
                      the Years 1822, 1823 and 1824*. 2 vols. London: John Murray.

Derrick, Jonathan

1975   *Africa's Slaves Today*. New York: Schocken Books.

Diarra, F. A.

1971   *Femmes Africaines en Devenir*. Paris: Anthropos.

DiDomenico, C.
1983   "Male and Female Factory Workers in Ibadan." In *Female and Male in West Africa*, ed. Christine Oppong, pp. 256–65. London: George Allen and Unwin.

Dikko, Saudc
1982   "The Role of Women Title Holders in the Zaria Political Setup." B.A. thesis, Bayero University, Kano, Nigeria.

Dinan, Carmel
1983   "Sugar Daddies and Gold-Diggers: The White-Collar Single Women in Accra." In *Female and Male in West Africa*, ed. Christine Oppong, pp. 344–66. London: George Allen and Unwin.

Dixon, Ruth B.
1982   "Women in Agriculture: Counting the Labor Force in Developing Countries." *Population and Development Review* 8 (September): 539–66.

Doi, Abdur Rahman I.
1984   *Islam in Nigeria*. Zaria, Nigeria: Gaskiya Press.
1970   *Introduction to the Hadith*. Lagos, Nigeria: Islamic Publications Bureau.

Dokaji, Alhaji Abubakar
1958   *Kano Ta Dabo Ci Gari*. Zaria, Nigeria: Gaskiya Press.

Dretke, James P.
1968   "The Muslim Community in Accra (An Historical Survey)." M.A. thesis, University of Ghana.

Dunbar, Roberta A.
1983   "Islamized Law and the Status of Women in Niger." Paper presented to the Southeastern Regional Seminar in African Studies, Charlottes-ville, Va.
1977   "Slavery and the Evolution of Nineteenth-Century Damagaram." In *Slavery in Africa: Historical and Anthropological Perspectives*, ed. Suzanne Miers and Igor Kopytoff, pp. 155–77. Madison: University of Wisconsin Press.
1970   "Damagaram (Zinder, Niger), 1812–1906: The History of a Cen-tral Sudanic Kingdom." Ph.D. diss., University of California, Los Angeles.

East, R. M.
1943   "Recent Activities of the Literature Bureau—Zaria, Northern Nige-ria." *Africa* 14, no. 1:71–77.
1936   "A First Essay in Imaginative African Literature." *Africa* 9, no. 3: 350–57.

Echard, Nicole
1989a   "Bori: Aspects d'un culte de possession hausa dans l'Ader et le Kur-fey (Niger)." Paris: Centre d'Etudes Africaines, E.H.E.S.S., working paper no. 10.
1989b   *Bori: Génies d'un culte de possession hausa de l'Ader et du Kurfey (Niger)*. Paris: Institut d'Ethnologie.

1986   "De la passion: Anecdotes du pays hausa de l'Ader (Niger)." In *Afrique plurielle. Afrique actuelle. Hommage à Georges Balandier*, pp. 127–36. Paris: Karthala.

1985   "Même la viande est vendue avec le sang: De la sexualité des femmes, un example." In *L'arraisonnement des femmes: Essais en anthropologie des sexes*, ed. Nicole-Claude Mathieu, pp. 37–60. Paris: Cahiers de l'Homme, Editions de l'Ecole des Hautes Etudes en Sciences Sociales.

1981   "La parole peule du porc-epic (Ader hausa, Niger)." In *Itinerances— en pays peul et ailleurs: Mélanges réunis parler chercheur de* l'ERA *246 du* CNRS *à la mémoire de Pierre-François Lacroix*. Société des Africanistes, Mémoires, 289–97.

1978a   "Mais où sont les sorciers d'antan? Note sur les sorciers hausa d'origine humaine en Ader (Niger)." In *Systèmes de signes*, pp. 121–30. Paris: Hermann.

1978b   "La pratique religieuse des femmes dans une société d'hommes: Les Hausa du Niger." *Revue française de sociologie* 19, no. 4:551–62.

1975   "Petites lectures sur des phénomènes de possession africains." *Archives de sciences sociales des religions* 40:145–56.

Echard, Nicole, Odile Journet, and Suzanne Lallemand
1981   "De l'obligation à la prohibition: Sens et non-sens de la virginité des filles en Afrique de l'Ouest." In *La première fois*, ed. Jean-Pierre Dordet, pp. 337–95. Paris: Ramsay.

Edgar, Frank. See Skinner, A. Neil, 1969, 1977a, 1977b.

Edholm, F., O. Harris, and K. Young
1977   "Conceptualizing Women." *Critique of Anthropology* 3, nos. 9–10: 101–30.

Entwisle, Barbara, and Catherine M. Coles
1990   "Demographic Surveys and Nigerian Women." *Signs* 15 (January): 259–84.

Esposito, John L.
1982   *Women in Muslim Family Law*. Syracuse, N.Y.: Syracuse University Press.

The Europa Year Book, Vol. 2
1988   London: Europa Publications.

Fapohunda, Eleanor
1983   "Female and Male Work Profiles." In *Female and Male in West Africa*, ed. Christine Oppong, pp. 32–53. London: George Allen and Unwin.

1978   "Women at Work in Nigeria: Factors Affecting Modern Sector Employment." In *Human Resources and African Development*, ed. U. Damachi and V. Diejomaoh, pp. 220–41. New York: Praeger.

Faulkingham, Ralph H.
1977   "Fertility in Tudu: An Analysis of Constraints on Fertility in a Village in Niger." In *The Persistence of High Fertility: Family and Fertility Change*, ed. John C. Caldwell, pp. 153–88. Changing African Family Series part 1. Department of Demography. Canberra: Australian National University.

1970   "Political Support in a Hausa Village." Ph.D. diss., Michigan State
              University, East Lansing.
Federal Electoral Commission, Nigeria
1979   Register of voters, General Election. Mimeograph.
Feinstein, Alan
1973   *African Revolutionary: The Life and Times of Nigeria's Aminu Kano.*
              New York: Quadrangle.
Ferguson, Douglas Edwin
1973   Nineteenth-Century Hausaland, Being a Description by Imam Imoru
              of the Land, Economy, and Society of His People. Ph.D. diss., Uni-
              versity of California, Los Angeles.
Fika, Adamu
1978   *The Kano Civil War and British Overrule, 1882–1940.* Ibadan: Oxford
              University Press Nigeria.
Fisher, Allan G. B., and Humphrey J. Fisher
1971   *Slavery and Muslim Society in Africa: The Institution in Saharan and
              Sudanic Africa and the Trans-Saharan Slave Trade.* New York (Lon-
              don 1970).
Flegel, E. R.
1985   *The Biography of Madugu Mohamman Mai Gashin Baki.* Trans. and
              annotated by M. G. Duffill. Los Angeles: Crossroads Press. Orig. pub.
              Hamburg, 1885.
Fofana, B. S.
1980   "Identification de projets de développement en faveur de l'association
              des femmes du Niger." In *Rapport de Mission*. Niamey: UN/CEA/
              Mulpoc.
Frishman, Alan
1982   "Small-Scale Industries in Urban Kano, 1973–1980: Success, Failure
              and the Availability of Capital." Paper presented at the annual meeting
              of the African Studies Association, Washington, D.C.
1979   *Small-Scale Industry in Metropolitan Kano.* Report to the World Bank,
              Washington, D.C.
Fuglestad, Finn
1983   *A History of Niger, 1850–1960.* Cambridge: Cambridge University
              Press.
Fyzee, Asaf A.
1955   *Outline of Muhammadan Law.* London: Oxford University Press.
Gaadoo Karhin Allaa (Waasan Kwaykoyoo na Zinder a 1973)
1977   Transcribed by Abuubakar Mahmman. Niamey: CELHTO.
Gaden, Captain
1904   *Residence in Zinder.* Paris.
Galadanci, Alhaji Shehu A.
1971   "Education of Women in Islam with Reference to Nigeria." *Nigerian
              Journal of Islam* 1, no. 2:5–10.
Gallagher, M.
1979   *The Portrayal and Participation of Women in the Media.* Paris:
              UNESCO, ref. no. CC79/WS/130.

Garba, Seydou
N.d.   "Exposé de psychologie: Condition de la femme nigerienne et la neces-
                    sité d'instaurer un *Code de la Famille.*" Paper presented to L'Ecole
                    National d'Administration, Niamey.
Geary, W. H. M.
1927   *Nigeria Under British Rule*. London.
Gilbert, A., et al.
1982   *Cities, Poverty and Development*. London: Oxford University Press.
Gleave, M. B., and R. M. Prothero
1971   "Population Density and Slave Raiding: A Comment." *Journal of Afri-
                    can History* 12, no. 2:319–24.
Goody, Jack, Joan Thirsk, and E. P. Thompson, eds.
1976   *Family and Inheritance: Rural Society in Western Europe, 1200–1800*.
                    Cambridge: Cambridge University Press.
Gramsci, A.
1978   *Selections from Prison Writings*. London: Lawrence and Wishart.
Greenberg, Joseph
1947   "Islam and Clan Organization Among the Hausa." *Southwestern Jour-
                    nal of Anthropology* 3:196–211.
1946   *The Influence of Islam on a Sudanese Religion*. New York: J. J. Augus-
                    tin.
Guyer, Jane I.
1981   "Household and Community in African Studies." *African Studies Re-
                    view* 24, nos. 2–3:87–137.
Gwaram, Hauwa, and Hajiya 'Yar Shehu
1983   *'Alƙalami a Hannun Mata'—A Pen in the Hands of Women*. Ed. and
                    annotated by B. Mack. Zaria, Nigeria: Northern Nigerian Publishing.
Hailey, Lord
1944   *Native Administration and Political Development in British Tropical
                    Africa, 1940–42*. London.
Hake, James M.
1972   *Child-Rearing Practices in Northern Nigeria*. Ibadan, Nigeria: Ibadan
                    University Press.
Hall, S.
1977a   "Culture, the Media and the Ideological Effect." In *Mass Communica-
                    tion and Society*, ed. L. Curran et al., pp. 315–48. London: Arnold.
1977b   "Rethinking the Base-Superstructure Metaphor." In *Class, Hegemony,
                    and Party*, ed. J. Bloomfield, pp. 43–72. London: Lawrence and
                    Wishart.
Hallet, Robin, ed.
1964   *Records of the African Association, 1788–1831*. London: Thomas
                    Nelson & Sons.
Hammel, E. A.
1984   "On the *** of Studying Household Form and Function." In *House-
                    holds*, ed. Robert M. Netting, Richard R. Wilk, and Eric J. Arnould,
                    pp. 29–43. Berkeley: University of California Press.

Harrington, Judith A.
1983   "Nutritional Stress and Economic Responsibility: A Study of Nigerian
              Women." In *Women and Poverty in the Third World*, ed. M. Buvunic,
              M. Lycette, and W. McGreevey, pp. 130–56. Baltimore, Md.: Johns
              Hopkins University Press.
Hassan, Alhaji, and Mallam Shuaibu Na'ibi
1962   *A Chronicle of Abuja*. Trans. Frank Heath. Lagos: African Universi-
              ties Press.
Hassan, Usman
1978   "Islamic Society in Nigeria: Its Implication for Education and Social
              Growth." Ph.D. diss., University College, Cardiff, Wales.
Hay, Margaret J., and Sharon Stichter, eds.
1984   *African Women South of the Sahara*. London: Longman.
Henn, Jeanne Koopman
1988   "The Material Basis of Sexism: A Mode of Production Analysis." In
              Patriarchy and Class: African Women in the Home and the Workplace,
              ed. Sharon B. Stichter and Jane L. Parpart, pp. 27–59. Boulder, Colo.:
              Westview Press.
Hill, Polly
1986   *Development Economics on Trial: The Anthropological Case for a
              Prosecution*. Cambridge: Cambridge University Press.
1977   *Population, Prosperity and Poverty: Rural Kano 1900 and 1970*. Lon-
              don: Cambridge University Press.
1974   "Big Houses in Kano Emirate." *Africa* 54 (April): 117–35.
1972   *Rural Hausa: A Village and a Setting*. London: Cambridge Univer-
              sity Press.
1971   "Two Types of West African House Trade." In *The Development of
              Indigenous Trade and Markets in West Africa*, ed. Claude Meillassoux,
              pp. 303–18. London: Oxford University Press.
1969   "Hidden Trade in Hausaland." *Man* 4, no. 3:392–409.
Hinchcliffe, Doreen
1975   "The Status of Women in Islamic Law." In *Conflict and Harmony
              in Education in Tropical Africa*, ed. Godfrey N. Brown and Mervyn
              Hiskett, pp. 455–66. London: George Allen and Unwin.
Hiskett, Mervyn
1985   "Enslavement, Slavery and Attitudes towards the Legally Enslavable
              in Hausa Islamic Literature." In *Slaves and Slavery in Muslim Africa*,
              ed. John Ralph Willis, 1:106–24. London.
1984   *The Development of Islam in West Africa*. London: Longman.
1975   "Islamic Education in the Traditional and State Systems in Northern
              Nigeria." In *Conflict and Harmony in Education in Tropical Africa*, ed.
              Godfrey N. Brown and Mervyn Hiskett, eds., pp. 134–51. London:
              George Allen and Unwin.
1973   *The Sword of Truth: The Life and Times of Usman dan Fodio*. New
              York: Oxford University Press.
1964–65   "The Song of Bagauda, a Hausa King List and Homily in Verse." *Bul-*

                    letin of the School for Oriental and African Studies (SOAS) 24 (1964):
                    540–67; 28 (1965): 363–85.
Hodgkin, T.
1960   *Nigerian Perspectives*. London: Oxford University Press.
Hogben, S. J., and A. H. M. Kirk-Greene
1966   *The Emirates of Northern Nigeria: A Preliminary Survey of Their His-
                    torical Traditions*. London: Oxford University Press.
Hogendorn, Jan S.
1980   "Slave Acquisition and Delivery in Precolonial Hausaland." In *West
                    African Culture Dynamics: Archaeological and Historical Perspectives*,
                    ed. B. K. Schwartz, Jr., pp. 477–93. New York: Mouton.
1978   *Nigerian Groundnut Exports: Origins and Early Development*. Zaria,
                    Nigeria: Ahmadu Bello Press.
Hull, Richard W.
1968   "The Development of Administration in the Katsina Emirate Northern
                    Nigeria, 1887–1944." Ph.D. diss., Columbia University, New York.
Hussain, Freeda, ed.
1984   *Muslim Women: The Ideal and Cultural Realities*. New York: St. Mar-
                    tins.
Ibrahim, J.
1983   "The Political Economy of Mass Communication in Nigeria: A Case
                    Study of Daily Times and New Nigeria." M.Sc. thesis, Ahmadu Bello
                    University, Zaria, Nigeria.
Ide, Adamou
N.d.   "Les règles générales de formation et de dissolution du mariage tradi-
                    tionnel du Niger (en comparison avec la legislation ivoirienne et
                    malienne)." Niamey. Mimeograph.
Imam, Ayesha M.
1988   "Women, Ideology and Mass Media in Kano State, Nigeria." Re-
                    search Report for Working Group on Women and Mass Media in
                    Africa, Association of African Women for Research and Development
                    (AAWORD), Dakar, Senegal.
1986   "Women's Liberation: Myths or Reality?" In *Women, Struggles and
                    Strategies: Third World Perspectives*. Rome: ISIS.
1985   "Ideology, Hegemony and Mass Media." Sociology Department semi-
                    nar paper. Zaria, Nigeria: Ahmadu Bello University.
1980   "An Analysis of the Structure of Racist Ideology in the Media." B.Sc.
                    thesis, Polytechnic of North London.
Imam, Ayesha M., and Renee I. Pittin
1984   "The Identification of Successful Women's Projects: Kaduna State
                    Nigeria." International Labour Organization Report, Geneva.
International Labor Organization (ILO)
1982   *Nigeria: First Things First*. Addis Ababa: ILO.
International Planned Parenthood Federation
1980   *A 1980 People Wallchart*. London.

Iwerierbor, I.
1981   "Image of Women in Nigerian Films." Paper presented to UNESCO
            Workshop on Women Media and Development, Lagos.

Jackson, Cecile (Sam)
1985   *The Kano River Irrigation Project.* Kumarian Press Case Studies on
            Women's Roles and Gender Differences in Development, no. 4. New
            York: Kumarian Press.

1978   "Hausa Women on Strike." *Review of African Political Economy* 13
            (May–August): 21–36.

Jelin, E.
1982   "Women and the Urban Labour Market." In *Women's Roles and Popu-
            lation Trends in the Third World*, ed. R. Anker et al., pp. 239–67.
            London: Croom Helm.

Johnston, H. A. S.
1967   *The Fulani Empire of Sokoto.* London: Oxford University Press.

1966   *A Selection of Hausa Stories.* London: Clarendon Press.

Kabir, Zainab
1985   "On the Women's Liberation Movement: Myth and Realities." Paper
            presented at the Conference of Muslim Sisters' Organisation, Kano,
            Nigeria.

Kaduna Polytechnic. Nigeria
1981   "Urban Renewal Study." Department of Town Planning. Kaduna,
            Nigeria.

Kano, Alhaji Abubakar Dokaji
1978   *Kano Ta Dabo Cigari.* Zaria: Northern Nigerian Publishing.

King, A. V.
1967   "A *Boori* Liturgy from Katsina." *African Language Studies*, supple-
            ment 7:1–157.

1966   "A *Boori* Liturgy from Katsina: Introduction and *Kiraarii* Texts." *Afri-
            can Language Studies* 7:105–25.

Kirk-Greene, Anthony H. M.
1970   *Political Memoranda, 1913–18, by Lord Lugard.* London: Frank Cass.

1968   *Lugard and the Amalgamation of Nigeria.* London: Frank Cass.

1965   *The Principles of Native Administration in Nigeria.* London. Oxford
            University Press.

1964   *A Preliminary Inquiry into Hausa Onomatology: Three Studies in the
            Origins of Personal, Title, and Place Names.* Zaria, Nigeria: Institute
            of Administration, Ahmadu Bello University, and U.S. AID.

Klein, Martin A.
1983   "Women in Slavery in the Western Sudan." In *Women and Slavery in
            Africa*, ed. Claire C. Robertson and Martin A. Klein, eds., pp. 67–92.
            Madison: University of Wisconsin Press.

Knipp, Margaret Mary
1987   "Women, Western Education and Change: A Case Study of the Hausa-
            Fulani of Northern Nigeria." Ph.D. diss., Northwestern University,
            Evanston, Ill.

Knowles, Carolyn
1985   "Women Under Development: Some Preliminary Remarks." In *Women in Nigeria Today*, pp. 68–81. London: Zed Press, for Women in Nigeria.
Lamphere, Louise
1987   "Feminism and Anthropology: The Struggle to Reshape Our Thinking About Gender." In *The Impact of Feminist Research in the Academy*, ed. Christie Farnham, pp. 11–33. Bloomington: Indiana University Press.
Lander, Richard
1830   *Records of Captain Clapperton's Last Expedition to Africa*. 2 vols. London: Colburn & Bentley.
Lanne, Bernard
1983   "Régime militaire et société de développement au Niger (1974–1983)." *Afrique Contemporaine* 125 (January–March): 38–44.
Last, Murray
1983   "From Sultanate to Caliphate: Kano ca. 1450–1800." In *Studies in the History of Kano*, ed. Bawuro M. Barkindo, pp. 67–92. Ibadan: Heinemann Educational Books.
1979a   "Historical Metaphors in the Intellectual History of Kano Before 1800." Paper presented at the Seminar on the History of the Central Sudan Before 1804, Ahmadu Bello University, Zaria, Nigeria, January 8–13.
1979b   "Strategies Against Time." *Sociology of Health and Sickness: A Journal of Medical Sociology* 1 (December): 306–17.
1967   *The Sokoto Caliphate*. Ibadan History Series. London: Longmans.
Leger-Hervieu, Daniele
1983   "Introduction." In *Oppression des femmes et religion*, pp. 1–5. Paris: Editions de la Société des Amis du Centre d'Etudes Sociologiques.
Legum, Colin
1984   *African Contemporary Record* 15 (1982–83). New York and London: Africana and Holmes & Meier Publishers.
Lemu, Aisha
1986   "The Ideal Muslim Husband," part 2. *New Nigerian*, Friday, May 16, p. 20.
1983   *The Da'awah Responsibilities of the Muslim Woman*. Minna: Islamic Education Trust.
N.d.   *A Degree Above Them: Observations on the Condition of the Northern Nigerian Muslim Women*. Islamic Education Trust, Minna; Zaria, Nigeria: Gaskiya Corporation.
Leroux, H.
1948   "Animisme et Islam dans la Subdivision de Maradi (Niger)." *Bulletin de l'IFAN* 10:595–696.
Levy, Reuben
1977   *The Social Structure of Islam*. London: Cambridge University Press.

Levy-Luxereau, Anne
N.d.   "Le petit élevage dans la société hausa de Maradi (Niger) et son évolution." Mimeograph.
1983   "Les femmes hausa du Sahel nigerien n'accédent pas aux nouvelles techniques agricoles." *Penelope* (Paris) 9:39–41.

Lewis, Bernard
1958   *The Arabs in History*. Rev. ed. New York: Harpers.

Lewis, I. M.
1971   *Ecstatic Religion: An Anthropological Study of Spirit Possession and Shamanism*. Middlesex, England: Penguin.
1966   "Spirit Possession and Deprivation Cults." *Man* 1:307–29.

Liser, Florizelle B.
1982   "A Basic Needs Strategy and the Physical Quality of Life Index (PQLI): Africa's Development Prospects." In *Alternative Futures for Africa*, ed. Timothy M. Shaw, pp. 201–36. Boulder, Colo.: Westview Press.

Longhurst, Richard
1982   "Resource Allocation and the Sexual Division of Labor: A Case Study of a Moslem Hausa Village in Northern Nigeria." In *Women and Development*, ed. Lourdes Beneria, pp. 95–117. New York: Praeger.

Lovejoy, Paul E.
1988   "Concubinage and the Status of Women Slaves in Early Colonial Northern Nigeria." *Journal of African History* 29:245–66.
1986a   *Africans in Bondage*. Madison: African Studies Program and the University of Wisconsin Press.
1986b   "Fugitive Slaves: Resistance to Slavery in the Sokoto Caliphate." In *In Resistance: Studies of African, Afro-American and Caribbean History*, ed. G. Okihiro, pp. 71–95. Amherst: University of Massachusetts Press.
1983   *Transformations in Slavery: A History of Slavery in Africa*. Cambridge: Cambridge University Press.
1981   "Slavery in the Sokoto Caliphate." In *The Ideology of Slavery in Africa*, ed. Paul E. Lovejoy, pp. 201–43. Beverly Hills: Sage Publications.
1971   "Long-Distance Trade and Islam: The Case of the Nineteenth Century Hausa Kola Trade." *Journal of the Historical Society of Nigeria* 5, no. 4:537–47.
1970   "The Wholesale Kola Trade of Kano." *African Urban Notes* 5 (Summer): 129–42.

Lubeck, Paul
1986   *Islam and Urban Labor in Northern Nigeria: The Making of a Muslim Working Class*. Cambridge: Cambridge University Press.

Lugard, Frederick
1970   *Political Memoranda: Revision of Instructions to Political Officers on Subjects Chiefly Political and Administrative, 1913–1918*. 3d ed. Ed. A. H. M. Kirk-Greene. London: Frank Cass.
1906   *Instructions to Political and Other Officers on Subjects Chiefly Political and Administrative*. London: Colonial Printing Office.

Mack, Beverly
1990   "Service and Status: Slaves and Concubines in Kano, Nigeria." In *At Work in Homes: Household Workers in World Perspective*, ed. Roger Sanjek and Shellee Colen, pp. 14–34. American Ethnological Society Monograph 3. Washington, D.C.: American Anthropological Association.

1988   "Hajiya Maɗaki: A Royal Hausa Woman." In *Life Histories of African Women*, ed. Patricia Romero, pp. 47–77. Atlantic Highland, N.J.: Ashfield Press.

1986   "Songs from Silence: Hausa Women's Oral Poetry." In *Ngambika: Studies of Women in African Literature*, ed. Carole Boyce Davies and Anne Adams Graves, pp. 181–90. Trenton, N.J.: Africa World Press.

1983   " 'Waƙa Ɗaya Ba Ta Kare Niƙa—One Song Will Not Finish the Grinding': Hausa Women's Oral Literature." In *Contemporary African Literature*, ed. Hal Wylie et al., pp. 15–46. Washington, D.C.: Three Continents Press.

1981   " 'Waƙoƙin Mata': Hausa Women's Oral Poetry." Ph.D. diss., University of Wisconsin–Madison.

1980   "Socio-Economic Profile of Residents in Kano, Nigeria (Old City)." Kano Water Supply/Sanitation Project Urban Poverty Background Study. Kano, Nigeria: Report to the World Bank; Washington, D.C.

Martin, B. G.
1976   *Muslim Brotherhoods in Nineteenth-Century Africa*. Cambridge: Cambridge University Press.

Martin, Carol
1983   "Skill-Building or Unskilled Labour for Female Youth: A Bauchi Case." In *Female and Male in West Africa*, ed. Christine Oppong, pp. 223–35. London: George Allen and Unwin.

Marx, Karl
1977   *A Contribution to the Critique of Political Economy*. Moscow: Progress Publishers.

1965   *The German Ideology*. London: Lawrence and Wishart.

Mason, Michael
1971   "Population Density and Slave-Raiding: A Reply." *Journal of African History* 12, no. 2:324–27.

1969   "Population Density and 'Slave Raiding'—The Case of the Middle Belt of Nigeria." *Journal of African History* 10, no. 4:551–64.

Matan Niger (Association des Femmes du Niger)
1980   Statut. In *Matan Niger*, no. 1.

Matlon, P. J.
1979   "Income Distribution Among Farmers in Northern Nigeria: Empirical Results and Policy Implications." *African Rural Economy* paper 18. East Lansing: Michigan State University.

Mattelart, A., and S. Siegelaub, eds.
1979   *Communication and Class Struggle*, vol. 1. Bagniolet and New York: 19/IMMRG.

Mba, Nina
1989   "Kaba and Khaki: Women and the Militarized State in Nigeria." In
            Women and the State in Africa, ed. Jane L. Parpart and Kathleen A.
            Staudt, pp. 69–90. Boulder, Colo.: Lynne Rienner Publishers.
Meillassoux, Claude
1986   *Anthropologie de l'esclavage: Le ventre de fer et d'argent*. Paris.
1983   "Female Slavery." In *Women and Slavery in Africa*, ed. Claire C.
            Robertson and Martin A. Klein, pp. 49–66. Madison: University of
            Wisconsin Press.
1975   *Femmes, greniers et capitaux*. Paris: Maspero.
Mernissi, Fatima
1975   *Beyond the Veil*. Cambridge, Mass.: Schenkman Publishing.
Miers, Suzanne, and Igor Kopytoff, eds.
1977   *Slavery in Africa: Historical and Anthropological Perspectives*. Madi-
            son: University of Wisconsin Press.
Miers, Suzanne, and Richard Roberts, eds.
1988   *The End of Slavery in Africa*. Madison: University of Wisconsin Press.
Mikell, Gwendolyn
1986   "Ghanaian Females, Rural Economy and National Stability." *African
            Studies Review* 29, no. 3:67–88.
Minces, Juliette
1978   "Women in Algeria." In *Women in the Muslim World*, ed. Lois Beck
            and Nikki Keddie, pp. 159–71. Cambridge, Mass.: Harvard Univer-
            sity Press.
Moody, J.
1967   "Staudinger: An Early European Traveller to Kano." *Kano Studies* 3:
            38–53.
Morgen, Sandra
1989   "Gender and Anthropology: Introductory Essay." In *Gender and An-
            thropology*, ed. Sandra Morgen, pp. 1–20. Washington, D.C.: Ameri-
            can Anthropological Association.
Morgen, Sandra, and Ann Bookman
1988   "Rethinking Women and Politics: An Introductory Essay." In *Women
            and the Politics of Empowerment*, ed. Bookman and Morgen, pp. 3–29.
            Philadelphia, Pa.: Temple University Press.
Moughtin, J. C.
1986   *Hausa Architecture*. New York: Lilian Barber Press.
1964   "The Traditional Settlements of the Hausa People." *The Town Planning
            Review* 35, no. 1:21–34.
Mukhopadhyay, Carol C., and Patricia J. Higgins
1988   "Anthropological Studies of Women's Status Revisited: 1977–1987."
            Annual Review of Anthropology (Palo Alto, Calif.) 17:461–95.
Murad, Khurram
1984   "On the Family." *Muslim World Book Review* 5.
Murdock, G., and P. Golding
1977   "Capitalism, Communication and Class Relations." In *Mass Commu-
            nication and Society*, ed. J. Curran et al., pp. 12–43. London: Arnold.

Nashat, Guity, ed.
1983   *Women and Revolution in Iran.* Boulder, Colo.: Westview Press.
Nelson, Cynthia
1974   "Public and Private Politics: Women in the Middle Eastern World."
               American Anthropologist 1, no. 3:551–63.
Nelson, Nici
1979   "How Women and Men Get By: The Sexual Division of Labour in the
               Informal Sector of a Nairobi Squatter Settlement." In *Casual Work and
               Poverty in Third World Cities*, ed. Ray Bromley and Chris Gerry, pp.
               283–302. New York: John Wiley and Sons.
Nicholson, Linda
1986   *Gender and History: The Limits of Social Theory in the Age of the
               Family.* New York: Columbia University Press.
Nicolas, Guy
1981   *Dynamique de l'Islam au Sud du Sahara.* Paris: Publications Orien-
               talistes de France.
Nigeria
1982   *Fourth National Development Plan, 1981–85.* Revised. Lagos: Federal
               Ministry of Economic Planning.
Niven, Sir Rex
1982   *Nigerian Kaleidoscope: Memoirs of a Colonial Servant.* Hamden,
               Conn.: Archon Books.
Nur Alkali, Mohammad
1978   "Kanem-Bornu Under the Sayfawa." Ph.D. diss., Ahmadu Bello Uni-
               versity, Zaria, Nigeria.
Ogunbiyi, I. A.
1969   "The Position of Muslim Women as Stated by 'Uthman b. Fudu.' "
               Odu 2 (October): 43–60.
Ogundipe-Leslie, Omolara
1984   "Aspects of Literature." *West Africa*, April 23, pp. 876–77.
Okonjo, Kamene
1983   "Sex Roles in Nigerian Politics." In *Female and Male in West Africa*,
               ed. Christine Oppong, pp. 211–22. London: Allen and Unwin.
Olayiwola, Peter O.
1987   *Petroleum and Structural Change in a Developing Country: The Case
               of Nigeria.* New York: Praeger.
Onwuejeogwu, Michael
1969   "The Cult of the *Bori* Spirits among the Hausa." In *Man in Africa*,
               ed. Mary Douglas and Phyllis M. Kaberry, pp. 279–305. London:
               Tavistock.
Orr, Sir Charles
1911   *The Making of Northern Nigeria.* London.
Ortner, Sherry B., and Harriet Whitehead
1981   "Introduction: Accounting for Sexual Meanings." In *Sexual Mean-
               ings*, ed. Ortner and Whitehead, pp. 1–27. Cambridge: Cambridge
               University Press.

Osman, Fathi
1986   "Muslim Women's Role in Society." *Arabia: The Islamic World Review*
                5 (April 1986): 11–13.
Paden, John N.
1986   *Ahmadu Bello Sardauna of Sokoto*. London: Hodder and Stoughton.
1973   *Religion and Political Culture in Kano*. Berkeley: University of Cali-
                fornia Press.
Palmer, H. R.
1928   *Sudanese Memoirs*. 3 vols. Lagos: Government Printer.
1914   "Bori among the Hausas." *Man* 14, no. 52:113–17.
Papanek, Hanna, et al.
1982   *Separate Worlds: Studies of Purdah in South Asia*. Delhi: Chanakya
                Publishers.
Parpart, Jane L., and Kathleen A. Staudt
1989   "Women and the State in Africa." In *Women and the State in Africa*,
                ed. Parpart and Staudt, pp. 1–19. Boulder, Colo.: Lynne Rienner Pub-
                lishers.
Peil, Margaret
1979   "Host Reactions: Aliens in Ghana." In *Strangers in African Societies*,
                ed. W. A. Shack and E. P. Skinner, pp. 123–40. Berkeley: University
                of California Press.
Pellow, Deborah
1988   "What Housing Does: Changes in an Accra Community." *Architecture
                and Behavior* 4, no. 3:213–28.
1987   "Solidarity among Muslim Women in Accra, Ghana." *Anthropos* 82:
                489–506.
1985   "Muslim Segmentation: Cohesion and Divisiveness in Accra." *Journal
                of Modern African Studies* 23, no. 3:419–44.
1977   *Women in Accra: Options for Autonomy*. Algonac, Mich.: Reference
                Publications.
Pellow, Deborah, and Naomi Chazan
1986   *Ghana: Coping with Uncertainty*. Boulder, Colo.: Westview Press.
People's Redemption Party (PRP)
1978   "The Platform of the People: The General Programme and Election
                Manifesto of the People's Redemption Party." Kano. Mimeograph.
Perham, Margery
1983   *West African Passage*. London: Peter Owen Press.
1937   *Native Administration in Nigeria*. London: Oxford University Press.
Pesle, O.
1946   *La Femme Musulmane*. Rabat: Les Editions La Porte.
Piault, Colette
1971   *Contribution à l'étude de la vie quotidienne de la femme Mawri*. Etudes
                Nigeriennes 10, pp. 110–12. Niamey: CNRS.
Piault, Marc-Henri, trans.
1978   "Mariage en pays Hausa." In *Systèmes de signes*, pp. 419–34. Paris:
                Hermann.

Pickthall, Mohammed Marmaduke
1953   *The Meaning of the Glorious Koran: An Explanatory Translation*. New
             York: Mentor.
Pittin, Renee I.
1987   "Documentation of Women's Work in Nigeria." In *Sex Roles, Popu-
             lation and Development in West Africa*, ed. Christine Oppong, pp.
             25–44. Portsmouth, N.H.: Heinemann; London: James Currey.
1984a   "Documentation and Analysis of the Invisible Work of Invisible
             Women: A Nigerian Case-Study." *International Labour Review* 123,
             4:473–90.
1984b   "The Migration of Women in Nigeria: The Hausa Case." *International
             Migration Review* 18 (Winter): 1293–1314.
1983   "Houses of Women: A Focus on Alternative Life-Styles in Katsina
             City." In *Female and Male in West Africa*, ed. Christine Oppong, pp.
             291–302. London: George Allen and Unwin.
1979a   "Marriage and Alternative Strategies: Career Patterns of Hausa
             Women in Katsina City." Ph.D. diss., University of London, School
             of Oriental and African Studies.
1979b   "Hausa Women and Islamic Law: Is Reform Necessary?" Paper pre-
             sented to the 22d annual meeting of the African Studies Association,
             Los Angeles.
1976   "Social Status and Economic Opportunity in Urban Hausa Society."
             Paper presented to the Conference on Nigerian Women and Develop-
             ment in Relation to Changing Family Structure, University of Ibadan,
             Nigeria.
Pokrant, R.
1982   "The Tailors of Kano City." In *From Craft to Industry*. ed. E. Goody,
             pp. 85–132. Cambridge: Cambridge University Press.
Potash, Betty
1989   "Gender Relations in Sub-Saharan Africa." In *Gender and Anthro-
             pology*, ed. Sandra Morgen, pp. 189–227. Washington, D.C.: Ameri-
             can Anthropological Association.
al-Qayrawani, Abu Muhammad 'Abdallah ibn Abi Zayd
1945   *al-Risala*. Ed. and trans. Leon Bercher. Arab-French ed. Algiers:
             Bibliothèque Arabe-Française.
Raynaut, Claude
1977   "Aspects socio-économiques de la préparation et de la circulation de la
             nourriture dans un village hausa (Niger)." *Cahiers d'études Africaines-
             68*, 17, no. 4:569–97.
1972   *Structures normatives et relations electives: étude d'une communauté
             villageoise haoussa*. The Hague: Mouton.
Remy, Dorothy
1975   "Underdevelopment and the Experience of Women: A Nigerian Case
             Study." In *Toward an Anthropology of Women*, ed. Rayna R. Reiter,
             pp. 358–71. New York: Monthly Review Press.

Research Bulletin
1972   Centre of Arabic Documentation, University of Ibadan, vol. 8, nos.
                1–2 (December): 33–34.

Riesman, Paul
1966   "Mariage et vol du feu: Quelques catégories de la pensée symbolique
                des Haoussa." *L'Homme* 6, no. 4:82–103.

Robertson, Claire
1987   "Developing Economic Awareness: Changing Perspectives in Studies
                of African Women, 1976–1985." *Feminist Studies* 13 (Spring): 97–
                135.

1984   *Sharing the Same Bowl: A Socioeconomic History of Women and Class
                in Accra, Ghana*. Bloomington: Indiana University Press.

Robertson, Claire C., and Iris Berger
1986   *Women and Class in Africa*. New York: Holmes and Meier, Africana
                Publishing.

Robertson, Claire C., and Martin A. Klein
1983   "Women's Importance in African Slave Systems." In *Women and
                Slavery in Africa*, ed. Claire C. Robertson and Martin A. Klein, pp.
                3–25. Madison: University of Wisconsin Press.

Robinson, C. H.
1896   *Hausaland, or Fifteen Hundred Miles Through the Central Soudan*.
                London: Sampson Low, Marston & Co.

Rosaldo, Michelle Zimbalist
1980   "The Use and Abuse of Anthropology: Reflections on Feminism and
                Cross Cultural Understanding." *Signs* 5, no. 3:389–417.

1974   "Woman, Culture and Society: A Theoretical Overview." In *Woman,
                Culture and Society*, ed. Michelle Zimbalist Rosaldo and Louise Lam-
                phere, pp. 17–42. Stanford, Calif.: Stanford University Press.

Ruxton, F.H.
1978   *Maliki Law. A Summary from French Translations of the Mukhtasar of
                Sidi Khalil*. London: Luzac. Orig. pub. 1916.

Le Sahel. République du Niger. Ministère de l'Information.
1984   Issues of January 4, 10, and 27; March 9–11, 19, 21, and 29; April 2;
                May 10, and 31; and June 13.

Sahel Dimanche
1989   Issue of December 15, pp. 12–13.

Sahel Habdo. République du Niger. Minstère de l'Information.
1984   No. 390 (January 16); no. 398 (March 12); no. 404 (May 14).
1982   No. 327 (September 6).
1978   No. 138 (August 3); special number, December 18.
1977   No. 70 (March 7); special number, April 15; no. 78 (May 16); no. 79
                (May 23); no. 80 (May 30); no. 81 (June 6).
1976   No. 14 (January 12); no. 33 (June 7); no. 46 (September 6); no. 57
                (November 22); no. 59 (December 6); special number, December 18.
1975   No. 11 (December 12).

Sa'id, Halil Ibrahim
1978   "Revolution and Reaction: The Fulani Jihad in Kano and Its Aftermath, 1807–1919." Ph.D. diss., University of Michigan.
Sa'idu, Abdulrazak Giginyu
1981   "History of a Slave Village in Kano: Gandun Nassarawa." B.A. thesis, Bayero University.
Salifou, Andre
1973   *Tanimoune*. Paris: Presence Africaine (Avant-Propos).
Sanday, Peggy R.
1981   *Female Power and Male Dominance: On the Origins of Sexual Inequality*. Cambridge: Cambridge University Press.
Sarly, R.
1981   "Urban Development Strategy in Metropolitan Kano." Report to the World Bank, Washington, D.C.
Saunders, Margaret O.
1980   "Women's Role in a Muslim Hausa Town (Mirria, Republic of Niger)." In Erika Bourguignon et al., *A World of Women*, pp. 57–86. New York: J. F. Bergin.
1979   "Hausa Women in Economic Development: The Case of Mirria, Niger Republic." Paper presented to Society for Applied Anthropology, Philadelphia.
1978   "Marriage and Divorce in a Muslim Hausa Town (Mirria, Niger Republic)." Ph.D. diss., Indiana University.
Schildkrout, Enid
1988   "Hajiya Husaina: Notes on the Life History of a Hausa Woman." In *Life Histories of African Woman*, ed. Patricia Romero, pp. 78–98. Atlantic Highland, N.J.: Ashfield Press.
1986   "Widows in Hausa Society: Ritual Phase or Social Status?" In *Widows in African Societies: Choices and Constraints*, ed. Betty Potash, pp. 131–52. Stanford, Calif.: Stanford University Press.
1983   "Dependence and Autonomy: The Economic Activities of Secluded Hausa Women in Kano." In *Female and Male in West Africa*, ed. Christine Oppong, pp. 107–26. London: George Allen and Unwin.
1982   "Dependence and Autonomy: The Economic Activities of Secluded Hausa Women in Kano, Nigeria." In *Women and Work in Africa*, ed. Edna Bay, pp. 55–81. Boulder, Co.: Westview Press.
1981   "The Employment of Children in Kano (Nigeria)." In *Child Work, Poverty and Underdevelopment*, ed. Gerry Rodgers and Guy Standing, pp. 81–112. Geneva: International Labour Office.
1980   "The Employment of Children in Kano, Northern Nigeria." In *The Economic Role of Children in Low-Income Countires*, ed. Gerry Rodgers and Guy Standing, pp. 81–112. Geneva: International Labour Office.
1979   "Women's Work and Children's Work: Variations Among Moslems in Kano." In *Social Anthropology of Work*, ed. Sandra Wallman, pp. 69–85. ASA Monograph 19. London: Academic Press.

1978a   "Age and Gender in Hausa Society: Socio-Economic Roles of Children in Urban Kano." In *Age and Sex as Principles of Social Differentiation*, ed. J. S. LaFontaine, pp. 109–37. ASA Monograph 17. New York: Academic Press.

1978b   "Changing Economic Roles of Children in Comparative Perspective." In *Marriage, Fertility and Parenthood in West Africa: Changing African Family*, ed. C. Oppong, G. Adaba, M. Bekombo-Priso, J. Mogey, no. 4, pt. 1. Canberra: Australian National University.

1978c   *People of the Zongo: The Transformation of Ethnic Identities in Ghana*. New York: Cambridge University Press.

1974   *Islam and Politics in Kumasi*. New York: American Museum of Natural History.

1970a   "Government and Chiefs in Kumasi Zongo." In *West African Chiefs: Their Changing Status Under Colonial Rule and Independence*, ed. M. Crowder and O. Ikimo, pp. 370–92. Nigeria: University of Ife.

1970b   "Strangers and Local Government in Kumasi." *Journal of Modern African Studies* 8, no. 2:251–69.

Schoen, Frederick

1885–86   *Magana Hausa*. London: SPCK. Reprint. C.H. Robinson, 1906.

Schwerdtfeger, F. W.

1982   *Traditional Housing in African Cities*. New York: John Wiley.

Silverblatt, Irene

1988   "Women in States." *Annual Review of Anthropology* (Palo Alto, Calif.) 17:427–60.

Simmons, Emmy B.

1976   "Economic Research on Women in Rural Development in Northern Nigeria." In Overseas Liaison Committee America Council on Education series, paper no. 10.

1975   "The Small-Scale Rural Food Processing Industry in Northern Nigeria." *Food Research Institute Studies* (Stanford) 14, no. 2:147–61.

Simms, R.

1981   "The African Woman as Entrepreneur: Problems and Perspectives on Their Roles." In *The Black Woman Cross-Culturally*, ed. F. Steady, pp. 141–68. Cambridge, Mass.: Schenkman.

Skinner, A. Neil

1980   *An Anthology of Hausa Literature*. Zaria, Nigeria: Northern Nigerian Publishing.

1977a   *Hausa Tales and Traditions*. Vol 2. Originally compiled by Frank Edgar. Madison: University of Wisconsin Press.

1977b   *Hausa Tales and Traditions*. Vol. 3. Originally compiled by Frank Edgar. Microfiche.

1969   *Hausa Tales and Traditions: An English Translation of "Tatsuniyoyi na Hausa," originally compiled by Frank Edgar*. Vol. 1. London: Frank Cass.

Sklar, Richard L.

1983   *Nigerian Political Parties: Power in an Emergent African Nation*. New York: Nok Publishers International.

Smith, Mary F.
1981   *Baba of Karo: A Woman of the Muslim Hausa*. 2d ed. New Haven,
               Conn.: Yale University Press. Orig. pub. London: Faber and Faber,
               1954.
Smith, Michael G.
1983   "The *Kano Chronicle* as History." In *Studies in the History of Kano*,
               ed. Bawuro M. Barkindo, pp. 31–56. Ibadan, Nigeria: Heinemann
               Educational Books.
1981   "Introduction." In Mary F. Smith, *Baba of Karo: A Woman of the
               Muslim Hausa*. New Haven, Conn.: Yale University Press.
1980   "The Jihad of Shehu 'Dan Fodio: Some Problems." In *Islam in Tropical
               Africa*, ed. I. M. Lewis, pp. 213–25. Bloomington: Indiana Univer-
               sity Press.
1978   *The Affairs of Daura: History and Change in a Hausa State, 1800–
               1958*. Berkeley: University of California Press.
1969   "Introduction." *Hausa Tales and Traditions*, vol. 1. Ed. A. Neil
               Skinner. London: Frank Cass.
1965a   "Hausa Inheritance and Succession." In *Studies in the Law of Succes-
               sion in Nigeria*, ed. D. J. M. Derrett, pp. 230–81. Oxford: Oxford
               University Press.
1965b   "The Hausa of Northern Nigeria." In *Peoples of Africa*, ed. James L.
               Gibbs, Jr., pp. 121–55. New York: Holt, Rinehart & Winston.
1960   *Government in Zauzzau, 1800–1958*. Los Angeles: University of Cali-
               fornia Press.
1959   "The Hausa System of Social Status." *Africa* 29, no. 3:239–52.
1955   *The Economy of Hausa Communities of Zaria*. A Report to the Colonial
               Social Science Research Council. London: Her Majesty's Stationery
               Office, Colonial Research Studies 16. Reprint. New York: Johnson
               Reprint Corporation, 1971.
1952   "A Study of Hausa Domestic Economy in Northern Zaria." *Africa* 22:
               333–47.
1951   "Social and Economic Change among Selected Native Communities
               in Northern Nigeria." Ph.D. diss., University of London.
N.d.   "Government in Kano." Manuscript.
Smock, Audrey C.
1977a   "Ghana: From Autonomy to Subordination." In *Women: Roles and
               Status in Eight Countries*, ed. J. Z. Giele and Audrey C. Smock, pp.
               173–216. New York: John Wiley and Sons.
1977b   "Bangladesh." In *Women: Roles and Status in Eight Countries*, ed.
               J. Z. Giele and Audrey C. Smock, pp. 83–126. New York: John Wiley
               and Sons.
Smock, Audrey C. and Nadia Haggag Youssef
1977   "Egypt." In *Women: Roles and Status in Eight Countries*, ed. J. Z.
               Giele and Audrey C. Smock, pp. 35–79. New York: John Wiley
               and Sons.
Spring, Anita
1978   "Epidemiology and Spirit Possession among the Luvale of Zambia."

In *Women in Ritual and Symbolic Roles*, ed. Judith Hoch-Smith and Anita Spring, 165–91. New York: Plenum Press.

Standing, Guy
1981   *Labour Force Participation and Development*. Geneva: International Labour Office.

Steele, W.
1981   "Female and Small-Scale Employment Under Modernization in Ghana." *Economic Development and Cultural Change* 30 (October): 153–67.

Stephens, Connie L.
1981   "The Relationship of Social Symbols and Narrative Metaphor: A Study of Fantasy and Disguise in the Hausa *Tatsuniya* of Niger." 2 vols. Ph.D. diss., University of Wisconsin–Madison.

Stichter, Sharon
1984   "Appendix: Some Selected Statistics on African Women." In *African Women South of the Sahara*, ed. Margaret Jean Hay and Sharon Stichter, pp. 188–94. London: Longman.

Stichter, Sharon B., and Jane L. Parpart
1988   "Introduction: Towards a Materialist Perspective on African Women." In *Patriarchy and Class: African Women in the Home and the Workplace*, ed. Stichter and Parpart, pp. 1–26. Boulder, Colo.: Westview Press.

Strobel, Margaret
1979   *Muslim Women in Mombasa, 1890–1975*. New Haven, Conn.: Yale University Press.

Sudarkasa, N.
1986   " 'The Status of Women' in Indigenous African Societies." *Feminist Studies* 12 (Spring): 91–103.

1981   "Female Employment and Family Organization in West Africa." In *The Black Woman Cross-Culturally*, ed. F. Steady, pp. 49–63. Cambridge, Mass.: Schenkman.

Suleiman, Ibrahim
1983   "On the Liberation of Women." Paper presented to the Muslim Students Association, Ahmadu Bello University, Zaria, Nigeria.

Tabet, Paola
1985   "Fertilité naturelle, reproduction forcée." In *L'arraisonnement des femmes: Essais en anthropologie des sexes*, ed. Nicole-Claude Mathieu, pp. 61–146. Paris: Cahiers de l'Homme, Editions de l'Ecole des Hautes Etudes en Sciences Sociales.

Tambo, David
1976   "The Sokoto Caliphate Slave Trade in the Nineteenth Century." *International Journal of African Historical Studies* 9:187–217.

Terray, Emmanuel
1982   "Réflexions sur la formation du prix des esclaves a l'intérieur de l'Afrique de l'Ouest précoloniale." *Journal des Africanistes* 52, nos. 1–2:119–44.

Thomson, James T.
1975   "Law, Legal Process and Development at the Local Level in Hausa-
                Speaking Niger: A Trouble-Case Analysis of Rural Institutional In-
                ertia." Ph.D. diss., Indiana University.
Tibenderana, Peter Kazenga
1985   "The Beginnings of Girls' Education in the Native Administration
                Schools in Northern Nigeria, 1930–1945." *Journal of African History*
                26:93–109.
Toledano, E. R.
1981   "Slave Dealers, Women, Pregnancy and Abortion." *Slavery and Abo-
                lition* 2, no. 1:53–68.
Trager, Lillian
1985   "From Yams to Beer in a Nigerian City: Expansion and Change in
                Informal Sector Trade Activity." In *Markets and Marketing*, ed. Stuart
                Plattner, pp. 259–85. Proceedings of the 1984 Meeting of the Society
                for Economic Anthropology. Monographs in Economic Anthropology,
                no. 4. Lanham, Md.: University Press of America.
Tremearne, Major A. J. N.
1914   *The Ban of the Bori: Demons and Demon Dancing in West and North
                Africa.* London: Frank Cass. Reprint, 1968.
1913   *Hausa Superstitions and Customs: An Introduction to the Folk-lore and
                the Folk.* London: John Bale and Danielson.
Trevor, Jean
1975a   "Western Education and Muslim Fulani/Hausa Women in Sokoto,
                Northern Nigeria." In *Conflict and Harmony in Education in Tropical
                Africa*, ed. Godfrey Brown and Mervyn Hiskett, pp. 247–70. London:
                George Allen and Unwin.
1975b   "Family Change in Sokoto, A Traditional Moslem Fulani/Hausa City."
                In *Population Growth and Socioeconomic Change in West Africa*, ed.
                John Caldwell, pp. 236–53. New York: Columbia University Press.
Trimingham, J. Spencer
1971   *The Sufi Orders in Islam.* London: Oxford University Press.
Ubah, Chinedu Nwafor
1973   "Administration of Kano Emirate under the British, 1900–1930."
                Ph.D. diss., University of Ibadan, Nigeria.
United Nations
1975   *Economic Bulletin for Africa: The Role of Women in African Develop-
                ment* 11, 1. New York.
United Nations Economic Commission for Africa (UNECA)
1972   "Women, the Neglected Resource for African Development." *Cana-
                dian Journal of African Studies* 6:359–87.
United Nations Educational, Scientific and Cultural Organization (UNESCO)
1985   *Statistical Yearbook.* Paris: UNESCO.
Vandevelde, Hélène
1985   "Le Code algérien de la Famille." *Maghreb Machrek* 107:52–64.

Veillard
1939   "Coutumier du Cercle de Zinder." In *Coutumier Juridique de l'A.O.F.*,
                vol. 3. Paris: Larose.
Wali, Isa
1956   "The True Position of Women in Islam." *Nigerian Citizen*. July 18
                (p. 6) and August 4 (p. 5).
Wali, Yusufu
1980   "The Translation of the Nur al-Albab (of Usman ibn Fudi)." *Kano
                Studies*, n.s., 2, no. 1, p. 14.
Wall, Roger
1982   "Merging Economic Growth with Political Rebirth." *Africa News* 18,
                p. 24.
Watts, Michael
1987   *State, Oil, and Agriculture in Nigeria*. Berkeley: Institute of Interna-
                tional Studies, University of California.
1983   *Silent Violence: Food, Famine and the Peasantry in Northern Nigeria*.
                Berkeley: University of California Press.
Watts, Michael, and Paul Lubeck
1983   "The Popular Classes and the Oil Boom: A Political Economy of
                Rural and Urban Poverty." In *The Political Economy of Nigeria*, ed.
                I. William Zartman, pp. 105–44. New York: Praeger.
Weekes, Richard V., ed.
1978   *Muslim Peoples*. Westport, Conn.: Greenwood.
Whyte, Martin King
1978   "Cross-Cultural Codes Dealing with the Relative Status of Women."
                Ethnology 17 (April): 211–37.
Women in Nigeria (WIN)
1985a   *Women in Nigeria Today*. Prepared for publication by the Editorial
                Committee of Women in Nigeria. London: Zed Books.
1985b   *Women and the Family*. Edited proceedings of the Second Annual WIN
                Conference. Dakar, Senegal: Codesria Books.
1985c   *The WIN Document: The Conditions of Women in Nigeria, and Policy
                Recommendations to 2000 A.D.* Zaria, Nigeria: Ahmadu Bello Univer-
                sity Press.
1983   *Proceedings: Second Annual Conference*. Zaria, Nigeria: Ahmadu
                Bello University Press.
Works, John A., Jr.
1976   *Pilgrims in a Strange Land*. New York: Columbia University Press.
World Bank
1988   *World Bank Development Report*. New York: Oxford University Press
                for the World Bank.
1986   *World Development Report*. New York: Oxford University Press.
Yakubu, Mahmood
1985   "A Century of Warfare and Slavery in Bauchi, c.1805–1900: An
                Analysis of a Pre-Colonial Economy." B.A. thesis, University of
                Sokoto, Nigeria.

Yanagisako, Sylvia Junko, and Jane Fishburne Collier
1987   "Toward a Unified Analysis of Gender and Kinship." In *Gender and Kinship: Toward a Unified Analysis*, ed. Collier and Yanagisako, pp. 14–50. Stanford, Calif.: Stanford University Press.

Yeld, Rachel
1960   "Islam and Social Stratification in Northern Nigeria." *British Journal of Sociology* 11:112–28.

Youssef, Nadia
1974   *Women and Work in Developing Societies*. Berkeley: Institute of International Studies, University of California.

Yunusa, Yusufu
1976   "Slavery in the 19th Century Kano." B.A. thesis, Ahmadu Bello University, Zaria, Nigeria.

Yusuf, Bilkisu
1985a   "The Rights of Women under the Shariah." Paper presented at the Muslim Students Society, Training Programme, Kano, Nigeria, December.

1985b   "Nigerian Women in Politics." In *Women in Nigeria Today*. London: Zed Press.

1985c   "Muslim Women Disown NCWS." Paper presented at Muslim Sisters Organization Conference, Kano, Nigeria, April.

Contributors

Janet Beik completed her doctorate in African Languages and Literature at the University of Wisconsin–Madison in 1984. Before that, she served as a Peace Corps volunteer in Niger (1976–78) and researched Hausa theater as a Fulbright scholar, also in Niger (1980–81). At present, she is a Foreign Service Officer in the U.S. Department of State, with tours in Sudan, Canada, and The Gambia since 1985.

Allan Christelow studies the social history of North and West Africa using Islamic legal records. His publications include *Muslim Law Courts and the French Colonial State in Algeria* (Princeton University Press, 1985). He taught at Bayero University in Kano, Nigeria, from 1978 to 1982 and is currently Associate Professor in the Department of History at Idaho State University.

Catherine Coles received her Ph.D. in anthropology at the University of Wisconsin– Madison and has taught at Ahmadu Bello University in Nigeria and at Dartmouth College. She has published articles on Hausa women as well as an extensive bibliography on Nigerian women and "Demographic Surveys and Nigerian Women" (*Signs* 15 [January 1990]) with Barbara Entwisle. Her research interests include Muslim women, urban life cross-culturally, processes of aging, and legal systems as they are embedded within particular cultures. She is currently attending law school in Boston.

Barbara Callaway serves as Acting Dean of the graduate School and Vice Provost for Graduate Education at Rutgers University in New Brunswick, N.J., where she is also a Professor of Political Science. She is the author of *Muslim Hausa Women in Nigeria* and of articles on political development, political change, and women and politics. During 1981–83, she was a Fulbright Professor at Bayero University in Kano, Nigeria.

Roberta Ann Dunbar is a social historian in the Curriculum in African and Afro-American Studies at the University of North Carolina at Chapel Hill, where she teaches courses on African women and on African art, literature, and civilization. Her original field research concerned the nineteenth-century history of Damagaram (Zinder, Nigeria). More recently she has focused her research and writing on the consequences for African women of the interaction of Muslim and civil law in francophone West Africa, especially Niger and Senegal.

Nicole Echard is an ethnologist and Directeur de recherche to the French National Center for Scientific Research (C.N.R.S.). She has done field research in rural Niger among the Hausa, Tuareg, and Songhaï peoples. Her research interests include history of settlement, iron metallurgy, religion, and gender relations.

289

Alan Frishman is a Professor of Economics at Hobart and William Smith Colleges. He has been researching the economic and spatial growth of Kano, Nigeria, for almost two decades. He has written numerous articles and chapters in books on small-scale enterprises, general economic activity, housing, squatter settlements, land tenure, population growth, and transportation in metropolitan Kano.

Ayesha M. Imam is a lecturer and researcher in the Sociology Department at Ahmadu Bello University, Zaria, Nigeria. Her main areas of work have been in gender relations, ideology, and mass communication. She is also active in the women's movement in Nigeria.

Beverly Mack lived in northern Nigeria for three years, where she conducted research on Hausa women's poetic artistry and the lives of women in the emir's harem. During that time she was a Fulbright scholar and taught at Bayero University in Kano. She has taught at Georgetown and Yale Universities and now teaches African literature and Hausa cultural studies at George Mason University.

Deborah Pellow is Associate Professor of Anthropology at Syracuse University. She has done field research in both Ghana and Nigeria. Her publications include articles on gender and ethnicity and the coauthored book *Ghana: Coping with Uncertainty*. Her current research interest is the interrelationship of social and physical space (cultural aspects of design) in Africa and Shanghai, People's Republic of China.

Priscilla Starratt taught African History from 1975 to 1989 at Bayero University, Kano, where she was Senior Lecturer. Since then she has been teaching Hausa Language and Culture at Boston University.

Connie Stephens is currently Deputy Chief of the African Division of Voice of America. When she wrote the chapter on Hausa *tatsuniyoyi* she was chief of VOA's Hausa Language Service. From 1981 to 1984 she worked with the National Languages Section of Niger's National Curriculum Institute (I.N.D.R.A.P.) on a maternal languages textbook project for Niger's experimental schools.

Balaraba B.M. Sule is a graduate of Bayero University, Kano. She taught Islamic History, Education and Social Studies from 1984 to 1989 at the School for Arabic Studies in Kano, Nigeria. Since 1989, she has been the Head of the Women's Programs Department of the Kano State Agency for Mass Education where she has organized literacy and vocational education programs for women.

Bilkisu Yusuf is the Deputy Editor-in-Chief of the *Citizen*, a Nigerian magazine of politics, economics, and culture. She has been editor of the *Kano Triumph* (1983–87) and the *New Nigerian* newspapers. Yusuf holds a Master's degree in political science and international relations from the University of Wisconsin–Madison and in 1986 completed a degree in Advanced Journalism from the Moscow Institute of Journalism. Her work has focused on matters of social relevance, with special concern for women's issues in Africa and internationally. In addition, she has long been an active member of the Nigerian National Committee on Women and Development, is Public Relations Officer for the Federation of Muslim Women's Association (FOMWAN), and has been a state representative of the Women in Nigeria (WIN) organization since its inception.

Index

Abbas, former Emir of Kano Muhammad, 131
Actresses: in Hausa drama, 24, 232–43
  passim; in Hausa radio, 244–52 *passim*
Adashi. See Savings, women's rotating credit
  groups for
Adar. *See* Ethnic groups
Ader region, 76, 207–20 *passim*
Adultery, 81
Ahmadu Bello University 96, 154
Agency for Mass Education, Kano State 93,
  94, 105. *See also* Education, adult women's
Agriculture, women as laborers in, 5, 8,
  18–19,
Aissata, Mrs. Moumouni, 88
Algerian Charter, 86
AlƘali courts. *See* Islamic courts
Amariya. See Wives, youngest wife
Amina, Queen of Zazzau, 111
Aminu Kano, Malam, 17, 94, 147–50, 152,
  153, 157
Aristocratic women. *See* Royal women
Armen kubble. See Seclusion in Hausa
  marriage
Arts, 26
Artists: creative Hausa women, 21–22; literary,
  23; performing, 23
Asante. *See* Ethnic groups
Asna, arne. See Hausa, pagan
Association of Nigerien Women (Association
  des femmes du Niger) (AFN). *See* Women's
  organizations
Auren kulle, auren tsare. See Seclusion in
  marriage
Authority and power, women's. *See* Royal
  women, authority and power
Avoidance, 124

Bako, Malam, 56

Bamidele community, women's position in,
  31–32
Baptism, 78
Basasa (Kano civil war), 133
Bayero University, Kano, 154
Bazawara. See Unmarried woman
Bello, Sir Ahmadu, 151
Biki. See celebration
Birth control, family planning, 101
Bori. See Spirit possession cult
Brides, 172. *See also* Marriage; youngest wife
Bridewealth, 75, 81. *See also* Dowry.
British overrule. *See* Colonial administration
Brotherhoods. *See* Mystical organizations
Budurwa. See Unmarried girl
Buzanga. *See* Ethnic groups

Celebration (*biki*), 73, 183
Chad, 185
Chamba. *See* Ethnic groups
Childbearing, 19, 171
Childcare, 8, 93, 97, 119, 126
Child custody, 9, 75, 81
Child support, 81
Christians, 4, 166, 169
Clan feeling (*zumunci*), 60–61, 67
Colonial administration (British overrule), 4,
  14, 16, 18, 128
Colleges d'enseignement generales (Nigerien
  secondary schools). *See* Education
Compound. *See* Household
Compurgation, oath of (*qasama*), 141
Concubine: contesting inheritance rights,
  16, 135–36, 140–41; in palace, 118, 126;
  who has borne her master a child (*umm
  walad*), 135
Constitution, First in independent Nigeria. *See*
  Voting rights

291